NOTES FROM A WAYWARD SON

GREAT CIRCLE BOOKS

Great Circle Books publishes literary nonfiction—including memoir, literary journalism, personal and lyric essays, and works that defy easy classification—by emerging writers. The Great Circle is the intersection of lines on the celestial sphere—lines overlapping and creating new entryways of understanding. In that spirit, Great Circle Books seeks, through innovative work, to merge the human experience with our relationship to place.

A complete list of books published in Great Circle Books is available at https://uncpress.org/series/great-circle-books.

NOTES FROM A WAYWARD SON

A MEMOIR

Adrian De Leon

THE UNIVERSITY OF NORTH CAROLINA PRESS
CHAPEL HILL

Designed by April Leidig
Set in Garamond by Copperline Book Services, Inc.
Manufactured in the United States of America

Cover art: torn paper © flas100 / Adobe Stock; bridge © Lisa Jager.

Library of Congress Cataloging-in-Publication Data
Names: De Leon, Adrian author
Title: Notes from a wayward son : a memoir / Adrian De Leon.
Other titles: Great circle books
Description: Chapel Hill : The University of North Carolina Press, [2026] | Series: Great circle books
Identifiers: LCCN 2026017307 | ISBN 9781469696638 paperback | ISBN 9781469696645 epub | ISBN 9781469696652 pdf
Subjects: LCSH: De Leon, Adrian—Family | De Leon, Adrian—Childhood and youth | Fathers and sons | Filipinos—Family relationships | Filipinos—Canada | Filipinos—United States | Filipino diaspora | Catholics, Asian—Canada—Social life and customs | BISAC: BIOGRAPHY & AUTOBIOGRAPHY / Personal Memoirs | FAMILY & RELATIONSHIPS / Parenting / Fatherhood | LCGFT: Biographies | Memoirs
Classification: LCC PR9199.4.D4264 Z46 2026
LC record available at https://lccn.loc.gov/2026017307

For product safety concerns under the European Union's General Product Safety Regulation (EU GPSR), please contact gpsr@mare-nostrum.co.uk or write to the University of North Carolina Press and Mare Nostrum Group B.V., Doelen 72, 4831 GR Breda, The Netherlands.

Dear Nanay—
I always understood.

Dear Balong—
I'm so sorry for the shrapnel.

Dear Lola Pet—
Agyamanak.

Dear Tatay:

My technique had been silence.

—James Baldwin,
Notes of a Native Son

CONTENTS

NOTES FROM A WAYWARD SON

WAYWARD

AT THE END of our relationship, as in the beginning, we had no words left.

You and I sat together on the porch like we used to, those summer afternoons when you and Nanay first planted the junipers, back when I'd make lemonade that was way too sour and not too sweet, and you preached to me. A good son, you used to say, loves his mother but listens to his father. Your political hero, Jesus Christ, was the best kind of son there was: an unparalleled devotee of his young mother, a Palestinian Jewish woman married to a local craftsman; and an unyielding servant of his father, the heavenly creator of everything in the universe. If I'd had the aggressive gumption of the Newfie kids at school, I'd have retorted that, technically, according to the Bible, Jesus didn't speak to God until he started his ministry in his thirties. By that logic, I had all my youthful years to love Nanay and learn how to take what you were saying seriously, so that, in adulthood, I could finally take the leap of faith and lay down my life for you. But, as with most things I tried to bring up, you would have hated that, so I kept quiet.

This was the fulcrum of our relationship's ritual: you spoke, the room went quiet, and I performed the act of listening. Your baritone voice, made hoarse from years of bellowing at platoons and screaming over jet engines, resonated with the Shakespearean cadence of classical Tagalog, even when all you were reciting was a prayer to bless our meal. It was a sort of spell whenever you pantomimed the bully pulpit, as father figure to the Scarborough kids, as a teacher each Saturday at the gym, as "Brother" in the weekly Filipino Christian group meetings, as "Father" when you led your first church.

Except when we sat together for the final time, the magic of Catholic fatherhood could no longer seal my lips. In truth, the magic had stopped working years before. Balong confessed to me that autumn that he had learned to keep his head down at home because, when I allowed myself to come of age, my natural disposition was to fight with you. Outside our suburban corner house, our vocations nurtured in each of us a gift for incantations, mostly from our own mouths, mostly upon distracted ears. But when we spoke to each other, we cast these spells against each other, and when I was younger, and I foolishly argued back, you used the magic of force. Each blow, first upon my naked skin, and later the clashing heft of our egos, must have been a detonation, because Balong and Nanay and Lola always cleared the blast radius.

That afternoon was supposed to be a quick visit. To show face, as my undergrad friends loved to say, at parties that none of us really wanted to go to but felt obligated nonetheless. Ever since I moved out in 2014, you and Nanay always suggested that I stay the night, to remind ourselves what a proper family should do. I did live with you again, technically, for four months, when the Canadian border tried to shut out an unyielding virus, except I insisted that you live elsewhere while I was there. This time, I was on sabbatical from work, living with my friend Minolta in a loft on Ossington and Dundas, and for the first time, I drove myself to my childhood home. I can't remember if I risked the crumbling Gardiner Expressway up to the Don Valley Parkway and east on the 401, or if I drove north to the Allen and took the 401 straight there. What I do remember is that my instincts must have told me to brace myself for some unspoken rupture, because my Honda blasted Protest the Hero on full volume. I was preemptively self-soothing with the mathcore metal I secretly listened to in high school. By the time I merged into the collector lane to exit at Morningside, I was headbanging to the introduction of "The Divine Suicide of K," a song you would never have approved for me, even if it didn't have any curse words. And when I pulled up to the garage, Spotify had brought me to my original queue, the latest Drake album, with the pregnant emojis on the cover.

The house was either the same but different, or different but the same. Most of the front yard remained, except that the little conifer I planted outside Lola's bedroom had become a terrifyingly tall evergreen. The pear tree that we tried to nurture on the south side of the yard still looked like a prop from the Charlie Brown Christmas special, and it never yielded any more fruit beyond the two it gave us a long time ago. Inside, you had redone the kitchen and the bathrooms and the living room, so that the interior looked like an incongruous blend of rustic cottage and shiny marble. The dining room kept its old wooden charm, the Last Supper painting still its most eye-catching feature. I was impressed, to tell you the truth. We had made it.

I rang the doorbell, and Lola answered, and I gave her a kiss, because I loved her the most, and you must have known this whenever you heard us speak in the native language you denied us. Then Balong came to say hi, in his cool-boy little-brother grunt. To greet Nanay and receive her blessing, I took her hand and pressed the back of her fingers to my forehead. Nanay had enticed me to drive to Scarborough with the promise of abundant leftover chicken adobo for my refrigerator. The price, of course, was that I'd have to talk to you. And when I tried to swipe the grocery bag and drive away, you stopped me at the door to collect the fee, a conversation on the patio.

You were opining about your line of work as a hospital chaplain in the palliative care unit, where you made the painful passage of death gentler with your soothing words. I never got to tell you how much I loved that you brought your guitar to the ward and serenaded the patients. You allowed your audiences a gentleness that no one ever gave you. I wanted to nod, wanted to commune in that softness, but I stared at my shoes, my right foot bouncing anxiously, the habit you hated so much, my body ready to run away.

That was the best kind of self-defense, you told me once: to run away. But that only works when the other person isn't your own father.

THAT AFTERNOON on the patio was our last-ditch effort to salvage a make-believe relationship. During the first pandemic summer, after I moved back to California, we joked about me finally becoming an adult. I bought my first piece of property, which, like yours, was a townhouse in one of the brownest neighborhoods in our respective cities. I learned how to drive, too. And when I got my license, you and Nanay were the first people I told because, like you, I passed on my first try, even when my exam center had the lowest passing rate (the Hollywood DMV) and my examiner had a tough reputation. You told me you were proud of me, and we joked that my devotion to public transit would give way to the pleasures of gas guzzling. Until then, I had never felt comfortable calling you, but it somehow felt right to put you on WhatsApp while I was driving down Sunset Boulevard. If you had gotten the chance to visit me, you'd have fallen in love with the westward drive like I did. Nanay told me then that we were so alike, in that we both loved to drive to calm our ruderous minds, and it didn't bother me. When I got behind the wheel of my Accord and spoke the spatial language of Los Angeles, I imagined that you must have felt this way when you first took our first station wagon for a cruise around Scarborough. The wide suburban streets must have felt like freedom compared to Manila's chronic congestion.

On those cruises, I used to call you for stories about your hometown in the Bataan Peninsula, and you'd tell me about the river that you swam as a kid. I remembered those rivers from my dreams, when you'd put me to sleep not with the lash of a leather belt but with a bedtime story about the Tenejero River that bisected your town. You told me that the nearby Rouge River in Scarborough, which had carved into the northern escarpments of the Leading Sea, the original and expansive Anishinaabe name for the diminutive "Lake" Ontario, was a gentle creek compared to the channels that webbed across the landscapes of your birth. I remember that river in a poem, and how we both expected its greeting when we went back to the Philippines together:

perhaps I'd finally find

the strong winding arms in bataan
the tenejero

this place could not be home
until I plunged my waist at the
depths

Along Riverside Drive, when the 5 was a sludge of crawling cars, you told me about the history of the peninsula, ravaged by Spanish and American and Japanese colonial wars, and about the cataclysms that cleaved short eighteen thousand lives when, in 1942, the

Japanese army forced Filipino and American prisoners of war to march to their deaths from Bataan to the base of the mountains in Tarlac. You recounted the water, which had once nourished the land but since receded into a trickle during the dictatorship of Ferdinand Marcos in the 1970s. Your estranged father, Ingkong, was one of the lucky few who managed to escape, hiding in caves and forests where he found a revolutionary front to join and cosplayed as a guerrilla, until he was ready to rejoin his rightful place in Bataan's civil society as a local elite. What you didn't mention was that the irrigated landscape before Ferdinand Marcos declared martial law in 1972 was not a commons but a plantation, namely our family's sugar plantation, the folly of our clan's stubborn reticence in a global economy that no longer rewarded the hacienda class. But I didn't say this, because I could see, even over the pixelated video call, how much you still mourned that buried river.

The last time we ever called each other, it was early 2021, a few months after the vaccines first rolled out in California, and my inoculated neighborhood buzzed with the delusion that everything was going back to normal. With an open city approaching on the horizon, we hoped that we could get our family's passion project, the Filipino martial arts gym, running again at last. Along with the rest of the world, you and Nanay made the difficult decision to close up our Midland Avenue martial arts gym in March 2020. Our family friends called you frequently to check in, wondering when the gym would reopen, and you always answered not with an estimate but with a prayer.

Sister Soon Lee, one of your favorite students and my former co-instructor at the gym, sent me a message with a link to a set of seminars that one of your former students, the one who lived in Buffalo, was conducting at his own dojo. That spring, on the twenty-third anniversary of our migration to Canada, he was relaunching his career as a martial arts teacher with a class called

AMERICANIZED ARNIS:
Is It Better than the Original Filipino Version?

"Interesting topic choice . . ." Sister Soon Lee captioned the screenshot she sent me. "Thought you'd get a kick from that."

"I'm ready to punch a motherfucker," I wrote back. Sister Soon Lee and I used to coteach with a sense of responsibility to the martial arts that you were passing down to us. At first, this former student's decision to open his own dojo felt like a violation of something sacrosanct to us as longtime practitioners and lifelong Filipinos. That student, in your long career of embodied pedagogy, was an insignificant fellow. He was one of many who had spent years training with you as a devoted student, driving across the border to visit Scarborough and learn martial arts from you, especially kuntaw, which you studied as a migrant worker in Saudi Arabia, and the style of arnis your father had taught you. I still hate that man. The thought of him stirred a maelstrom, my mind trying to claw furiously out of my body, and I dialed whatever home number I could find.

Nanay picked up, and I demanded that she put you on the phone. It must have been confusing to hear, on the other side of the line, my rage over some stupid Facebook post. I think I was expecting you to validate me. He made these trips across the Niagara Falls bridge, stayed in our home, enjoyed your private sessions at the gym, dined with the families of the other kuntawistas, and pretended that I, your son, didn't exist. This last point lingered in me. I never knew if it was because I was fat, and thus unworthy of being a martial artist, or if it was because I could always see through his bullshit. Instead, you gently, gracefully even, reminded me that the politics of Filipino martial arts was not a world that you wanted for me. What I wanted you to see was that it was a race war, the audacity of white American ex-soldiers to take upon themselves the mantle of the traditions of the savages their country colonized. What you wanted me to know was that you were a conscripted veteran of that battlefield, and that you wanted peace away from it.

I HUNG UP, and texted you a day later to apologize for my outrage. Like a true Canadian, I said sorry without feeling sorry. You accepted the apology, and assured me that of course you treated me differently: I am your flesh and blood.

I hated you for saying that.

And I held that grudge against you six months later, when I drove my Honda from LA to Boston and then to Toronto, a car which I had sacrilegiously named Hybrid Jesus, because I had adorned it with American flags and a Jesus fish magnet on the back, talismans to protect me and my driving companion from the vicissitudes of Middle America. Those talismans were in my glove compartment when I drove up to see you that September because I was neither American nor Christian anymore. The former had been a possibility, if you and Nanay had decided to move us to the United States instead of Canada. The latter, you're both still in denial about.

ON MY TWENTY-NINTH BIRTHDAY, two months after I abruptly left and drove away, after I left you and Nanay dumbfounded on the patio, you greeted me on WhatsApp. Thirty messages must have come in at the same time, and I tried to convince myself that I would answer yours after I responded to the rest of them. Above a bookstore, in my Las Vegas apartment, on my first literary fellowship, where I learned how to write a novel and where I learned how to fail at writing a novel, I ignored everyone. That night, I promised myself that I'd try to compose a response after a sushi dinner. After ten pieces of nigiri and a drive home in my rented douchebag car, a Hellcat, I didn't know what to say.

this will be the last message I send you

You texted me the day after. I deleted our chat and blocked your number, and scrambled to text everyone else. For my lateness, I apologized to everyone, and especially my homeboy Lasagna, who, to this day, somehow always knows to check in when I'm feeling like shit, even if he was a whole continent away, and even if I kept forgetting to add his number on my phone, even though he was one of the few remaining people back home with a 416 area code.

"My bad, bro," I said. "Been a hell of a week. Appreciate you."

As usual, Lasagna responded in ten seconds. In his words I could hear the gentleness of his cadence, the steady timbre of a man who offered safety.

"Say less, fam."

PART ONE

NAME

1992–2000

FOOTWORK

THE FIRST TIME WE MET, my feet were covered with fire ants. I was sitting on the ground, exploring the concrete crevices that lined our family's compound, a complex of cousins and aunties and uncles, high above the blaring Manila street. My toddler toes were still plump, the nails well groomed by my doting mother. I stretched my legs forward and moved my ankles around. The corrugated steel roof across the street glinted dully from the smoggy sky. I curved my legs inward into a fold. In single file, red dots marched from a crack in the ground under my pinky toe. Then more red dots, from other cracks, found their brethren. I watched them march between my toes and to the tops of my feet. And then a burning.

I wailed.

"*Psst*!" an uncle hissed at me. A swift, voiceless fricative, snapping like a whip. It shut me up at once. I bit my lower lip with my uneven baby teeth and rapidly sniffed to calm myself down. The ants had dug their way into my flesh, finding its delicious capillaries.

"Don't cry," the voice continued sternly. "He's about to come home."

I didn't know how to ask the voice what he meant. I rubbed the burning spots on my feet. Red dots constellating the pink streaks drawn by my fingernails. Other red dots crawling up my ankle, around the sole, into the heel. I pressed down on the fire ants and crushed them into a dark dye.

Down below from the street, footsteps gathered at the base of the stairs. The scurrying of hard wheels. The steps clamored upward, slow, methodical, labored.

"*Allah*," the voice said menacingly. "That's him now."

Ascending the stairs was a man with a military haircut and a collared shirt, its creases sharpened as if by whetstone. I had never met the military man before. I looked down at my feet again, streaked so deeply red that they looked like a bloodbath. Or a map in red ink. I tried to follow its myriad routes until a long shadow shrouded my legs in darkness. From above, I smelled the military man's approach: the musk of sweat and the cologne cloud of an acrid department store. I kept my eyes fixed on the stinging map.

From above my head, your voice.

Psst.

UNDER THE COVER of a dark November morning, in a hospital in Manila's Mandaluyong district, Nanay pushed me out into the world, surrounded by underpaid and overworked clinicians, with you on the phone, calling in from the Middle East. At 5:45 a.m., due to complications, they dug me out of her with the precision of zoologists. When the wretched child came out of the womb, I had shit myself. You loved to tell this story. I always hoped Nanay hadn't gotten infected or necrotic.

Like a melodramatic cliché from those Philippine soap operas, it might have been easy to say that you were never around. But even at that early age, I understood that your way of taking care of us was to live halfway across the world, in a compound in the Arabian Desert, the best possible place of employment for a Filipino man who needed sufficient wages to support a family in the early 1990s. Despite your pedigree as a military officer and a religious scholarship to study in Manila, your utopia of comfort—being together as a family—was just out of reach. In the aftermath of Ferdinand Marcos's dictatorship in the 1970s and 1980s, the coffers of the country were all but emptied out. All that was left to earn was abroad.

In our east Scarborough home, over Saturday brunch, you narrated your travels to Saudi Arabia as a bildungsroman: a small-town expat goes first to Manila, and then to the grander world, coming of age through a dizzying set of adventures. In Tanyag, an aunt once gifted me a travel book, and I imagined seeing the world like you did. I marveled at the Eiffel Tower, all one thousand six hundred and sixty-five steps to the top, and the Grand Canyon, a ten-mile hike to the depths of its ancient rivers. From the other room, I could hear you two murmur about saving enough so we could all see those sights together.

MIGRATION IS SO ingrained in the Filipino condition that, according to our common sense, rootlessness might be our birthright. As evidence of our coerced globalization, those of us abroad love to point out that every country in the world is bound to have within its borders a single Filipino, because the world wouldn't function without deracination. Not even those who never left the Philippines could be free from the throes of migration. Cans of Spam and corned beef, University of Toronto sweatshirts, Tim Hortons merchandise—they adorn the homebound care packages we send to our families as gifts. Even the barangay, a self-governing neighborhood in the Philippines, takes its name from a precolonial outrigger, a waterborne vessel upon which ancient chiefs, their warriors, and their clans sailed between the islands, long before a European armada landed on their shores in 1521.

But the water lily, that hitchhiker of the freshwater lake, rarely relinquishes its tendrilous grip into the sand. Nor is a dandelion, its stubbornness a homeowner's affliction, ever truly unyielding as it seeds across the summer's air. The barangay of old, no matter how itinerant, spoke the language of the shore upon which it anchored. And in those times, "the archipelago" not only signified the islands but also meant the water between the shores, long before a colonial government partitioned the country into its three official regions: Luzon, the Visayas, and Mindanao. Each island, each channel, and each outrigger—a world unto itself, constellating in the saltwater universe we now call Southeast Asia.

The first colonizers—the Catholic Church and the Spanish Empire both—could not control where our forebears stayed and went, even as they forced them to build and live in parish towns, even as they massacred the forest folk and the Chinese boatmen, even as they classified the islanders with the nomenclature of a distant peninsula. And the wealthier children of the nineteenth century, whose parents had made their money in sugar, and who would have been perfectly comfortable in the hacienda, doted upon by servants, caught the travel bug.

They, too, could not let the homeland go, and in every literary genre they could get their hands on, they penned odes to the Philippines from their travels in Europe. A deep love for country, as you know, plunges the passion-stricken patriot into the nation's death drive. The most famous uprising, the Philippine Revolution in 1896, began in part because the ophthalmologist and nationalist writer José Rizal—your other political hero, exiled from his native Luzon after his own homecoming—dared to dream of a free homeland. His execution by a Spanish firing squad, on the morning of the second-last day of the year, sparked a revolution. And across uncommon islands and languages, the archipelago's own people, in those unfinished insurrections against three centuries of occupation, mothered a country into being.

Every colonizer afterward tried to adopt, or abduct, that infant by force. The Philippine Islands, first and westernmost overseas colony of the United States from 1898 to the eve of the Second World War, a laboratory experiment for modern torture and modern medicine both. Then the Second Republic of the Philippines, the puppet state of the Japanese Empire during World War II, and the whipping boy of Yamato military discipline. And then the liberated state after 1946, an American colony in all but name, the domain of despotic families, the postcolonial parasites of the islands' riches.

The old-school nationalists might say that, like its people, the country came of age in shackles for half a century. The sympathizers might retort that those shackles were good for the nation, and the jailer and judge were benevolent actors. The whips, they'd say, taught us how to speak English, the chains taught us Western freedom, and the pistols taught us how to be obedient—all suitable behaviors for a civilized race. Others might say that the nation matured with its people, and like a kind of messiah, each Filipino carries the promise of the revolution, inside and outside of the archipelago, and swells and moves with the places that we labor into being.

For me, the Philippines exists today as a monster: a tiyanak, the reanimated body of a stillborn or abandoned child. In the forest, the tiyanak coos like an infant to lure an unsuspecting wanderer and, if it doesn't devour them immediately, chases its prey at breakneck speed. And like the tiyanak, the Philippines exists because something exhumes it from its grave and denies it rest. Even José Rizal, freshly dead from the bullet of a firing squad, was paraded around by the Americans to become the theology of the new country, the martyr whose scholarly life served as our model, the migrant who watches over all migrants. And while Rizal's reanimated spirit lures the patriot with his poems and his mythology, his corpse is bound forever to the base of a monument, an obelisk in a park by the sea, a single bronze middle finger, cursing the smoggy sky.

AS A CHILD OF an old landowning clan, you once led an opulent and worldly lifestyle, lavishly cradled in a household that imagined itself as one of the last bastions of Hispanism in the faraway boondocks of Southeast Asia. But in the 1970s, these luxuries met their end. The global sugar market crashed, draining any last viable source of income for the Tenejero branch of the clan. To make ends meet, your family's land was sold off in parcels, until only the least fertile plots were left. The house, once an elegant hacienda, began to fall to ruin. In its grand halls, Lola Isabella, once doted upon by an army of servants, was reduced to bowls of rice and ketchup for dinner.

The family's fall from grace landed them in such abject poverty that the local religious orders considered them worthy of charity. With the financial help of nuns, you left Tenejero for the bustle of Manila, arriving in the metropolis during the throes of the Marcos regime. On the television, the Philippines gleamed, a modern first-world country in a sea of communists. On the ground, in the inner-city slums where you first lived, the Philippines reeked of ruin.

You reminded me that your scholarship was meant for a degree in engineering, because you were something of a math and science whiz—an aptitude that your benefactors at the nunnery noticed. One Sunday afternoon, when I was at the cusp of becoming a teenager, after a lunch of corned beef and garlic rice, you sat me down at the dining table and pulled out a piece of Xerox paper and a pencil. In your arthritic penmanship, you drew a box.

"When I was your age," you opined, "I won a national award for designing an underground incinerator." With a twitch of eidetic memory, you filled in the box with a labyrinth of passages and devices. A chute from the top left of the box. Chambers and tubes above an open flame. An aperture for smoke, released from a chimney protruding just above the ground's surface. My eyes darted across the sheet of paper, following the tip of your pencil.

Abruptly, you placed the pencil down, and your eyes still sparkled with the magic of an entrancing memory, as if telling me how exciting it might be to become an engineer. I didn't have the heart to tell you that I didn't know what *incinerator* meant.

AT THE UNIVERSITY of Santo Tomas, one of the oldest universities in the world, even older than Harvard, you began your lifelong obsession with postsecondary education. Before I received my bachelor's degree, I visited UST on my first research grant, in the summer following my junior year, shortly after I had given up on student activism, when I decided I wanted to learn to not hate being Filipino.

For reasons I could never learn, you dropped out of UST's engineering program and moved to Adamson University, a 1930s institution founded by a Greek chemist. Then the military as a captain, and then a maelstrom: deep-sea fisherman, jeepney driver or fare collector or both, and then public servant. Your multiple sojourns, a million timelines lived.

At Adamson, you met Nanay in a graduate school classroom. She wanted to be a dancer, but she was too dark-skinned for the television and too poor to pursue a career in performance. You wanted to be a great scientist or pious pastor, too unruly for the technocracy, too impure for the priesthood. After school, Nanay had found a job as an office clerk at Sharp, the Japanese tech company with Southeast Asian frontier ambitions. After your former boss, the president, left office, your career options had worn thin. Caught between staying home with no prospects and going abroad, you submitted an application to fly to a place called Dhahran, in the dry heat of Saudi Arabia, to work for a company called Aramco. With your overseas job looming on the horizon, you quickly married. A few weeks later, you boarded a cab to Ninoy Aquino International Airport and flew west.

Nine months later, past the midnight hour, somewhere in a compound in the Arabian desert, you pressed your ear to the telephone. A sob of relief, a faint shrill wail. At the other end of the line, the sound of your wife holding your newborn son.

YOUR JOURNEY HOME from Saudi Arabia would take you from the Ninoy Aquino International Airport to the barangay of Tanyag, a neighborhood in the inland city of Taguig, just south of Manila. Cabs to Tanyag always drop you off as close as possible to the tight alleyways of Taguig, where you might have ridden something called a tricycle, a rickshaw with the side cabin, deeper into the city's passageways until not even the most compact cars could pass through without some difficulty. Sitting in a tricycle always meant crouching in the sidecar. You, unlike your siblings and your sons, were blessed with average height, and found the tiny bench more manageable than my own misadventures in tricycle rides. At the end of the commute, you'd disembark under a metal arch, painted red and white, that announces the name of the neighborhood:

BARANGAY TANYAG

The alleys were adorned with every permutation of cement. Concrete below as above, along the walls, up the steps, down to the ground beneath the makeshift shelters of corrugated metal. Storefronts packed together, sharing canopies of tarp and steel to keep them dry from the typhoons. Narrow stairs up to housing clusters in the floors above. In the absence of horizontal space, Tanyag's people built toward the sky, as far as they could go, before the floors creaked and swayed.

Almost everyone in Tanyag was a member of my maternal family. Before my grandmother and her children moved into the neighborhood in 1974, Nanay's uncle had already established roots there. He was a part of a wave of emigrants from the base of the Northern Luzon mountains, ravaged and destitute by a tanking agricultural economy. That uncle settled in Tanyag and slowly brought his family to join him.

Lola Pet had been living just west of Taguig in a municipality called Pasay. In the 1970s, her husband left the family behind to start a new one. Lola's brother offered to move her and her young family east to Tanyag. To sweeten the deal, he built them a house.

Long after we had already moved to Canada, you told me that if I saw what my childhood home looked like, I would cry out of pity. But I remember that house well, two stories and cozy rooms, built lovingly by an ancestor who wanted little else but to take care of his kin.

At sixteen years old, when I first returned to the Philippines, I saw that neighborhood and my childhood home again. It was smaller than I thought. But no less beautiful.

What Tanyag lacked in range, it more than made up for in depth. Every corner of the neighborhood held a set of surprising smells, a distinct blend every ten steps. For the first few paces when you walked past the arch, you might have smelled the gasoline from the tricycles. Further in, perhaps a tire fire or the mucky odors of deep potholes. Then the titos and titas selling some drinks and skewers, and my favorite snack, grilled quail eggs.

I craved those quail eggs, but I didn't know how to get them. I tried asking the tita down the concrete steps if I could have some of her wares. "Wala kang pera, anak?" she responded in feigned pity, waving me away: *No money, my child?*

The neighborhood kids taught me how to get money. Sometimes, taller-than-average men and women would hang around in Taguig's malls or lurk around the outskirts of the barangay. Pale as eggshells—the chicken eggs, not the speckled ones of quails. Some, like you, had specks on their face, but against a canvas-white backdrop instead of your gentle brown. My neighbors told me to watch for their pastel bags, if they had open zippers, or otherwise their thighs, if their jeans bulged at the sides. Ready-made banks on their person, ready for withdrawing.

My second technique for acquiring quail eggs was less frequent and more difficult. I'd ask Nanay to get me some when she came home—while she was still awake. I had about fifteen minutes between her return and her naptime.

Nanay loved buying me treats. Just outside of the barangay was the Burger Machine, a revered neighborhood institution, cheap and convenient nourishment for a community on the move. When she could leave work early enough, she picked me up from school and we took the jeepney back to Tanyag, but not before making a detour to the chromelike outdoor booth with diner stools and picnic tables. I clung onto her cardigan while she ordered to a disembodied voice from above. A couple of minutes later, an arm would descend from the booth and hand me a slim burger wrapped in off-white paper. I unwrapped the burger, and it oozed with a sweet nuclear-red sauce.

"Eat it quickly, anak," Nanay reminded me. "We should get home before it's dark."

I wolfed the burger down, my first bite yanking off a third of the sandwich.

"Huy! Chew your food!"

In a smog-covered city of nine million people, Tanyag was a village, close-knit because everyone was related to each other in some way. In Nanay's immediate family, I was the oldest child, so the entire barangay doted on me. The rainy season was my favorite time of the year. Whenever the canopy leaked, someone would leave out a bucket to catch the water right outside of the house. I hopped into the bucket and splashed around, waving my arms, imagining that my little vessel was the wide-open sea. After I'd had enough, Tita Cathy, Nanay's youngest sister, made sure I had dry towels waiting for me inside.

Tanyag was my first institution of higher learning. Nanay's cousin Tito Randy left me books to read. My favorite book was the dictionary, and my favorite word was *accommodate*. My fingers traced the letters as they bounced in gentle curves, occasionally punctuated by straight lines, with a Christian cross just before the end. *Accommodate*.

The neighborhood school was my second institution of learning, a modest building with a flagpole outside. Tita Pina, Nanay's cousin, taught us the wonders of the English language. Once, Tita Pina held a spelling competition. We could choose any word we liked from a dictionary and had to memorize it and then recite it in front of the class. I studied my favorite word religiously that night. The next day, the day of the spelling competition, Tita Pina asked me what word I brought to share. *Accommodate*. A, K, O, M, O, D, E, I, T. *Accommodate*.

In my only picture of Tita Pina, it is commencement season. I know this because of the foil letters hanging behind me on a white curtain. I also know this because I am wearing a white gown—my first piece of academic regalia, too big and flowy for my tiny frame, adorned with two ribbons and a leafy brooch. Nanay, the former stage performer, is beaming at the camera, and I am staring at the lens, mouth agape. Behind her, Tita Pina is speaking into the microphone.

In 2022, two days before Halloween, I texted Nanay that I had been asked to interview at Yale University. A dream job, to have the opportunity to work in the rarefied halls of the Ivy League, in a postindustrial town along the salty shores of Long Island Sound. A place teeming with books and archives, and brilliant and interesting people who would read alongside me.

"I have news of your junior kindergarten teacher in Tanyag, Tita Pina," Nanay responded. "She passed away yesterday. She had stage four breast cancer." My heart dropped.

Nanay remembered her cousin for her mirthful laughter and her love for our little family. I remembered the picture, the grin on Tita Pina's face as she announced my graduation to the audience. Tita Pina, who taught me how to study, taught me the shapes and sounds of the English language. Tita Pina, who showed me how to devote myself to the pursuit of beautiful words.

I never got to thank her.

I DON'T REMEMBER your younger face. Only synecdoches of your presence: a luggage bag, a stray photograph, starched and ironed slacks, and your feet. Always your feet. Sometimes they were adorned with fine leather oxfords, polished into a muddy mirror, or in "rubber shoes," our Manileño slang for sneakers. I'm certain that you often wore slippers, but your visits were so short that I could never have imagined you inside our house, let alone walking around with exposed toes.

Only once, in those early years, did I catch a glimpse of your bare feet. It was a cloudy weekend, at the precipice of rainy season. You asked me to follow you around the back of our lot to a sturdy ladder of two-by-fours nailed together by a skilled craftsperson. "Stay right behind me," you warned, and stepped onto the ladder.

I wrapped my hands around the rung directly underneath your heel, trying to avoid the mud marks left behind by your sneakers. Tied to your back was a long fabric case with a Velcro top, the contents of which I had never seen. We climbed to the very top of our compound, a concrete roof that miraculously never caved into itself. You hoisted yourself onto the platform and pulled me up from behind you.

Until I climbed the compound that day, my sense of Manila stopped at the edge of the barangay. Atop the roof, I could see the towering concrete and glass north of Taguig, in Manila's commercial districts. A gray and orange haze intermittently covered the blue sky, wrapping around the skyscrapers, beyond which was the muck of the South China Sea.

"It's time for you to learn how to fight, anak."

The sticky wind blew frigid. Here, high above our slice of the city, I would have to fight *you*?

"No, we're not going to fight each other!" you guffawed, more so at my relief that I wasn't actually going to have to size up a gigantic man three times my height. "I'll teach you how fighting *works*."

You bent down and untied your sneakers. I looked at my own feet, still gentle and plump from toddlerhood, and my eyes followed your newly exposed digits. Your big toes bent in an acute angle, and the others seemed to follow no logic. Like me, you had flat feet, no curve. Along the edges of your soles, calluses that had crystallized into an impenetrable layer. Scars and the remnants of old bruises speckled the tops of your extremities. I felt ashamed of the softness of my body, compared to your toes, each of which seemed to keep an archive of a difficult life.

You took off the crossbody strap and opened the flap of the fabric case. Two rattan sticks slid out. You gave me one to hold. My tiny fingers just barely wrapped around it. I gripped the stick as tightly as I could. It wobbled out of balance.

"This is called *kali*. This one is made of wood, and it's how Filipino martial artists first learn how to use weapons."

To support the heavy stick, I held on to the middle with my left hand.

"*Psst,*" you reprimanded me, and smacked my hands. I flinched and dropped the stick. You picked it back up.

"Ay, naku. No. Even though the stick is made of wood, imagine it's a blade. A sword. You can't hold a sword by the middle. You'll cut yourself."

You learned how to use sticks from your father, Lolo Malaya, a village patriarch in the Bataan Peninsula. Malaya was a fighter—Ingkong, they called him, meaning "great master"—and was known for being pedagogical and violent in equal measure. Everywhere Lolo Malaya went, he was armed with a bolo, a machete he forged himself. At the river's edge, you and your father practiced combat techniques together. You practiced without shoes, your feet sliding against the wet earth, repeating the choreography until perfect. When you fucked up, Lolo unsheathed his blade and chased you home.

On the rooftops of our Taguig compound, it was my turn to inherit your father's techniques. We faced each other, feet shoulder width apart, rattan stick in right hand, left hand open, its outer edge rested atop the other end of the pretend-blade.

Then left foot forward, right hand and stick cocked at the hip. Left hand open close to the chest, to guard the body from any incoming attack. I held my hand against my body, clutching my shirt.

"No, no." You pulled my hand forward until it was a foot away from my chest. "Keep your fingers pressed against each other, as few weaknesses as possible."

Step forward with the right foot and strike the opponent's left temple. My wobbly stick could only reach your shoulder. You mirrored me, stepping backward, meeting my swing with yours.

One!

Step forward with the left foot, bringing the fighting arm above the left shoulder, then backhand, striking the enemy's right temple. Again, you mirrored my strike, blocking the swing with your weapon.

Two!

Forward with the right foot, right arm cocked again around the left shoulder, then striking the opponent's right shin. I could reach your shin this time, but you responded with another block.

Three!

And for the fourth step, a quick jump, switching the feet around, so that the left foot is back up front. The right arm swings above the head and targets the left shin. You block this strike, following my footwork with a swift hop more elegant than my clumsy attempt.

Four!

"And that's the first four moves!" you beamed. "There's twelve altogether, but that's for another lesson." I handed you my stick. You slid the weapons back into their sheath and ruffled my hair. I shut my eyes.

On that roof, you told me that I should always practice, even if it were only those four moves, because one day, I might be the one teaching my own kids. From the bottom of the ladder, Nanay hollered at us, kain na tayo, because dinner was ready, and if we delayed any longer, it'd get cold and the neighborhood would finish it before us. Down the rungs, I asked you if your mother, Lola Isabella, supported your learning how to use weapons from Lolo Malaya, and you grunted something half-hearted about how grateful you were that she always took care of you. For a moment, you floated away into another time and looked up at the roof, suspended midclimb. You winced yourself back into the present. At last, on the descent, my flip-flops slapped against bare concrete, and I changed the topic.

"When will I learn the other eight moves, Tatay?"

"I'll teach you the whole thing when we finally live together, anak."

ABROAD, YOU GAINED access to incomes that would never have been available if you had stayed home. Through your combined salaries, I was moved from my neighborhood school—little more than a concrete warehouse—and enrolled in a fancy new private school.

Every morning, as a four-year-old, I walked from our flood-proof compound down to a pothole-ridden street, past the storefronts and street vendors, until I reached the colorful arch at the end of the barrio. There, I waited for a red bus to pick me up along with other young pupils on its rounds, until we reached the shiny edifice of St. James College of Parañaque.

St. James was a rarefied space, fanciful with the money it flaunted from new donors, which meant that new wings on campus were almost always under construction. As a kid from Tanyag, I was one of the charity cases, the kids on the red bus, who were shuttled to the school gates from the city's back alleys. My fellow red-bus kids must have come from other neighborhoods like mine. But I never knew, because we could never see outside in the rocking of the windowless vehicle. So instead, we stared down at our knees.

When you lived in Saudi Arabia, you would send back two kinds of remittances: financial aid, and the photographs and medals that you earned in your competitions. While I never saw the remittance receipts, I noticed Nanay's growing collection of portraits from the Middle East. Since you were abroad when I was born, my first pictures of you were in a martial arts uniform, heel raised, about to strike at your opponent's chin. Nanay kept them all and, in exchange, sent pictures of me with love notes on the back.

Your wanderlust was infectious. Ate Rose, your niece, bought me a shiny new present: a children's SUV that I could pedal like a bicycle. In my new mini-Humvee, I pedaled into the street. I swerved around the potholes, brown ponds brimming with rainwater and sewage, and drove to the end of the barangay. The river of cars was still a trickle, maybe one or two vehicles at once. I turned into the street to join. I must have been doing something right, I thought. The drivers behind me were honking. I honked, too, a squeak from the horn on my wheel.

"*Huy*! *Huuuuuy*!" In the distance, a familiar man was running toward me.

In my next memory, I was sitting on our living room floor, my feet touching together, my knees butterflying out. I was playing with my toes again, and in my peripheral vision, a larger pair of feet. I could feel the man glaring at me from above. Fatherlike, but not you; the aura of Nanay's brother.

Despite my shame, I came to crave that taste: Manila's streets, the world between and beyond my barangay and my school, no concrete walls to cover my view.

I wanted to leave home.

One day, an amusement park came to St. James. A towering Ferris wheel and a two-minute roller coaster replaced the picnic benches in the courtyard. We were supposed to spend our recess periods enjoying the rides with our class. But we hadn't even made it past the first period when a boom outside rattled our desks. I couldn't move. Minutes later, my teacher was waving at me to stand up and follow her. "Look down. Keep your shirt over your nose." The ceiling started to crumble, and I kept following the teacher's feet, past the soot and the burnt black flakes on the ground, until we reached the courtyard.

Sometime after the fire, you came home again. I still remember your dazzling smile, announcing that it would be the last time you'd have to return home. "We'll be leaving here soon, anak." Your brow furrowed. I think I was crying. "A better home is waiting for us. We'll be going to Cah-Nah-Dah."

I ran back into my room and grabbed the encyclopedia. Cah-Nah-Dah. *Canada*. Mountains capped with a brilliant white ice, lakes as blue as the water bodies in cartoons, cornfields, a big concrete penis that prodded the sky. And on the eastern part of the country's map, a large swath of land in the shape of a flu-ridden dog's head. The eyes, nose, and dripping snot were called New-Found-Land and Labrador. The rest of the skull, *Kwee-Beck*.

"That's Kueh-Back, anak, so we'll need to learn how to speak French!" Nanay exclaimed, peering over my shoulder. I asked her what *prents* was. "French, French. Frawn-sayze. *Français*. Zhu-zhu-zhu!" she imitated, in jocular fricatives, *zhu-zhu-zhu*. I joined in, and we pretended to be cosmopolitan francophones. *Zhu-zhu-zhu*.

THE NIGHT BEFORE we left for good, my feet began to itch. I dreamed that the great brown sea beyond the bay was gasoline. It stung my feet, callused and bent out of shape. Your voice, panicked: "Keep running," you say. "Tumakbo ka, anak. Run away, my child. Takbo. Run."

When I awoke, my feet were on fire again. Climbing my toes, a cockroach. I froze. In the early morning blear, the cockroach and I stared each other down. It wiggled its antennae, almost a shrug, almost a nod, and crawled down to the floor, not to be seen again.

From between the blinds, the first stray bits of sunlight caressed my feet. Downstairs, a hasty rustling. It was time to leave.

FLIGHT PATHS

IN THE BOOK PAGES sprawled across my Tanyag bedroom floor, the ocean was a blue lake on a map. It seemed small and tame on paper. Two decades later, when I lived in Hawai'i, I learned that our Austronesian ancestors navigated the boundless seas on outriggers, using a rich and vast knowledge of the stars. The sea is a giant duvet: it smothers you if you don't fold yourself along its soft edges, it blankets you with life-giving fish, it buries you within its trenches, it bubbles your final breath.

We continue that tradition, even if that stargazing is replaced with schedules and travel points. From the discomfort of the skies, the sublime and frightening magic of the ocean is gone. In its place, a small airplane window, a portal to water's ephemeral state.

In May 1998, at the precipice of the long tropical rainy season, we left the Philippines for good. I was only five and a half but can still remember the first few hours of that journey with the clarity of a chronicler. We arrived at Ninoy Aquino International Airport, named after a senator who, just fifteen years prior, was assassinated on the tarmac. I knew none of this history, of course. All I knew was, once we were past customs, there was no turning back to the city I had once called my home.

The first leg took us to Hong Kong, a brief two-hour flight to a metropolis that, in many ways, mirrored Manila. Like the Philippine capital, the former British colony spread out across a bay along the South China Sea (or West Philippine Sea, depending whom you ask). At the airport, we stopped at an Italian restaurant and ordered a large plate of spaghetti with diluted red sauce. I dug around to find my favorite part, the diagonally sliced morsels of hot dog that adorned the Filipino version of the dish. Instead, the plate offered me gray-brown orbs of ground beef. I poked at them, and they quickly fell apart.

"Those are meatballs, anak," Nanay reassured me. "You'll have plenty of those in your new home."

I hated the meatballs. They didn't have the same satisfying crunch of a hot dog. The red sauce, I was told, was made of tomatoes, not like the sweet nuclear-red banana ketchup that we used at home. But the noodles, long and al dente, transcended the glutinous Jollibee version.

Then I was on a flight to Vancouver. We spiraled up above the clouds. A blonde woman approached me and asked what I'd like for breakfast. "Eggs!" you exclaimed, remembering my favorite food. The flight attendant arrived with some wrinkly yellow rubber, steaming out of a rectangular plastic plate.

Half a day later, we landed at Toronto's Pearson International Airport, in a strange and cold land called Cah-Nah-Dah. Ninang, a godmother I had never met, had come to pick us up. We loaded our bags into her sedan, and Ninang wound through a rainstorm into the city's east end, an assemblage of low-rises and strip malls called Scarborough.

Shortly after we unloaded our belongings, we huddled together in an unfurnished basement that we would call home. Here, underneath the earth, wrapped in a pile of animal-print blankets, I felt cold to my bones.

Ninang's house was a "semi-detached" property, popular in Toronto's post–World War II period for their cheapness to build. The lot was split right along the connecting wall. I learned this because I accidentally walked into the neighbor's place, thinking the door was Ninang's. Inside, gingerly stepping through its uncluttered hallways, I snuck into a fully furnished basement. From the darkness, a child stared back at me, pale as a sheet.

AFTER NINANG'S BASEMENT, we jumped around between other basements and spare bedrooms, some colder and dustier than others, in an effort to find a place to call our own. I can only remember a couple of them. There was the public housing high-rise above a squeaky railroad track, overlooking the chrome complex that was the Lawrence East train station. Some other relatives who weren't really relatives housed us, their faces now eluding me, but I remember the massive bed, the one with the canopy over it, the regal drapes at the four edges, and the view of the train tracks and the Lawrence Avenue overpass. From south of the bridge, four pillars around my newfound nest, I felt like a king.

After the bedroom above Lawrence East, we moved into a jaundiced basement apartment on Scarborough's Danzig Street, an enclave of quiet bungalows and public housing. Compared to the concrete Tanyag compound, Danzig was amazing. There were trees—every house had at least two standing tall in the yard. There were yards. Each yard boasted an expanse of grass, verdant sod that neatly tapered away in garden plots. There were gardens. The residential streets had a single car pass by every minute, and they steered clear if the neighborhood kids swatted their street hockey balls too far out. Across Morningside Avenue, the main corridor that Danzig feeds into, there was a basketball court, improvised out of the concrete of an abandoned lot. And to the south, past the convenience store, across the train tracks, the aquamarine waters of the Leading Sea.

St. Martin de Porres, the local school to the north, began as a brief footnote, a few months at the tail-end of a school year, before it became the epicenter of my preadolescent life. I remember precious few moments: the classroom sandbox, the eggshell-white hallways, the faded pink tiles, the semicircular sink with the pedal, the strange porcelain rectangles along the walls, the Canadian boys skillfully aiming their piss at them, the drenched jeans, the ammonia-scented walk of shame at the end of the day.

IN OUR TINY new apartment, with a calling card to the United States, you dialed a 619 area code. That call opened a channel between Scarborough and San Diego that would irreversibly change our families for the next twenty years.

A few hours later, you finally hung up. "You have a new Lolo, anak."

In your stories about your tatay, Lolo Malaya, the mysterious guerrilla fighter from the Bataan Peninsula, was a man of legend:

a survivor of the Bataan Death March, a patriarch to the village, a prodigious fighter. He had died long before I was born, with a hint of a smile after you forgave him on his deathbed. I wondered if his estranged widow, your mother, had remarried.

It was your longtime dream to start a martial arts club, you said, should you have the opportunity to start a new life with your family. Now that we had moved to North America, it was time to make it happen. You told me whom you'd called: the founder of a martial art called kuntaw, your favorite combat style, which you learned in the Middle East. You asked him for permission to teach his techniques in Scarborough, and he gave it to you.

"That's your Lolo Kuntaw," you said.

He was the father you never had. A surrogate grandfather when my direct ancestors were either estranged or dead. Lolo *Kuntaw* because he and his martial arts inheritance were one and the same. A few days a month, you'd sprawl out on the couch, the receiver to your ear, grinning like a born-again son.

WHEN I TELL my students in my Asian American history classes about our family lore, especially when my Canadianness baffles their nationalism, especially when I mention how often you'd drop Arabic phrases into your everyday lingo, I lecture about kuntaw. Like my students' own family histories, ours is a story of labor migration.

On the weekdays in Dhahran, I tell them, you fixed airplanes, and during the weekends, your own body would take flight. Your opponents couldn't do much but watch as you soared six feet into the air before your jump kick sent them suddenly collapsing to the ground. I imagine the masterful rotation of your hips, summoning the momentum into a spinning back kick, your starched white top and red pants whipping the air, a loud *snap* before the *thud*, your heel on your opponent's chest—or face. In Scarborough, you'd teach me that style, the Tagalog martial art of sikaran. The flavor of tae kwon do's kicks, but pummeling the opponent at close range. In the Saudi Arabian circuits, as an honored black belt in sikaran, you were a champion.

It was one fight, you tell me, that changed the course of your practice forever. The opponent, also a young Filipino man, wore a red and white outfit, much like your own. But that's where the similarities ended. In sikaran, the fighting position was loose and springy, ready to leap at a moment's notice. Across the ring, the other man anchored himself into a deeper stance: his legs were spread further apart, his feet perpendicular to each other, and his knees bent lower. His hands stayed close to his body, one open-palmed into the shape of a knife, parallel to his front leg. The other curled into a fist, tucked away below his right breast, hidden from plain view.

"I fell in love with kuntaw when I beat my opponent, a kuntawista," you boasted.

It was a close match. You swiveled out of the kuntawista's line of attack and dug your heel into his chest. You won the fight, you'd remind me for the tenth time. But something about that man's movements enchanted you. His punches were swift and precise, and his blocks could switch from brute-force strikes to graceful and circular parries. Despite the sturdy bend in his knees, his stance was deceptively light, and he could sweep the opponent to the ground at a moment's notice. Economical and graceful. Hard and soft, at the same time.

After the fight, the soaring kicker approached the grounded puncher. "What style was that?" you asked him, offering your hand.

"Kuntaw," the other responded proudly, returning the handshake. "I'd love to teach you."

Unlike sikaran, kuntaw is grounded. Patient. Not qualities that you had developed naturally as a child in Bataan or as a soldier in the Philippine military. You welcomed the challenge. In a few short years, you pivoted to kuntaw and earned a black belt. From that point on, after a voracious sojourn across different styles, you became a devoted kuntawista. That martial art, an obscure practice from the Southern Philippines, became your primary craft, trading high-flying kicks for economical and practical movements, open palms and sturdy stance when in defense, closed fists, a barrage of punches, low kicks.

Despite your prodigious rise to the top, there was no chance for you to open a studio in Saudi Arabia. The labor compound in

Dhahran was a caste system, with white Europeans and Americans and Arab technocrats on top, and the vast array of migrant workers at the bottom: Indians, Filipinos, East Africans. You came to Saudi Arabia with two degrees and could only get as high up as aircraft mechanic. You considered going back to the Philippines, where, like millions of others before, you and Nanay could make a bid to go to the United States—perhaps Chicago, where your brother lived, or California, where all the Filipino Americans were. Your boss, a thickly accented blond Swedish man named Anders, convinced you to go to Canada instead. Universal healthcare and cheaper housing, even if it was colder than the deserts or the rice paddies. There, he said, you could raise your child, build a life, and one day open a dojo of your own.

You took the Swedish man's advice. An immigration application to Canada would be easier, because you and Nanay would both come in with degrees and international recommendations. Each signature was a brain drain. After saving money in Saudi Arabia, you resolved to chase your dream to open a gym, and be with your family for good.

You told me about the Swede only once. When my youngest brother was about to be born, I suggested the name Anthony, after the dashing singer Marc Anthony, with whom I was enamored every time he appeared on the TV. You vetoed my name suggestion in favor of a Swedish name, after your former boss in Saudi Arabia, the man who brought us to Canada.

WHEN I CAME home from St. Martin's, an L-shaped brownstone building next to the neighborhood church, you'd sit at the dining table, filling out stacks of forms to submit to the government. Nanay told me that the gym would be registered as a small business. I nodded along, pretending I knew what *registration* and *business* meant. For the forms, you had to pick a name for the club. At the time, you spent your nights packing boxes for Zellers, a Canadian department store, whose distribution center was wedged underneath a freeway overpass.

Once, you came home smelling like the stale gasoline of a jalopy. I thought it was from a rough shift at Zellers, until you brought me outside to meet a faded brown station wagon that, in the wrong light, looked like a hearse. I called that hearse Monster, because it was the biggest car I'd ever been inside. After a couple of key turns, Monster roared to life. We turned left on the stoplight at Morningside Avenue, a north-south road that ended at a fenced-in ravine at the edge of the Leading Sea. Then north, past the church and the school, past an imposing brown edifice emblazoned with MORNINGSIDE MALL in rounded yellow font. Further up, the suburban streets gave way to a breathtaking valley, a deep fissure in the landscape that reminded us that our houses were on top of a cliffside. At the bottom of the valley, we turned left onto a gravel road, winding through the thick trees lined with tall dog-strangling vines, until we found the parking lots at the edge of a wide field. Dotting the meadows were picnic tables and rusted grills for families to use.

You backed up into a parking spot next to the grass and opened the hatch. Inside, a familiar slender fabric rectangle, a flap Velcroed to the top to keep it shut. Two rattan sticks slid out—the same kali you had used to train me on the rooftops of Tanyag, when you came to visit from Saudi Arabia. My fingers were still too small to grab the stick. I had to hold it an inch above the base, but my wrist wobbled from the imbalance. "Don't sacrifice proper technique," you reprimanded me. It would build strength in my wrists, and when my grip wasn't flimsy anymore, I would be a full-fledged kali fighter.

At the park, you taught me the last eight of the twelve strikes we started in Manila. I still remembered the first four, to the left and right temple, and then to the sides of the legs. After the tame precision of the first four strikes, the other eight techniques were gorier. The fifth strike was to the left shoulder blade, a vertical slice from above my head. The sixth strike was a stab to the torso, thrust into the opponent's body with full force, and the seventh was a backhanded wide slice across the neck. For the eighth strike, a wide cut along the torso, from left shoulder to right hip. Number nine was backhanded again, bent low, to target the shins. For ten, a two-handed upward slice, cleanly along the torso from left hip to right shoulder. Number eleven was a two-handed swing to the temple, followed by the last strike: a powerful thrust into the enemy's stomach.

With each of my swings, you conjured a response, matching each bloody slice with a gentle block. Against the ninth strike, when you couldn't bend down to stop the swing, you jumped. I was entranced. I wanted to learn those moves.

"I'll teach you the defenses when I promote you to yellow belt," you assured me.

"Does that mean I'm a white belt right now?" I asked breathlessly.

"It does. We'll get you a full uniform when we can afford it, anak."

WHEN THE WEEKEND weather was bad, or when you had energy after work, you'd clear out our basement living room so we could practice downstairs. "No kali in the house!" Nanay insisted, our ceilings too low for us to safely swing our sticks. Your compromise was that you'd teach me a martial art that didn't need very much space to practice. I remember our first lesson well. Feet shoulder width apart. Fists closed, hands extended, parallel to the toes. "Humanda sa pagpupugay," you'd say, towering over me. Ready for bowing. "Pugay, ta!" Bring left foot beside the right, drop the left hand to the side, right hand open and placed atop the left breast. Open back up again to ready stance. For the next hour, after a quick warmup, I practiced kuntaw.

My kuntaw lessons were markedly different from my armed fighting classes. A different philosophy altogether, punctuated not by immediate combat but instead by a practitioner's relationship to history. Without a physical archive, we martial artists are the carriers of our cultural history, writing the past anew with every performance. Instead of written documents, we tell our stories through anyo, or what Okinawan karate calls kata, or form: a series of movements that rehearse a fight scenario, carried out with perfect poise, delivered as a repertoire from memory. Every rudimentary anyo introduces the hard and soft variations of each movement we do. Through anyo, we learn stance and balance, strikes and blocks, and the logic of how we should move in combat. A set choreography of patterns that is supposed to synchronize us, each offering the same lessons to our body and mind, until we could move together across space and time. As if we could aspire to face the same way, deliver the same movements, regardless of language and region. As if we could dream up an archipelago of anyo.

From ready stance, move your left foot forward to left forward stance, left hard downward block. Next, bring your left foot back to a back stance, right hard inside block. Shift to a right forward stance, left-right double punch. Then left frontal kick, landing on left forward stance, lunge punch, with a sound off—kiai!

These movements make up the initial sequence of the inelegantly named X-Form, the first of over fifty anyo that the kuntawista learns over the course of their career. Students go through great pains—and frustrations—to learn this sequence, since it demands a certain patience with themselves. The learner stretches their capabilities, reorienting for themselves what it means to maintain balance when each stance demands that you shift your body weight at a moment's notice. The other sequences become more difficult, all the way up to the last one, when your legs are crouching like a cat—literally, tayong pusa, or cat stance. The feet stand closer together, left foot on tiptoe, and left hand mimicking a knife shape and later a chicken beak.

But that patience pays off. To close out the anyo, the performer launches from the cat stance into a sturdy left forward stance and downward chop, to the side of the imagined opponent's neck. This move is followed by a right elbow to the enemy's face, then a right knee that knocks them down to the floor. Finally, the finishing move: a punch to the opponent's gut, when they are already flat on the ground.

The pummeling brutality of X-Form has a twin, clumsily named X-B-Form, which you assured you would teach me after I earned my yellow belt. Unlike its ironlike sibling, X-B-Form opens its blocks from clenched fists to outstretched palms, quick jabs to circular movements. Here, in X-B-Form, brute force gives way to grace and flow, the water to X-Form's metal. Hard and soft ways.

When I finally mastered X-Form, you and Nanay surprised me with a gift: a matching pair of white trousers and a gown, to be tied diagonally at the hip, and a white belt. You taught me how to tie it: one foot hanging off of the left side of the waist, kept in place by the left hand. Wrap the belt around twice, and once the other end is in front, let the hanging side loose, and adjust them until they're even. Loop the outer end underneath the belt and tie them tight. I think you did this for me, because my hands could hardly grasp at the dense fabric with enough grip.

"I have another surprise for you." From the bag, you produced another belt—a yellow belt made of the same cloth of my white belt, but with a sheen that gleamed dully in the jaundiced basement light. "This is your promotion day."

There is a ritual that accompanies every promotion. It is not my story to tell. What I will say is that after I stood up, yellow belt around my waist, white belt scattered loosely on the ground in front of me, a part of my body stung from pain. At the tender age of six, in the low ceilings of our Danzig dwelling, I became a real martial artist.

DISSATISFIED WITH OUR solitary training, you signed me up for a weekend karate class at the community center. I would finally be around other kids who had been studying martial arts, but in a style not my own. "Stick to your kuntaw training," you reassured me. "They'll try to make you bow in the Japanese way. Do the pugay instead."

At the community center, I felt underdressed. The other students had sharper uniforms, made of red and black fabric, flashier than my all-white attire. We stood in single file along the walls of the gym, and the master, standing in the middle, stood at ready stance. Except his ready stance was off. His feet were shoulder width apart, but his hands were extended further out toward the sides of his body. The students followed suit, and I instinctively copied them. At the corner of the gym, you glared at me. I readjusted my stance to the familiar kuntaw one.

"Sensei ni rei!" the instructor cried out. The students brought their feet together in one sharp movement, a *snap* echoing in the gym. They bowed deep. *Osu*. I rushed through my kuntaw bow in shame. The student next to me looked at me like I was a foreigner.

Some of the techniques in the karate class matched my own, at least at the basic level. The straight punches were the same, as were the frontal and side kicks. But that's where the similarities ended. They had a technique called the Tiger Claw Punch, where your palms are open but your fingers are curled in. I wasn't sure if I was supposed to strike with my knuckles or my palm, which would be, technically, not a punch. The sensei adjusted our hands into place and forced my fingers apart. We should never spread our fingers apart, you taught me, because an opponent could twist them out of place.

I went to only a couple of sessions at the community center before you pulled me out. The language might have been too foreign for you, too.

PUNCTUM

IN ONE OF MY most treasured photographs of us, our legs are raised in two different ways. I am delivering a snap kick, the ball and heel of my right foot at a ninety-degree angle to the ground, the two impact points at my imagined opponent, the camera.

Your technique, a side kick: left leg raised, and right before you extend forward, your hips turn right. The foot angles inward, its outer edge making the shape of a blade.

Balong stands in between us, the patriarch's facsimile, mimicking your side kick, hips twisted to maximize the surface area of his tiny feet. Behind us, our trophies glisten in the living room light, hard-won at a martial arts tournament from which we had just come home.

In *Camera Lucida*, his reflection on photography and grief, the French philosopher Roland Barthes identifies two ways that we make meaning when we look at images. The studium includes the most obvious signifiers of a picture. In my photograph, it might be the hypermasculinity of the image: the trophies, a father and his two sons, a gesture of combat. Perhaps it might also be the class signifiers of the living room: outdated floral furniture, a faded brass mirror, a ten-dollar Ikea lamp.

By contrast, the punctum is an element of the image that speaks for itself, without any analytical context. It pierces the viewer, almost like a force of nature, reaching from the past moment of the photograph to the present. Before you know it, the punctum envelops the entire image, until it becomes difficult to think about it in any other way.

My punctum—that which punctures me in this image—isn't your kick. The side kick pushes away the opponent, who might stumble and fall, or recover and run away. By contrast, the frontal snap kick knocks someone *down*. I know this, because I have known this feeling since I was thirteen years old.

In this image, my punctum is my smile. Everyone I've shown this photo to, without fail, has remarked on how cute we look. Underneath my unkempt hair, I wear a goofy grin that stretches my lips into a thin line across my plump cheeks. I am struggling with my weight. I am also trying to fix my face. I remember feeling like a disappointment. My best guess is that the smallest trophy, second from the bottom right, was mine. No goblet on top, just a skinny pillar wrapped in cheap multicolored foil. It was nowhere near the many accolades that you had brought over from Saudi Arabia, long before you materialized as my Canadian father.

MY LAST MEMORY of the Danzig apartment is a scar on my right leg. You had just signed a lease all the way on the other side of the city, in a brownstone mixed-income mid-rise across from Scarborough's northernmost hospital. We'll love our new area, Nanay reassured me. Until our move, we should say our final goodbyes to the neighborhood, you concur. None of us knew that, in four years, this southeastern suburb would pull us back home for good.

A late summer, when late summers stuck to your skin like film. Humid, not searing. Water balloon weather, rubber Molotovs that detonate on unshorn lawns. Nanay had prepared a fried tilapia in tinfoil, and a Tupperware of soy sauce and a spritz of concentrated kalamansi juice from the ethnic grocery aisle at the No Frills. In a reused yellow plastic bag, you carried three bottles of water, a tub of steamed white rice, a Ziploc of pico de gallo, mistakenly mixed with red onions instead of the traditional white. I only had to bring our spare blanket, a discounted perk from your Zellers job.

On Morningside Avenue, if you walk down five blocks from Danzig Street, the land drops at a razor's edge. Down the first block, a church and a strip mall compete for traffic, neon lights trying to drown out the old-fashioned bold font. The strip mall, too, waged its own civil war. In the southernmost storefront was Joe's Convenience, the Goliath of corner stores, where at twelve years old I would bum my first cigarette. Over the years, the eponymous Joe (no one knew the man's real name) filled every inch of the glass with signs for sales, and kept them up long after the terms had expired.

But not to be outshone, the more modest Sunny Variety, run by a Korean woman the neighborhood kids called Sunny, boasted a well-organized pantry with an abundant stock of Freezies. Soon enough, Joe caught on and stocked his own shelves with chocolate-covered Drumsticks.

Two blocks south of the cold dessert arms race, a train track bisected the land. Past the tracks, the houses tripled in size and halved in average occupancy, the biggest mansions pressing themselves as far south as possible, away from the rabble, monopolizing the Leading Sea. Where Morningside ended, a boundary, reinforced with loosely corrugated steel, lazily barred our access from a well-lit woodsy clearing, past which another fence of cross-hatched metal, with a half-open gate, led into a dark ravine.

It wasn't until the forest path sloped down, and the greenish blue of the sea came into view, that I winced. My knee had scraped against the corrugated metal, puncturing the thin denim, the blood hardly visible through the dark dye. The wound burned. I limped down after you two, watching to make sure you didn't turn around and catch me in pain, downhill, deep into the winding path etched along the bluffs, onto a stretch of white sand. "Spread the blanket out, anak," Nanay said as she unpacked her food, and you took off your sandals and gingerly stepped over to the water. Nanay followed suit, and you two bent down in synchrony and washed your hands in the lake.

For two hours, on that empty beach, we made believe that we were home. Nanay raised the tilapia from its aluminum blanket, the freshwater turquoise in the backdrop, like she'd just snagged a catch from a Pasig River long gone. You pretended that the soy sauce, hinted with kalamansi, tasted like Tenejero's brackish waters, just a bit sourer. I squatted on the sand, still nursing the cut on my leg, and for an ephemeral moment, I wasn't there. It was a date that you two wished you could have had in Manila, had a dictator not plundered our city of everything you loved, had there been no secrets between you two, had not the Arabian Desert, which stretched the sinews of our family to its most gossamer threads, lured you away to make the money we needed to survive.

I don't remember how we got home. Did you carry me up the steep path, between the oaks, past the gap in the woods, through the gate, over the offending steel? Did I hobble up Morningside Avenue, the west side of the street, never the east, because you were too scared of the ghetto, even if we lived on the next block and we'd move to that side of the street in a few years? Or did we take the bus, the smoky guzzlers with the rounded tops, four steps up the door, and crusty seats? Did you hoist me up and pay my fare?

At night, one of the last ones we'd spend in that basement with the jaundiced walls, it must have been three in the morning when I rolled to the edge of the floor mattress and I came to. Beside my lamp, an opened tube of antibiotic ointment. On my knee, a dully glistening clear film, numbing the throbbing pain I tried to wish away.

A MONTH AFTER I started first grade, still at the school where I had once infamously pissed myself, you pulled me out of class and picked me up in a U-Haul truck. Nanay was already in the passenger's seat, but she stepped out and I sat in between you two. Over the next hour, we made our own northwest passage, to Scarborough's opposite end, where, you said, we'd be surrounded by more Asians. For all my bladder's unruliness, I had never felt out of place as a Filipino at St. Martin's, even if my English was still atrocious. Even then, I doubted that a new school would have urinals that I understood.

In the U-Haul, we drove north along Morningside, past the mall into the stretch of avenue that bisected the Rouge Valley, turning into the cloverleaf to go westbound on the 401 freeway. While you steered, Nanay unfolded a pamphlet she'd bought at the Ministry of Transportation, a detailed map of the entire City of Toronto, all six boroughs, and fringes of the hinterlands outside of the 416 area code. She pointed out where we'd turned in—Morningside Avenue just north of a street called Military Trail—and I clung to her to keep myself upright in the g-force of the cloverleaf turn. You stomped on the pedal and the engine roared, and the truck rattled with the weight of the little life we carried in it: our clothes, the second-hand dining table, and the mattress we laid out on the ground. Scarborough's landmarks blurred past us: a forest-green Rainforest Café next to the Famous Players theater, a massive white plastic dome with the words METRO GOLF, the freight trucks that lined your workplace. At the Kennedy Road exit, just north of a beige building whose red sign declared it a Chapters bookstore, you veered right and drove north to Finch Avenue, which hardly looked any different from the city's southeast, except that there were more signs in nonromanized scripts. In the same block, Devanagari competed with traditional Chinese and Tamil, with the occasional Cyrillic or Hangul. "We're almost home," you grinned, dropping the window and turning the radio volume up, Delilah's sultry voice announcing the Barenaked Ladies. You had done your studying—you reminded me that the band was formed right here, in Scarborough, Ontario.

After half a year of jumping between basements and spare bedrooms, we'd finally landed our very first real apartment, a fourth-floor unit in a brown public housing complex along Scarborough's Silver Springs Boulevard. I always thought that Silver Springs was an idyllic place. Whenever we'd walk home, we would take the long way around, strolling through an orchard of boysenberry trees and snacking on bounteous fruits before stepping into the building. Each floor boasted the scents of myriad spice blends, or the grilling aromas of different kinds of fish. Down the street, a couple of blocks from the hospital where Balong would be born, was a plaza with every culinary necessity imaginable for the Tamil, Filipino, and Cantonese families in the area. In the basement of the plaza, an elder sold Pocky sticks and Sky Flakes crackers between VHS rentals of Filipino melodramas from the 1970s and '80s, at the height of martial law.

Almost every piece of furniture in that Silver Springs apartment was financed. I know this because I learned as a kid to hate Leon's, a Canadian furniture company. Having been lured by the flashy Leon's commercials (not to mention how similar the name was to our own), you and Nanay put in an application to finance their furniture. But without sufficient Canadian credit history, the company rejected us.

A week later, you two returned home, beaming and professing your love for the rival furniture company, the Brick. *Nobody Beats the Brick!* the commercial proclaimed—as did we, its newest customers, its newest citizens. Triumphantly, you declared that, from here on in, our hatred for Leon's would know no bounds. Our genealogy would furnish itself with the wares of the Brick, which, in its Canadian goodness, welcomed us with open arms. From now until our clan's dying days, every time we drive by a Leon's, we would jeer at the evil furniture overlords behind its lemon-yellow sign.

To this day, every time I visit Toronto and pass a Leon's, I can't help but yell out a *boo*. Instead of blowing a raspberry, I flip my middle finger out at the logo. As a ritual, this Ten Seconds of Hate had become a moment of warmth through which we, ardent devotees of the Brick, could reaffirm our worship. And how much of a pedagogy of Canadianness this was, to relate to my settlement through the arbitrary love or hatred of a corporation that didn't give two fucks about us. I never asked you what interest rates the Brick offered us.

In 2012, Leon's bought out the Brick for seven hundred million.

ON A CHILLY FRIDAY, after a grueling week at work, you came home with Nanay bearing exciting news. You two had been scouting the strip malls of Scarborough for more established martial arts gyms. On the southeast corner of Brimley Road and Lawrence Avenue—a few blocks away from Ninang's house, where we first lived—you found a Shotokan karate club led by a man who looked like Stone Cold Steve Austin. Over coffee and donuts from the Tim Hortons nearby, you and Canadian Stone Cold worked out a deal so that we could sublet his dojo on Saturdays, when there weren't any other classes going on.

The Shotokan master checked with his landlord, and when it was confirmed that the arrangement would work, the papers were quickly signed. You were over the moon. We finally had our first gym. Another basement, in the grottoes underneath a Tamil bakery and a fish market. The pungency of mustard seeds and stale tilapia lingered long after we went downstairs on our first visit to the location. Underneath the strip mall was a mirrored dojo, lined with blue, red, and gray carpet. At one end of the basement was a spectators' room behind glass, for any parents who wanted to wait for their kids to finish class. At the far corner was a thick kicking bag wrapped in burlap. And at the very end of the complex, we had two changing rooms, a table for Nanay to do her administrative work, and a few pieces of gym equipment for anyone who wanted to warm up.

A dojo, you remind me, is nothing without its students. But outside of the family friends who had generously hosted us in those first months in Scarborough, we had very few connections. To anchor ourselves in a community, we began to attend the local Catholic church, St. Aidan. There, through the other Filipino parishioners, you started to go to something called "household meetings" every two weeks, at some of your new friends' much nicer homes. You called these friends "Brother" and "Sister." Not kuya and ate, not kapatid, but English kinship terms that meant a different kind of relationship altogether. But, you said, I was to call your new friends tito and tita, uncle and aunt. They were our family now. "You can practice your English!" Nanay said, when I balked at the thought of meeting other kids. A foreign language still, even stranger as I tried to join the well-dressed children poring over their brand-new Nintendo 64s in their unjaundiced basements. Upstairs, in the reverent silence, someone would start to play guitar, and the crowd would sing musical renditions of Bible verses.

Couples for Christ, your new Filipino Catholic community, became our world. We children had our own catechism lessons, and we learned the choreographies of happier-sounding songs about Moses and the prophets while our parents swayed and belted mournfully in the main room. As you two immersed yourselves into lay Christian life, you also found that your brothers and sisters might be interested in sending their children to martial arts. You had a ready-made pitch: martial arts would teach their troublemaking kids discipline and obedience to their parents, while connecting them with their Filipino culture. The marketing tactics worked; at every church hall gathering, you added one or two new names to your list of future students.

In the weeks that followed, we prepared for our opening day. While Nanay was at work at her new office job downtown, you and I made periodic trips to Home Depot, where we shopped for wooden dowels to fashion into kali. A natural carpenter, you cut them into three-foot sticks, thirty of them, and wrapped them in black electrical tape for extra padding and to protect our hands from blisters. "Watch me, anak," you said, when I twiddled my thumbs and paced in the corner. At the ends of the thinner rods, with a Sharpie, you wrote *Y*, for Youth, and for the thicker ones, *A*, for Adult. For me, you set aside two sticks and wrote my nickname at the ends.

Armed with a full list of potential students, Nanay made the fateful calls to the parents she had met at the Couples for Christ meetings. She also called up any relatives that Ninang had to see if they had any kids they wanted to enroll in the gym. Tuition would be dirt cheap, she assured them—we weren't in this for the money—and the commitment was only three hours every Saturday. We had insurance for any injuries, and under the watchful eye of a seasoned master, there was very little risk of serious hurt.

Over thirty parents called Nanay back. They would drop their kids off early, and some would watch class, while others would come back after their work shifts. On the first day of class, it felt like we had over forty students, all Filipino.

In full gi, you waited in front of the class. I'd never seen you in this outfit before, a red tunic adorned with a Filipino flag and championship honors, paired with starched white pants that shrugged and snapped every time you took a step. Your black belt, the thickest and sturdiest belt I'd ever seen, had five stripes at the end.

Two claps. The new students froze in place, mid-chatter, and fell silent, not knowing what the gesture meant. "When I clap twice, it means you come up in front of me and line up in three rows." You clapped again.

I was to stand at the front row to set an example, the most senior member of the class in my white uniform and yellow belt. The students gave me a strange look, wondering who I was, already further advanced in my training.

"We'll begin with learning how to bow," you bellowed.

I stood at ready stance and fixed my gaze forward, hoping that my classmates would follow. When they did, you spread your feet shoulder width apart, arms parallel with your toes.

"Humanda sa pagpupugay."

FOR TWENTY YEARS every Saturday, as if doing household chores, we assembled foam mats and combat equipment into a gym, our slice of immigrant economic life. Our neighbors had turo-turo ("point-point") takeout restaurants, or remittance and grocery storefronts. We had our dojo. Sometimes in a community center, sometimes at the back of any one of our neighbors' small businesses. During good times, you managed to scrounge together enough for a repurposed office space. In our last location before the pandemic, we practiced paces away from a freeway overpass, in the confines of an old warehouse that was now an immigrant services center.

The gyms, ephemeral locations all, became extra wings of our home, unfurling from the front door and spreading across an archipelago of martial artists across the city. Our students, young and old, comprised its islands: Filipino, Tamil, Jamaican, Palestinian, Syrian, Nigerian, and more. Sometimes, visitors came from the Philippines, the Middle East, the US South, the Rust Belt, and Western Canada.

No matter where they were from and who they were outside of our dojos, they lined up in the same "ready stance": feet shoulder width apart, closed fists, arms in front of thighs, eyes straight ahead, ready for your opening command:

Humanda sa pagpupugay. Prepare to bow.

In your signature booming voice, you could silence an entire crowd into total decorum. Nanay, yards away in a makeshift administrative space, hissed a piercing *shush* that settled down any lingering audible chatter. Years later, when a struggling heart prevented you from doing your second-favorite thing in the world—after preaching—that booming voice was replaced by the voices of your senior students. And when those students stepped away to have their own families, the voice that boomed from the front was my own.

Pugay, ta!

From ready stance, left foot meets the right foot. Right fingers together, right palm up to left breast. Say *kuntaw*: the name of the martial art we practice. Then back out to ready stance. Every Saturday afternoon, at the beginning and end of every session, and every time a student stepped out of the hallowed space we designated as a dojo.

Years later, I can still name the exercises off the top of my head. *Hands on your hips*. Elbows out, and arms curved into an obtuse angle, the students follow. *Head exercises, up and down—ONE.* Ten counts each, exercises that loosen the student up from head to toe. Shoulder and hip rotations, to slowly unlock mobilities beyond our bodies' expectations. By the time we are stretching our legs, our breathless gasps echo from the mats below our hanging heads.

To finish off our opening exercises, a meditation. Deep breathing to synchronize our lungs back into our bodies, and to each other. *Inhale*—the panting of a chest steadied into a single motion. *Exhale*—the heart pounding in the ear, slowing down into a steady metronome. Inhale through the nose, exhale through the mouth.

Then ready stance, fists parallel to our shoulders, back straight, gaze forward. Stillness with our now-steadied heart rates. At the front: guro, sensei, master, then grandmaster, you. Tatay.

PART TWO

FATHER

2000–2005

PEDAGOGY

EVERY DAY, you reminded me to pray, and every other day, you reminded me that we were poor. I had just learned what an inheritance was at the public library, where the staff showcased the abridged children's versions of Victorian novels. My favorite among them was *The Count of Monte Cristo*, the ur-text of every revenge plot I've ever dreamed up since. The story's Byronic hero, Edmond Dantès, is a young and eager crew member working on a homeward-bound ship. He docks in Marseille, the Scarborough of France (or the San Francisco of France, depending on whom you ask), ecstatic at the thought of finally marrying his beloved, Mercédès. But the night before his wedding, he is arrested and falsely tried for treason, framed by his jealous crewmate.

For his alleged crimes, Dantès is condemned with a life sentence in the Château d'If, an Alcatraz off the coast of Marseille. After six years without human contact, he digs through the prison walls and reaches his neighboring cell. The dingy quarters house an Italian abbot, Faria, who gifts the sailor with a clandestine education. At the priest's deathbed, Dantès learns of a treasure hidden away at the island of Monte Cristo, bequeathed to him by his dying mentor—an inheritance. A decade later, Dantès reinvents himself as an aristocrat and seamlessly integrates himself into Parisian upper-class society.

"Tatay, will I inherit anything?" I asked you at our regular meeting place, mandatory meals at the dining table, over a bowl of white rice and soupy corned beef, Nanay's favorite version of the dish, with tiny cuts of potatoes, so that the rice is flavored throughout with MSG and soy sauce.

"Blessed are the meek, for they shall inherit the earth," you joked—one of your favorite beatitudes. I pursed my lips, not understanding that you had been speaking in jest.

My first thought was that my literary hero, Edmond Dantès, was punished for meekness and his innocence. His bildungsroman wasn't his self-motivated transformation from a naive teenager to a vengeful aristocrat. He was perfectly content with his life as a sailor, and motivated by a romance denied to him by embittered coworkers. More than the dragon's hoard left to him by his teacher, the twenty-four years that followed his incarceration were his pedagogy.

"Education is your inheritance," you reassured me, catching my reaction. "It's the best thing we can give you."

To this day, this adage still shapes me. Dantès, after all, was a sailor like you. And like you, he was drilled with rigorous lessons from the devoted pedagogy of a clergyman on an island school with beautiful views of the water. Except his island wasn't his homeland; it was a prison. Unlike the debonair protagonist, you had no buried treasures awaiting you at the volta of your journey. And Dantès's escape wasn't an airborne adventure to the desert but a plummeting dive into the sea, where he was assumed to be dead.

EACH SUNSET ON LABOR DAY, my legs quivered. The dilated twilight of the late summer meant no more cartoons after nine, and it was time to break out the pencil case and the backpack and fantasize about the new classroom I'd step into. You found my trembling endearing, well into high school, when I tried to hide it behind a fitted cap and black Air Force 1s, and into my college years, when the only evidence you saw of my educational progress was the bill we had to pay every August. Every year, on the night before the first day of school, I still get the jitters, even when I'm on the other side of the lectern.

Next to St. Aidan, our neighborhood church, was a school of the same name. Because we moved into the area halfway through September, a fortnight into my first grade, I didn't get the usual privilege of Labor Day's anticipatory excitement. I may have pissed my pants at St. Martin's, but now I was nervous enough that I might have shit myself if you hadn't soothed my nerves by volunteering to walk with me to the new school. With her suave English, Nanay had just landed a job downtown, working in a government office whose function I wouldn't really understand until my late twenties, when someone unsuccessfully tried to teach me what a mutual fund was. Meanwhile, you were still at Zellers, and at the encouragement of a recruiter, enrolled yourself in elocution classes. I didn't know this until you came home one day to rant about your Guyanese teacher.

"That woman has no idea what she's talking about."

Nanay grunted and scooped a heap of white rice topped with monggo into her mouth. I mimed her motions, but in reverse, the stewed mung beans at the bottom of my spoon, and a little rice on top.

"Anak," you pressed, "you know how to speak English. Let me spell a word, and you tell me how to say it. Get me a pen and paper."

Nanay began to get up. "Sit down, he needs to learn," you reprimanded her.

"Di na, I'll get it, kumakain pa siya," she snapped back with a wince, and she fetched a pencil and Xerox paper from a stack across the living room and handed them to you. On the page, you wrote eleven capital letters, spaced out for emphasis, still just barely legible from your rushed and scratchy script: COMFORTABLE.

"Sige, anak, how do you say that?" You turned the Xerox paper around and slid it across the table. I swallowed my monggo hard and scrunched my face from the mass struggling to push down my esophagus. I pored over the word—not a word I had ever personally used—and tried to remember where I might have heard it before. The answer came not from the game shows and cartoons that we watched on the chunky cathode ray tube TV but from an older program, one I used to watch in Taguig with my cousins, a British show with anthropomorphic bananas wearing cozy sleeping garments. I cleared my throat and softly mouthed it to myself, with the breathy roundness of an English accent, a rehearsal in a new language not my own.

"Comfortable," I recited, the emphasis on the first syllable, the "for" hushing into an unvoiced labiodental fricative, my top buck teeth gently biting down on my plump lower lip, before stumbling through a schwa, hastily broken apart by consonants.

"See? *See?*" You slammed your hands on the table, and Nanay and I—and the thin metal cutlery—jumped. "COME-fortable. My '*teacher*' said it wrong. Come-for-TAY-bull. *ComforTAble*! Foolish!

Unqualified! Who is *she* to think that she could be *my* teacher?" I kept stock of three new words I learned that night: *comfortable*, *foolish*, and *unqualified*.

From then on, *comforTAble* became one of our running jokes. But it was this intramural humor, in which we were trying to make this strange and inconsistent language familiar to ourselves, that terrified me about going to St. Aidan. Our first language joke, which you used to repeat until the day you collapsed, was *welks*. You found it amusing how Canadians shorten a perfectly good and polite phrase, "thank you," into its truncated abomination: *thanks*. Finding ourselves struggling to learn the vernacular, you took it upon yourself to speak back on behalf of empire, and coined a postcolonial neologism, *welks*, for "you're welcome." Snappy, you'd say, and efficient. A single syllable in exchange for a single syllable.

The kids in the first grade didn't think so. My first December in that school, back when Decembers still brought real snow, the kind that my tiny body could sink into neck deep, I waddled into the classroom, a marshmallow of fake down and sheer white polyester. Mrs. Frigidaire, who always brought herself a Tupperware of leftovers, had mastered the exquisite art of Southern Ontario winter preparedness: a long gray jacket down to her ankles, a hood lined with fur, and a large knitted hat with a pom-pom on top. "This is a *tuque*," she'd teach me, when I referred to the chapeau as a bonnet. *Tuque*. I made sure to bring the word back to Nanay, for our growing collection of francophone phraseology.

In those stormy weeks, Mrs. Frigidaire made sure to give us extra time to put our winterwear on. My marshmallow jacket and boots were next to those of Sour Cream, a Cantonese girl who styled herself in vests and always wore her hair in a tight ponytail, her scalp and her roots playing tug-of-war with her forehead. She had forgotten where she had put her boots. I had recognized hers beside mine, for they matched the rest of her lavender outfit. I handed them to her.

"Thanks," Sour Cream said.

In response, I offered your clever neologism. The offending word rippled out to every child within earshot. The nape of my neck itched, each confused glance an irritant on my skin. Sour Cream tilted her head and asked what language I was speaking.

That night, I ran into bed, shoved my face into the mattress, and sandwiched my head with a pillow. Before going to sleep, I lifted the thick Merriam-Webster dictionary from your bedroom, the one with the red hard cover, and pored over it until my eyes grew heavy. I vowed never to say *welks* again.

ON MY SEVENTH BIRTHDAY, a monster was sleeping in my bed.

You reminded me to come home as soon as possible that afternoon, no lingering with friends, no hanging out at the Filipino video store. With a backpack half my weight, I sprinted home, along the same path where the school's cross-country runners practiced. Around the brownstone school and the ragged parking lot, over the channelized reservoir that smelled like damp towels, beneath the burgundy trees, behind the pale-fenced townhouses, across Birchmount and to the north side of Finch, to the opening of the fence. I jogged a lap around the building, through the orchard of boysenberry trees, and entered through the door between the garbage cans at the back. Then the elevator button, rounded at the edges and faded from generations of skin oil, that archive of residency. I sprinted through the hallway that smelled of cumin and ghee and opened the apartment door.

At my bedroom door, I froze. A man-shaped lump had curled up in my bed, underneath the covers. Its head was covered in a bonnet—a *tuque*, Mrs. Frigidaire would remind me—and its legs were gathered into an unnatural mass two-thirds of the way down the mattress.

"Nanay! *NANAY*! *TATAY*!" I screamed in a panic, howling into the living room, my voice straining from the urgency.

"Open it," you told me through your beaming smile, "don't be scared," even though something was in my bed. From the corner of my eye, I thought the body was shuddering. I took two steps forward, and one back, my feet quivering at the uncanny presence. When I pulled back the man's hat, the beady black of a blue teddy bear's eyes stared at me. I tugged at the rest of the blankets until they fell to the ground. Underneath its ursine head, the bedridden monster's body was a Yamaha keyboard, sixty-one keys, with a cushioned bench.

Behind me, you two cackled. I couldn't help but laugh, too. My heart, pounding irregularly in my throat, steadied itself.

The second part of the birthday gift was that, every week, you would enroll me in piano classes in the neighborhood. East of our apartment, on Wayside Avenue, was a strip mall and medical office complex, and a music store called Unison Piano Company. Inside, the tiny space felt like an expansive warehouse, lined to the brim with polished upright pianos of all colors. Even with my smaller frame, I had to squeeze through the merchandise, afraid that any wrong turn would scuff up the wood. Toward the back of the store were closet-sized rooms for lessons, with a piano and bench, and a chair for the teacher to watch. One room had no piano inside and was reserved for students of guitar.

The day of my first lesson, a tall Cantonese boy, around twelve years old, brought a nylon-string guitar. I had never seen anything like it. It sounded so different from your guitar at home, which had steel strings, the kinds that made my fingertips ache whenever I tried to press on them, or the instruments that the musicians at church would bring to Sunday mass to guide the congregation into hymns. The boy had no strap across his body, and he opened his legs, nestling the wide body between his thighs, and tilted the neck upward at a forty-five-degree angle, unlike the Catholic players, who stood up and strummed solid chords while their instruments hung down their necks and torsos. Years later, when I briefly flirted with piano virtuosity, you liked to tell your friends that you'd convinced me to take piano when I first wanted to play guitar. Piano, you'd opine, would teach the musical fundamentals that all other instruments followed. After teaching myself how to play a few other instruments, I agree with you, except that I really don't think I asked to play guitar first. When I played my first melody in Mrs. Chu's studio, and then replicated what I had learned at home, I fell in love.

The Yamaha, though, instilled a series of terrible habits that, to this day, I can't quite shake off. The plastic keys had no weight sensitivity, so it didn't matter how hard or soft I pressed, the note was the same volume. To prepare for Friday night classes at Unison, I had to imagine the minute dynamic difference between medium soft, or mezzo piano, and soft, or piano. But on Fridays, Mrs. Chu gave the same comment: "Too loud, not forte! Piano! *Piano*!" As a result, the difference between playing hard and soft was easier at the gym, and damn near impossible on the instrument anciently called a pianoforte.

This didn't stop me from trying to learn above my skill set. The Yamaha had preset tracks that I could scroll through, and an accompanying score sheet of abridged versions of pieces that couldn't fit within the truncated set of sixty-one keys. The first one I learned was a waltz, which the Yamaha's blue LED called "Chopsticks," using only the white keys, whose melodic line and primary harmony could be played with two index fingers, the distance between them oscillating from claustrophobically close to a perfect octave. There was a left-hand accompaniment, too, that demanded a leaping agility I didn't have, so I saved it for when my fingers could reach better. To get to that point, Mrs. Chu recommended that I practice my scales, repetitive cascades along the keyboard, so that my fingers could naturally grow into the choreography. Or chords, to build strength and grace. In half a year, I could imperfectly play "Chopsticks" with both hands, its crunchy melody with my right, and the waltz rhythm with my left.

Those preset tracks were my skill targets. My next milestone was a piece written by a dead German man who shared the name of a fictional dog. In class, I asked Sour Cream how to pronounce the name, which I had rehearsed in my head as *beath-oven*. The aggressive inconsistency of the English language warned me to shut up before I could confirm.

"Bait-owe-vin!" Sour Cream said. An appalling difference from its spelling. She, too, disclosed that it couldn't have possibly been in English, but she learned the word from a movie that her family had watched recently, about a giant slobbering St. Bernard named Beethoven. *Who on earth names their dog Beethoven?* I thought. Sour Cream admitted that she found the movie boring.

When I went home, I tried to learn the piece by a man who was also the namesake of a Hollywood dog. The real Beethoven was a young virtuoso from Bonn, given the name Ludwig. Like me, his first teacher was his father, and like me, he was terrified of this man. To push young Ludwig to play piano, Johann, often half drunk, dragged his son out of bed to play until he felt satisfied with his student's performance. Sometimes, as motivation, the father would lock the son in the closet.

If Johann had lived long enough to see Ludwig make his high-society debut, would he have given himself credit, even when his son had long wanted to run away from home?

The piano felt safe. My mind would quiet, and my fingertips conducted their own colloquium. At school, when I couldn't sit still in class, I'd tap on the desk, pantomiming a keyboard on the laminated wood. My right pinky and ring fingertips oscillating first, then a circular descent to my thumb, the opening theme of "Für Elise." Then thumb to pinky, ascending arpeggios, and repeat the opening. My left hand, at the gaps, would respond with broken upward triads. Call, response, an argument, an elaboration, in a casually somber A minor.

Outside of our family and Mrs. Chu, only one other person knew I played piano. In the Silver Springs complex, but in a different building, Curtis, a head taller than me, a year older than me, with an unkempt lineup and a backpack half his body weight, asked if he could walk with me to school. He carried a blue basketball with him and dribbled it down the sidewalk, trying to bounce it on every crack, while prattling on about a new game his parents bought him called *Pokémon*. When he figured out that I'd never played a video game before, the next day he brought his Game Boy, a pistachio-colored rectangle with plastic buttons and a dim screen. He handed it over to me.

"Go ahead and play while we walk to school!" he'd say on the days he had his Game Boy, and when he didn't have it, he'd say the same thing if he wanted us to bounce the basketball to each other. His toys were only for recess, those precious unstructured minutes, simulacra of freedom, but never after school, he'd say ominously, as if he'd disappear the next morning if he didn't come home by 3:30 p.m.

Only once did Curtis tell me he could break curfew, which was also the last day I ever spoke with him. I wore a golf shirt to class, Nanay's attempt to match my wardrobe to yours: a starched collar, a cotton and polyester mix wrapped around my belly, punctuated with pinch marks where I picked at the fabric. Curtis wore a black oversize shirt emblazoned with a picture of his idol, Allen Iverson. And per tradition, he was dribbling his blue ball up the hill.

"Do you want to come over and play *Pokémon* later this week?" he asked. I told him that I didn't have a Game Boy. "That's okay, we can play it like a tag team. My mom is making bake and saltfish." I didn't know what saltfish was, but it sounded like the fried smelts Nanay cooked that you hated stinking up the apartment, so we'd only eat it as takeout. I asked Curtis when.

"Friday after school!"

I told him that I had to be home early enough to practice piano. His brow furrowed, and he walked a little ahead of me.

"Piano? That's pretty gay, man. Are you gay?"

I didn't know enough to figure out what Curtis's tone meant, except that I knew he no longer wanted to be friends. I had told Curtis that I didn't know what the word was. He kept his gaze forward and dribbled his ball home, elongating his strides, outpacing me, disappearing into the gate to the neighboring building.

When you got home that night, over the dinner table, I asked you what *gay* meant. You dropped your utensils and met my glance. Nanay kept her eyes on her plate.

"Where did you learn that word?"

I told you about Curtis, who had never come over to meet you. Your breathing dropped to a shudder. You squeezed the table's edge. Arthritic knuckles pushing out from underneath your skin.

"Don't you *ever—EVER*—let anyone call you gay."

A restrained rage exhaling through your nostrils. With trembling voice, you pointed to my instrument: "Go practice."

"Let him eat, mahal," Nanay said.

"After you finish your food," you revised, your eyes still on me.

After dinner, I sat at the bench and closed my eyes, and sniffed hard, to drown out the living room around me, to eradicate all discourse and immerse myself in the space of music. "Für Elise," Mrs. Chu would remind me, was a piece dedicated to Beethoven's object of affection. *Close your eyes and think of someone who's caught your eye.* Beside me, still hauling his giant backpack, adorned with his prematurely chiseled face, joining me on the bench, was Curtis.

WHEN MONSTER, our station wagon, broke down, you replaced it with a leased Plymouth Voyager, a forest-green seven-seater marvel with sliding doors and a body as curvaceous as Ditto, a Pokémon that looked like a blob. Unlike its rickety predecessor, the Voyager didn't have a badass nickname like Monster did. I tried pitching nomenclature along the same wave. For about half a second, you mulled over the name I offered (*BEAST!*—with the requisite exclamatory enthusiasm), which was inspired by an American spinoff of the *Transformers* anime franchise.

While Monster remains in our family lore, the name *BEAST!* never had a chance to shine. *BEAST!* was the perfect vehicle for the gym. When our family was still a modest number of three, we could keep the gym mats and arnis sticks at the back to use every Saturday, without having to overfill the storage unit in the apartment. And even with this traveling dojo in the trunk, *BEAST!* would have enough seats left over for one or two other people.

Sometimes, on the way to the gym, we'd pick up a student whose parents couldn't make the time to drop their kids off. Often, it was your best student—your favorite student—Bing, the stepson of Ninang, our first caretaker, whose basement was our first Canadian home. Bing looked like a Filipino Lance Bass: high eyebrows and a defined squint, broad and chiseled jaw, stiff hair petrified into porcupine spikes, religiously frosted tips. And like the singer, he climbed into the minivan with an unshakable broad-shouldered charisma, the quality that your workplace self-help books called "executive presence."

Among all the students, you loved Bing for the rawness of his talent and the natural magnetism that he brought every week. For warmups, he pushed the limits of his endurance and his flexibility, visibly straining to push his hips to the ground for a full split, even as his adolescent knees protested. For drills, Bing's horse stance was immaculate, an exquisite straddle, his calves and his thighs at a perfect perpendicular angle, fists cocked at the waist, fingers curled into his palm so that his wrists couldn't wiggle at the impact of his imaginary punch. Unlike the rest of us doing punching drills, which you counted for us in groups of ten, Bing gave each punch his full power, in his best mimicry of your desert-polished technique: his shoulders perfectly still, his arms alternately striking the sides of an isosceles triangle, the vertex of impact at the mental opponent's chest, the punch's power mustered from the hips. And his *sai*—his emphatic combat scream—shook the whole dojo, reverberating to the locker rooms and down the long hallway to the stairs beneath the fish market.

Then there was Shane, *my* favorite student of yours, who took two buses to the gym every weekend. The complete opposite of Bing, no flying kicks, no preemptive strikes. Shane was shorter than the rest of the students his age, his demeanor a perpetual poker face, betraying nothing but the contours of his skin, a calculated inscrutability so polished that the rest of us thought he hated being at the gym. Even his *sai* was muted, a staccato of a hum, as pointed and parsimonious as the thrust kick with which he struck his opponent's solar plexus. Inside and outside of the dojo, not a single gesture or word was wasteful; he spoke few words, his steps gentle and stealthy, the kind of movement prized in the ninja society of my favorite anime, *Naruto*. Shane's beauty was in his economy.

From those early years, other students threaded the lore of our dojo's tapestry: Past-Life Pastor, the suave teenager from your Couples for Christ meetings, whose mushroom haircut shook in time with his focused strikes; Future Monk and his two brothers, regular parishioners at St. Aidan, whose father became a priest after Future Monk retreated into the New York mountains to join the Franciscans; Right Elbow, who later became our gym's mythical hero for defending a young woman at the north Scarborough McDonald's by knocking out a would-be assailant with his bony joint. And there were the brothers Freedom and Redemption, whose silky shoulder-length hair I envied, who could never move gracefully enough for forms but were high-flying monsters in the ring.

You and Nanay, intrepid and entrepreneurial, recruited not only individual students but entire families to the gym, all of the children, the cousins, the family friends, the entire barkada. Before the Filipinos excommunicated us for heresy, you practiced your calling as God's shepherd with your students. After warmups, you'd sit us down on the mat and deliver a sermon disguised as a lesson plan. One of your longer homilies was to endear us to the idea of competing at a regional martial arts tournament. The room murmured, a fluttering din of anticipation. Future Monk's youngest brother, Beloved Disciple, one of my St. Aidan classmates, stretched his torso and arms over to me, his legs still crossed, and whispered, "It's just like *Dragon Ball Z*!" To humor us, you said that it'd be just like Bruce Lee's *Game of Death*, except that no one would die. Quickly, though, your sermon switched directions, and you laid bare the real agenda behind our first tournament foray: it'd give all of us a real goal to work toward, and remind us that our families were inseparable from our success. You would send every student's parent a personal invite, so that when we won our medals, they could watch us with pride.

Since most of us were too junior, our club could compete in only three tournament events. I recognized some of the Japanese words from my community center karate lessons: solo kata, group kata, and kumite—or sparring. For three months, we trained. As your anak, Nanay reminded me, I was to compete in all three events, and work extra hard to make sure that I could set an example for the other kids, most of whom could already kick my ass. Beloved Disciple, closest to me in age, was half a head taller and a trillion times more flexible. He would beat himself up for not being able to grasp your sparring lessons or not being able to catch up to his older brothers, prodigious maulers both. I would assure him that he was doing well, secretly jealous that he was actually an excellent student and was on pace to get promoted past my yellow belt in shorter time. To encourage ourselves to practice, we assigned each other *Dragon Ball Z* roles. He would be Tien, the even-keeled three-eyed monk, and I would be the green alien Piccolo, a diasporic citizen of the planet Namek. In our corner of the moldy dojo, close enough to the bathroom, in case either of us got too nervous, we made believe that we were in our tournament arc and were training in a Gravity Machine, a space-age capsule in the *Dragon Ball* universe that allows the fighter to practice combat in exponential multiples of Earth's gravity. Neither of us felt heroic enough to call dibs on Goku, or grungy enough to claim his embattled rival, Vegeta.

"Two times!" I'd say, and the ground felt like Jupiter. Our ankles carried the entire mass of our bodies. We pressed our heels against the dusty carpet. I steeled myself against the planet's pull and shifted my weight to my front leg, lifted the rear knee, and delivered a sluggish kick, my heel aimed at Beloved Disciple's chest. He stumbled out of the way and gathered himself, throwing a lethargic punch to my exposed gut. I parried it out of the way, and we tried the routine again.

"A hundred times!" Beloved Disciple announced, and we keeled over, struggling to hoist ourselves up from the surface of a star. No Filipino resilience could help me muster the strength to stand up. Not even Goku, the great Saiyan warrior, was able to overcome gravity without tapping into his supernatural powers. Beloved Disciple dragged himself into a back stance, his palms aglow with his aura, congealing into a ball of pure energy. I was done for.

"Ka . . ." Beloved Disciple gasped, "me . . . ha . . . me—"

Noticing our fantastical distractedness, you'd trot over to yell at us. "*Huy*! You two—*focus*!"

On the morning of the tournament, we unloaded the mats from *BEAST!* and in their place stacked the van with huge duffel bags of sparring equipment: foam helmets, punching gloves, shin and foot guards, jockstraps, fresh mouthguards. We didn't really need them at the event, you told me, as I tried to help you hoist the bags into the van, but it was better to be safe than sorry. You shut the liftgate, *BEAST!* filled to the brim with combat equipment, and we drove out of the parking garage, east on Silver Springs Boulevard to Kennedy, south to Highway 401, and east again to Markham, in the farthest lane to the right, so that the cargo that *BEAST!* carried wouldn't topple over. You exited at Markham Road and took the winding road east to Centennial College, a vocational school in the trades and technical skills, to the parking lot of a gymnasium, emblazoned in blue and white: HOME OF THE COLTS.

Of the tournament itself, I can't remember a thing. My only memories of it were developed in Shoppers Drug Mart, a collection of images Nanay sent me on WhatsApp decades later, when the event had dissolved into phantasmagoria.

"You're not imagining," she wrote to me, with these images attached. "Very cute photos."

Unlike my piano classes, where my performances tended to be way too loud, I was much too soft at the gym. The fine precision that a pianoforte demanded seemed to be antithetical to the pummeling force of a sparring match.

Fortunately, you told me, not every martial art needed brute force for the fighter to decapitate his opponent. And for every martial deficiency, you had a cure. "You're getting taller," you observed, "so it's time to learn something new."

When you declared your dream to open a kuntaw gym, you said nothing about any of the previous styles you had learned. Until then, your first love, sikaran, was a mystery to me. In a few years, when I turned sixteen, we'd finally return to the Philippines together for the first time and pay a visit to Meliton Geronimo, the grandmaster of sikaran, on the slopes of the hills in Antipolo. Even in his advanced age, he limped soundlessly, as if his toes just caressed the earth, ready to spread his wings at any moment and take to the smoggy Manila sky. The only sound that betrayed his arrival was the clapping of his flip-flops against his heels. There, I learned why you loved these arts. If kuntaw taught you to be a patient and steady frog, with sikaran, you became a heron.

North of the Silver Springs complex was L'Amoreaux Park, a hinterland of sod that blankets over the remains of a Haudenosaunee village. A channelized creek runs through L'Amoreaux, winding between three hills where we'd toboggan in the winter, up to the northern expanse, a children's water park that smelled like an open-air sewer. In L'Amoreaux's southern parking lot, you opened *BEAST!*'s liftgate, strung the door's interior handle with some twine, and looped the ends around the neck of a Kirkland Signature water bottle.

Today's lesson was the biakid, the pinnacle of sikaran, and the foundational kick from which every other technique is derived. You began from an inscrutable fighting stance, so casual and nonchalant that the opponent can't possibly predict that you'd dig your heel into the top of their spinal cord in half a second. When they approached, at about an arm's length away, your body turned, your head dipped as low as possible behind you, your free hand balancing your body on the ground, and your rear leg whipped into the air, striking the back of the head from point-blank range. You demonstrated the biakid with the bottle strung as high as possible, uncomfortably close to the door's metal, but with enough slack that it still swung freely upon impact. I worried for your ankle in the way that I'd have worried about mine—but unsurprisingly, you heeled the bottle with precision.

The biakid was the heron's nest: the rehearsal for babies to teach them to take to the skies. Still, I wasn't confident that I could fly as you did. But like a proper striking technique in kuntaw, sikaran's strength came from the hips. I'd learn how to exploit the momentum of my body, my anchoring foot the fulcrum, my spinning heel drawing its force from a three-sixty turn. And I'd only get better with height, you reminded me. You said nothing about weight.

"Your turn." You loosened the knot and slid the bottle down to what you claimed was a manageable level for me, a head above my own. First, I needed to learn how to ikot, the initial pivot from which the kick would naturally fly. But my heel refused to turn, and I stumbled to the ground. Again. I turned and swung my head and torso down, raising my leg. My foot pivoted at last, and my other leg took flight: it unwound from my body on its own, soaring above my head, pummeling into the Kirkland Signature bottle. Midflight, I realized what I had done and fell down, scraping my palm against the coarse asphalt.

"Ang galing!" you exclaimed, catching and steadying the bottle, and caressed my head. My hair curled into a messy bundle.

That was the only kick I landed that day. All afternoon, I tried to biakid the bottle again, but the best my foot could do was graze its toes against the bottom. We'd try again at the apartment, you comforted me, when I grew frustrated in myself. But Nanay hated it when we practiced at home, and for good reason: as we got more settled into the neighborhood, the living room also served as my playing area, as your home offices, and as our entertainment center. The chunky white Hewlett-Packard computer and the sluggish printer were right next to the chunky television. It became too dangerous to practice in our cramped apartment, so L'Amoreaux became our personal classroom.

In the warmer seasons, I learned how to bike in that parking lot, while you sat at the back of the van, or tied a bottle up for yourself to practice your biakid. In the colder months, when Scarborough got bombarded with waist-high snow, the three of us dragged some folded-up cardboard boxes to the top of a hill. We sat down, me in front, you holding on to me from behind, and Nanay with her own makeshift toboggan, and you pushed us down the slope. The snow hit us in the face, seasoning us with its frigid bounty, and at the bottom of the hill, we were a family of snowpeople.

When my kick was practiced enough, we drove to the martial arts supply store to get some new kicking pads, foam tennis-racket-shaped doohickeys with two sturdy layers that collided with a satisfying *clap*. At the gym, you called me forward to demonstrate a new skill that the class would learn: the biakid. You explained that from here on out, we'd be venturing into the terrain of another martial arts style from the Philippines, sikaran, the kicking games of the Tagalogs of Central Luzon, who sparred in the wet and spongy earth of the rice paddies. I didn't know any of this from when you taught me the kick.

You extended a clapper forward, a head above my own. I visualized the Costco-brand bottle dangling from *BEAST!* and focused my energy on my front leg. "Too far," you said, and I nudged closer, much closer than we had practiced, until the clapper was a foot away from my face. I'd have to bend down as low as possible for the ikot, and stretch my legs higher than I had at L'Amoreaux. I steadied my breath and spun as quickly as I could. But my foot struck something harder than the clapper, more metallic than the bottle, more painful than the dangling twine. I had hit your Seiko watch.

"Aray!" you winced, nursing your wrist, and everyone laughed. My face warmed, and I bit my lip, my ankle throbbing. It was unbecoming to cry, your voice cautioned me, *Because you are my son.*

ELDERS

AT SOME POINT, the uncomfortable English lessons must have paid off. Nanay had landed a job in the provincial government, something about mutual funds (which I still don't quite understand), and you snagged a position in an investment funds certification company, whatever that meant. But you were so proud to announce the name of your new company—*IFIC*!—that we were in a celebratory mood for months. Back then, with some work, coupled with a savvy placement officer, your degrees from that Catholic university in Manila got your foot in the door of the rarefied realms of Canadian finance regulations.

Now that you both worked nine-to-five jobs, neither of you could take care of me at home. At St. Aidan, you met our neighbor on the ground floor, Lola Aling, a stern elderly woman with gray bangs and a graphic tee who kept her screaming granddaughter, Sarah, on a tight leash. Lola Aling, an entrepreneur herself, looked at me after mass and asked if you needed someone to take care of me while you were at work. After church, you announced our new schedule. Nanay's new job was at the glass building above the Eaton Centre, in the heart of downtown Toronto. After work, she would take the northbound train on Yonge Street to meet you in North York, where you'd pick her up after you were done at IFIC. After class, instead of taking the elevator up to our unit, I would stay on the ground floor, walk down the foreign hallway, and knock on the fifth apartment on the right, where Lola Aling would let me in. Until you could come home, at about 6:30 p.m., I would spend the afternoon at Lola Aling's apartment with other kids my age.

Lola Aling's unit had the same configuration as ours, except that it was darker. Her two bedrooms doubled as storage closets, so that the tall beds were squeezed in between half-packed balikbayan boxes, like she was always ready to leave Canada within twenty-four hours. Instead of a tasteful couch and television arrangement like ours, she had a matted play area for all the children that came to visit every weekday. Where our pigeon-stained balcony would have been, she had an open patio that led into the boysenberry orchard at the side of the Silver Springs complex. Sarah, the sweet screaming kid from church, was now free to bellow into the trees.

Restrained anarchy is the best way I can describe afternoons at Lola Aling's place. She had her hands completely full with Sarah, who loved to pick her nose and fling the crust at her grandmother, but politely and mercifully no one else. When Sarah hollered for her mom, whom I never met, Lola Aling would yell right back, a Dadaist dissonance of the highest aesthetic order. Their volume would scare the rest of us into submission—or feigned apathy.

Eventually, I got to know the other children who would call this place their afternoon home. Most of us lived in Silver Springs, but a good number lived in any of the surrounding blocks around St. Aidan, the washed brown townhomes along the reservoir, the other apartment complexes that looked identical to ours, the bungalows closer to the radiating hydrofields. One of the kids, Shrimp Chips, was someone I recognized from Couples for Christ, at weeknight church assemblies. I considered her to be one of the cool kids who hung around the children's ministry. She was tall and slender, demonstrably deferential, and always lined up first to meet the elders, to take the back of their hand between her fingers and press it against her forehead. "Mano *po*," Shrimp Chips, in her sweetest voice, would ask for their hand, emphasizing the honorific particle *po*. The adults would swoon over her.

When she wasn't around CFC people, Shrimp Chips was a proud tomboy. In her backpack, she stashed a change of clothes for Lola Aling's place, loose sweatpants and Paul Pierce's Boston Celtics jersey. When we gathered in the dining room to eat, I gingerly picked at the galunggong's spiny bones, while she crunched away at the fried daing. At Lola Aling's, her voice dropped an octave, and when Sarah climbed the couch to smack her head, she slapped her right back.

Shrimp Chips immediately took a real liking to me. At first, her English was way too fast for me to follow, a barreling snowball of discourse careening downhill with preadolescent fluency, so I tried to stay away and retreated to the bedroom, too awkward to speak, but she followed me in. Within a month, we had established a ritual at Lola Aling's: whoever would come in first would call dibs on the smaller bedroom, turn on the TV, and flip the channel knob to the soap operas. Our fixation was a show called *Passions*, set in a seaside town where each denizen lived in a beige manor and concealed some inexplicable superpower. Shrimp Chips pointed out how thick the men's eyebrows were. She licked her thumb and flattened my own anemic eyebrows. "You'll grow into them," she smirked.

In *Passions*, everyone in their twenties drove a convertible car, Mustangs and Camaros with miraculous tire traction, cruising over asphalt then veering off-road right onto the New England beach. Towels spread like their naked bodies against the sand, faces pressed against each other, fingers snaking along wispy blond hair, moaning accentuated by a sliver of a visible boom mic. When the camera cut to beachside scenes like these, Shrimp Chips sat up on the bed, her eyes bug-wide, her fingers miming the movements against an imaginary head of hair. I lay down underneath the blanket and half-closed my eyes, covering my face with the edge of the sheet. At home, you never let me watch the raunchy scenes. *Not until you're older, anak.*

"We have to try to do this scene."

"How?" I wondered aloud, not wanting to get myself covered in sand, or the makeshift beach I imagined in the dirt outside.

"We can do it right here," she said matter-of-factly.

Instead of a New England seashore, we could reenact the make-out scenes on Lola Aling's bed. Like a seasoned actor-director, Shrimp Chips choreographed our film shoot. She would play the svelte brunette man on top, crawling from the sand to the beach towel, then atop my legs, upon which she'd sit and embrace my back. I would be the blonde girl at the bottom, breath fluttery and soft, and wrap my arms around her back. "Scratch me!" she snapped, when my palms held her too wimpily.

"You're so sexy," my cue, to be delivered with breathy tone, from my lips to her ear. Shrimp Chips was anxious to capture the gravity of that scene. She hated when I grunted from the impact of our fall into the mattress. We rehearsed over and over again, every day after school, for some unknown performance in the far-off future.

At school, I asked Sour Cream what *sexy* meant. I think she figured out that I was new to the language and, absent the earlier confusion, decided to become my first friend. After Sour Cream, who was rather popular, others followed suit: the two Josephs, Egyptian (who called me "Maree," an affectionate truncation of the part of my name you and I shared), and Tamil (who fed me savory snacks his mom packed him in abundance); and the Serbian kids, Ube Cake and his twin, the former a ready-made chatterbox, the latter a silent enigma. Beloved Disciple, from the gym, sat with us, too.

"I've never heard that word before," Sour Cream said, eating her fries. "Let's go look it up." With her greasy fingers, she took my hand and we walked to the book corner. On top of the low shelf was a blue tome on a wooden bookstand, the *Oxford English Dictionary*. "Sexually attractive or alluring." My eyes darted upwards to the word *sex*, meaning "physical contact between individuals involving sexual stimulation, or to identify as male or female, esp. to determine the sex of (an animal, an individual from skeletal remains, etc.) by examination."

After that, I found myself hesitating before knocking on Lola Aling's door, and felt at ease only when the living room TV was on and Shrimp Chips wasn't around. Sometimes, I wanted her to be there, because she'd press herself against me and push my torso down. Underneath her body, I felt slim.

One day, Shrimp Chips disappeared. Her family stopped coming to church; Nanay told me that they had moved to a wealthier neighborhood to the southwest. New kids joined Lola Aling's posse, also from Couples for Christ, also recent Filipino arrivals whose parents left them for their new jobs. None of them wanted to watch *Passions* with me, so I stopped hiding in the bedroom altogether.

The start of the new millennium greeted us with a new arrival to our family, Nanay's quiet and soft-spoken mother, Lola Pet, destined to be your live-in mortal enemy, but as we'd all agree years later, an infinitely better choice than your own mother, Lola Isabella. Lola Pet was to be my new roommate and my replacement babysitter. On the opposite side of my bedroom, you laid down another single bed and a second nightstand identical to mine, where she could put her belongings. The room would no longer smell only like my juvenile body odor but would be joined by a mélange of Vicks VapoRub and baby oil. In passing, you enigmatically mentioned that she was there to take care of your children, in the plural, a conjugation I allowed to linger with me. After Lola Pet moved in, I never saw Lola Aling again. As for her posse, I couldn't say the same.

IN OUR SHARED SPACE, my new roommate and I practiced a delicate choreography. After three blasts of the alarm clock, I groggily awoke, while it took Lola Pet another two to crack her eyes open. Our morning greetings were little more than grunts—my Tagalog, by then, had begun to wane into mere aural comprehension, and her English was virtually nonexistent, except for a few choice phrases quilted between her second language of Tagalog and her occasional slips into her native tongue, Ilokano. Yet in the time I took to ready myself in the morning, she had already microwaved a glass of milk and laid out some bowls of boiled dilis and ampalaya slices with scrambled egg, and we sat together and ate in silence, a ritual we continued during my weekend and overseas visits in my late twenties, until I stopped visiting you altogether.

After school, in the numerical new year, our last year and a half in the Silver Springs apartment, I'd look forward to coming home to these same Ilokano goodies, not because I had a particular taste for eggs and bitter melon, but because Lola Pet was fun to hang around with. When she wasn't on the couch and watching *The Jerry Springer Show*, sporting her *Matrix* sunglasses and a moist face towel over her forehead, she was unloading her grocery bag of Goodwill clothes, her expert thrift hunts occasionally yielding choice pieces for my haphazard wardrobe: technicolored tuques with snazzy pom-poms, knitted sweaters with a slight turtleneck, patched vests and graphic tees.

The best part of my afternoon hangouts with Lola Pet was that we could distractedly watch trash TV together, *JERRY! JERRY! JERRY!* at full volume, while I sat on the floor with an open box of Nanay's Xerox papers for kuntaw paperwork. At school, we were making our way through our first novel, *Sadako and the Thousand Paper Cranes*, a Japanese Canadian classic that I realized later was written by a white woman from Saskatchewan. In *Sadako*, the titular character, a leukemic survivor of the atomic bomb in Hiroshima, set out to fold one thousand origami paper cranes, in the hopes that she would recover well enough to join her track and field team. On her deathbed, she had managed to fold only 644 cranes, and after she passed, her loved ones completed the other 356.

With a box of Xerox papers and Lola Pet's American English lessons on the television, I set out to fold my own thousand. It was you who helped me find the best instructions to fold the birds, after you sat me down one evening and taught me how to use the search engine Ask Jeeves. Because the Xerox sheets were 8.5 by 11 inches, unlike the delicate square papers that origami artists used, I folded one corner down to the natural edge, pressed the excess rectangle down at the bottom, licked my finger, and drew a moist line along the crease, before tearing the rectangle away to leave myself with a perfect square, bisected with a single diagonal fold. This was your trick, and one I never forgot; today, I can still fold a paper crane from memory, with any non-square sheet handed to me. An origami paper, with its dainty print on one side and a silken off-white on the other, felt like cheating.

Each *Jerry Springer* segment was just over ten minutes, with commercial breaks in between, so initially I tried to fold one crane every two minutes. Lola Pet never visibly reacted to the episodes, and at first I didn't really understand why the show was entertaining to her. But she'd always shift slightly when Mr. Springer, the former mayor of Cincinnati, cleared out of the way as two cousins started to maul on each other. These were my favorite parts, even though I didn't understand that these cousins were also illicit lovers, because I could assess the inefficacy of their combat technique. Skinny white men loved to throw hook punches, swinging from behind their shoulder to the side of their opponent's head, leaving their entire torsos open. Most times, the scraps devolved into inchoate slapping, sometimes a grapple down on their knees, and when someone got into a headlock, the skinhead guards half-assedly strolled over to break them up.

When I realized that these fights transfixed me, my crane folding got faster and sloppier because I tried to cram it into Mr. Springer's interview portions and stopped when someone looked like they were about to throw a chair. Like any work of origami, a perfect crane depends on the preparatory work done beforehand, with precisely angled folds so that the final product's wings can flutter if one tugs at the tail while holding the bottom together. Your square paper trick was a perfect preamble, bestowing upon the sheet an ideal diagonal, and my first step was to cross the other corners together and fold them down to make an X. Then turn the sheet over, so that the creases protrude upward, and fold opposite lengths together to make an eight-point star of creases. Spread the paper flat again, and along the natural indentations allow the sheet to collapse into a smaller square. Fold the extended edges into the center, meeting at the bottom corner, into an isosceles triangle atop a parallelogram, and do the same on the other side. Press down the protruding top triangle to prepare it for the final phase, to open the layers upward to form an intricate diamond. The bottom bits of the diamond can then be folded inside out, forming the head and the tail, the upper half the wings, which you shape into a crane. With enough practice, this could take me at most two minutes.

At first, I didn't have a wish ready for when I finished my thousand cranes. You reminded me that I had to make a wish, when you and Nanay came home one day and I, surrounded with a mass of off-white birds around me, didn't hear you come in. By then, Lola Pet had already turned off the TV and retreated into our room to take a nap. I never mentioned *Jerry Springer* to you, a gut instinct that you might not have liked the fuller picture of my afternoon recreations with your mother-in-law.

"What about a sister?" you suggested, while Nanay grinned on her way to the kitchen. I had noticed that her belly looked rounder than usual.

"A brother!" I blurted out.

"But you're already a boy!" Nanay chimed in from the dining room, setting the placemats. "Don't you want a sister instead?"

"A brother!" I firmly reiterated.

"That's a good wish, then," you said.

By early June, I had decided that I had finished a thousand cranes, even though I didn't bother to count them, or perhaps because I grew bored of my months-long fixation. Those crane heaps you packed into plastic bags and kept in my bedroom for good luck. I still wished for a brother, and you and Nanay stopped bothering me to change my mind.

Nanay had started to join Lola Pet and me at home because she had grown too rotund to go to work. Lola Pet watched *Jerry Springer* a lot less by then, and at a lower volume, and only when Nanay was in the master bedroom sleeping. After I declared my origami hiatus, I sat at the computer instead, and for hours into the afternoon played *Neopets*, an HTML game where you raise fantastical pets and explore an alternate posthuman universe containing ancient omelets and secret mountains of Jell-O.

In mid-June, late into Gemini season (a cosmology I had learned from TV), you and Nanay were nowhere to be found. I wondered if Nanay felt well enough to have gone back to work. Taking advantage of your absence, Lola Pet sat at the TV and cranked the volume up to full. It was too early in the day for *Jerry Springer*, so she flipped the channel to CablePulse24, the local news. Neither of you were around to log me into the computer. Instead, I sat at the keyboard, and at max volume I practiced "Für Elise."

Shortly after three in the afternoon, the telephone rang. You were on the other line, and for the first time, I heard your voice tremble.

"Your wish came true," you murmured, trying to suppress a squeal of happiness and relief. "You have a new brother."

AS AN OLDER BROTHER, I found the new baby a joy to care for. When you two brought him home, you kept him in a white wooden crib next to your bed, where I'd pull up a stool and watch him wriggle around in his bear-printed straitjacket. When he let out a toothless cry, I rocked him back and forth, rolling him like a burrito, and he fell right back asleep. Then I'd go back to the living room and sit at the piano and, at the lowest audible volume, practice my scales.

Lola Pet came to call the little cooing bundle Balong, meaning "little boy" in Ilokano. When Balong could speak and Lola Pet acted as his main caregiver, those two became thick as thieves, despite the oceanic chasm between their discursive worlds. Now in his mid-twenties, Balong still bickers with Lola Pet, and he FaceTimes me from across the border to complain about her notorious habit of microwaving milk at four in the morning.

My only worry was whether or not Balong's good behavior would translate to Sunday mass, where babies loved to scream over the sermon and the altar servers could barely conceal their disdain even though they had been infants only a decade and a half before. The priest, whose face I can't remember because we always sat in the pews farthest away from the altar, especially after we started bringing the baby to the service, existed for me only as an echoey voice, at once indiscernible and soothing. According to the Catholic liturgical calendar, it was one of the days in "Ordinary Time," which I interpreted as Christianity's filler arc. He read the gospel with an animated countertenor while clutching the bully pulpit, less televangelist and more humanities keynote lecturer. Even the most adorable gospel, Jesus's sermon about the heavenly favor of children, couldn't escape our priest's scholarly cadence. *Let the LITTLE children. Come to me. And hinder them NOT. ForthekingdomofheavenbelongstoTHEM.*

Today's homily, fitting for a filler episode of ecclesiastical time, was about the duty of parents to their children, even if they cost half a million dollars (a figure the pastor repeated) on average to raise to eighteen years old, even if most of his audience lived in public housing. After the homily, the congregation rose together and recited the Apostles' Creed, a lengthy prayer that listed every belief that any good Catholic should have, and after another blessing, we sat down once again, and the ushers passed around woven baskets to collect our spare change. You always made a point to give more than the bare minimum, making sure that everyone around you saw the envelope of cash you dropped into the basket.

Nanay, the intrepid home accountant, took the priest's lessons to heart. At the dining table, she could sit for hours with printed spreadsheets and a calculator, upon which she would rapid-fire sums and differences and figure out our family's long-term budget with two kids, a mother, and a husband. I figured that with five mouths to feed she predicted that we'd be stretched thin, so while you were at work, she searched for other streams of income. Kuntaw wasn't an option, you emphasized; it was your form of community service, to teach Scarborough's youth how to mediate a violent encounter with mediated violence, so by design the gym should never be profitable. Now and then, Nanay would suggest that you consider an advertisement campaign, but you always refused, fearing that we'd sell out.

But some parts of Nanay's gym campaign were better received. You promised to be more entrepreneurial in recruiting students outside of the church, including non-Catholic and non–Couples for Christ families and, should the opportunity present itself, non-Filipinos. As a compromise, you refused to pass out flyers, though in a few years you'd ask me to design our gym's website for some online presence. The market was out there right under our noses, you promised, and we wouldn't have to do anything drastic to augment our everyday life.

Your recruitment strategy proved to be right. On the northeast corner of Markham Road and Lawrence Avenue, beside the Shoppers Drug Mart and its white sans serif font, was Soon Lee—every Filipino's favorite Chinese supermarket, which became obvious to anyone trying to do their weekly groceries on Sundays. The building was clearly a converted warehouse, with bare steel beams on the ceiling before industrial core became cool, and faded yellow walls that wrapped around the aisles and the wall-to-wall fishmonger. Across from the register, plastic crates of live crabs wriggled from the box and snapped at unsuspecting passersby. Down the dried food aisle, you spotted a family of five, a handsome couple with two elder daughters and a wailing son. More accurately, you heard the family, because the son was stomping his feet and bellowing at his mother to get him candy. I was at the end of the aisle, poking around at the crate of live crabs with plastic tongs, and peeked my head around to watch your advertising genius unfold. The signature sign of your efficacy was that, after your elevator pitch, the parents felt emboldened to shut their child up. The sisters, preteens both, covered their faces in embarrassment.

With a squinting smile, you waved us over to introduce us to your new friends, Tito Art and Tita Science, and their daughters Sister Soon Lee and Cop City, and the screaming kid, Brother Side Kick. When I didn't respond, you dropped your grin and flashed an eye that you'd cash in that evening for the lash's sting. I took Tito Art and Tita Science by the hand and pressed the back of their fingers to my forehead, before retreating to Balong's babbling side.

Now a one-man marketing firm, you turned every interaction into a possible sales pitch: the bakery where we'd get pandesal; the turo-turo store when no one at home was willing to cook; the bank line; the Manchu Wok at the Scarborough Town Centre food court; the Rainforest Café, where the carpets smelled like feet. Still, these new recruits meant only that the gym, not us, would break even. Nanay's opportunity for her own side hustle came in a serendipitous playdate. During recess, I was spending more time with Ube Cake and his twin brother, short-haired Serbians with the same permanent blush, and my first basketball teachers. Each twin was one half of a cohesive basketball player. Ube Cake, with a penchant for flair, never wanted to play defense but could dribble dizzying circles around a defender and lay the ball up close into the net, while any shot attempt further than two feet away fell short like a thrown brick. By contrast, his twin flickered with the possibilities of a valuable 3-and-D player, an off-ball specialist in long-range three-pointer shots, and a sticky defender who never let his man cross him without barreling through his unusually broad shoulders.

After school, our mothers surprised us outside the front doors. The three of us, who had spent all recesses playing pickup, smelled like the sun, as the Filipino adage goes. The moms were chatting, Nanay in her most comfortable but presentable blouse, the Balkan woman in a blazer and a sweater underneath, with a dazzling rhinestone necklace.

"How about a playdate?" Nanay suggested.

"A *date*?" Ube Cake spat out. His twin looked away, distracted by the masses of students spilling out of the doors. I followed his cue. Ube Cake looked incredulous. "Ew!"

A playdate, I learned later, was a prearranged block of time that parents organized to hang out with each other while making sure that their kids didn't need childcare. Lola Pet was on Balong duty, and Nanay clearly wanted a break. "How about this afternoon?"

In Mrs. Ube Cake's mom's minivan, we drove west on Finch Avenue, past the giant Zellers department store, to their bungalow in a winding neighborhood of identical bungalows. The house boasted an expansive living room; I marveled at the fireplace because I had never seen one before. In their bedroom, the twins wanted to show me their new computer game, *Counter-Strike*, a first-person shooter where you could either lay out a bomb as a terrorist or diffuse it as a counterterrorist. "Always play the terrorist," Ube Cake remarked. "It's more fun."

Nanay brought home a souvenir from the playdate, an orientation packet for a nutrition supplement company. Over the next few weeks, we received shipments of branded shake mixes and vitamin pills, Thermoses and cups, and swag bags. Our already strained dining room doubled as a storage closet for the material, with which Nanay would try, like her playdate co-supervisor, to preach its nutritious gospel to her friends at church. And when it didn't work, the shipments kept piling up, as did Nanay's spreadsheets, as did your silent treatment.

The play dates with Ube Cake and his twin stopped altogether. We still sat together in class and played basketball at recess, but when I tried to say hi to their mom, she averted her gaze, scurrying her children out of the school grounds before I could wave goodbye. Shortly thereafter, the nutrition supplement deliveries ceased, and the quietude of home dissipated into its usual rhythm. The one piece of paraphernalia Nanay kept around was a white shaker, because it was a great vehicle for the morning smoothies that you two had replaced breakfasts with. When you tried to get me to drink a diluted blueberry concoction, I protested, wanting to eat eggs instead. That hunger strike, which lasted a week, was broken by Lola Pet, who shared her sticky Quaker Oats with me after you two left for work.

Fifteen years later, when acquaintances tried to sell me their own irrefutable opportunities for residual income ("I did it, and you can, too!"), I remembered the clutter of nutrition supplements and walked away, never to speak to them again.

SLEEP

AT LEAST ONCE A MONTH, you'd beat my ass, and shortly after, you sung me a lullaby to help me fall asleep. For each whipping session, I sat at your bedside, while you stood over me and screamed my sins back at me. There were several running themes behind my transgressions, such as a bad report card or my having stayed on the computer too long playing *Neopets*. My favorite theme, however, was my lethargy around chores. You told me to take out the trash every day after school, but I'd never listen. I'd lie to you and say I forgot, and you would blame it on the television I watched with Lola Pet after school, so you reminded me that I would be banned from English-language programs for a month and was only allowed to turn my attention to French TV, so that I could learn how to be a proper Canadian. What I didn't tell you was that the garbage chute always made me puke whenever I opened it, and I preferred your consequences to my disgust.

When you finished your lecture, you told me to lie on my stomach, removed your belt, and lifted it above your head. Then a series of whips against my buttocks, each one more punishing than the last. In the early days, I made the mistake of wearing nothing but my pantulog shorts, the same ones I'd wear to sleep, a thin faux-satin layer that barely kept my genitals warm, let alone concealed. The more sins I committed, the more I adapted, and years into our Silver Springs sojourn, I learned to wear at least two layers of underwear underneath my shorts for the nights I knew that an ass-whooping was coming. You must have adapted, because you'd occasionally whip me on my lower back or the backs of my thighs, targets guaranteed to leave me in a limp.

After your beatings, I retreated to my room, and on your behalf continued the afflictions on myself: I'd try to tear my hair from my head, or slap and punch myself in the jaw, or bash my head against the wall, always in a spot covered with hair, so that you wouldn't inspect my face and find anything else that would earn your whips. I locked myself in my room and, until my bedtime at 9:00 p.m., retreated into any of my favorite books. As my curfew crept up, I preemptively turned off the lights and blanketed myself from head to toe. Miraculously, Lola Pet never came into the room those nights, and gave me my space.

I liked to pretend that my stinging eyes were just my body getting sleepy. As I started to drift off, you slowly opened the door and sat down beside me in bed.

"Anak," you muttered in your dulcet baritone, "would you like me to sing you a lullaby?" I nodded. You cleared your throat and stroked my hair. I choked and began to cry.

Your go-to lullaby was a ballad by a Filipino priest, "Sino Ako?" or "Who Am I?" Back then, we'd call it "Hiram sa Diyos," after the first line of the song, a reminder that, in the end, our lives are only borrowed from God. As I finally gave in to sleep, you'd whisper in my ear, "I love you, anak."

I wanted to be a good Christian like you, so I started paying more attention at church. But the acoustics at St. Aidan remained terrible, and the priest's voice still a garbled keynote, so I watched instead for the altar's choreography. Accompanying the priest was either another junior pastor or a deacon, which was something like a priest's butler, the highest rank a married man could reach in the Catholic clergy. Flanking them were gowned boys and girls, dressed like acolytes, who performed all the ceremonial tasks of a Catholic mass: processing up with the crucifix and candles, washing the priest's hands, setting the table with a plate and goblet, and clearing the altar after communion. On special occasions, one of the acolytes swung a brass flail from which a smoky frankincense wisped, filling the church with an olfactory flair. I knew how to do most of those tasks at home anyway, I figured, and so I asked you if I could enlist in the altar servers' ranks.

"When you're older and mature enough," you'd tell me, "you can be an altar boy."

To enter into altar service, I had to be inducted into the church itself. Baptism, which I had undergone as a baby in Manila, was only the first step. After I had been ritually purified in the metonymic waters of the Jordan River, my sins thereafter had tainted the sanctity of my soul, once I had gained sentience. The next steps were called sacraments, and would set me on the path toward another paternal relationship, not to my biological father, but to the Father in heaven. Atoning to God for a borrowed life of sin was, naturally, a lifelong journey, which began with the sacrament of confession. Like our kuntaw drills, which built my physical aptitudes, your beatings were meant to train me in the spiritual skills I needed to become a full-fledged Catholic. And because I was such a fantastic liar, I needed the force of your remediation. Above all, the sacrament of confession demanded from the faithful one thing: the ability to tell the truth.

The ceremony for the sacrament of confession was a muted affair. On an afternoon at St. Aidan, I joined other kids my age in line, almost a hundred of us, and sat social-distanced on the pews so we could take the requisite space and silence to reflect on everything wrong we had done. The head priest, whose face I couldn't bring myself to look at, solemnly stepped out of a door to the side of the church and called upon us to join him one by one. Another pastor opened an adjacent door to help with overflow. The deacon would usher us to the confessional. When it was my turn, he led me to the second door, a spare chamber with an empty chair, across from which the pastor—a handsome blond man from Newfoundland—waited for me.

"Have a seat, my son," he murmured, a yellow-tinted smile flashing across his face. "Don't be scared," he reassured, and gestured to the empty seat. He glanced at my hands; my fingernails, cut short, were trying to dig into the flayed skin along my cuticles.

I sat across from him. I recalled the script we had learned from the coordinators earlier that day, who reminded us what we had to say.

"B-bless me, Father, for I have s-sinned," I blurted out. "It has been . . ."

"This is your *first* confession," the pastor coached me in a whisper.

"T-this is my first confession."

"What are your sins, my child?"

I listed some worldly afflictions I had enumerated in the pews. My list was compiled from all the times you beat my ass. I lied often. I watched television shows that I shouldn't have (though I never did tell the priest that it was *Jerry Springer*). I didn't do my chores in a timely manner. I didn't listen to my parents at home. And worst of all, my grades weren't all that great. Above the hum of the air conditioner, I thought I heard the good pastor stifle a chuckle.

"Listen to your parents, according to our Lord's second commandment, and you will learn how to prepare yourself for a good relationship with God Himself. Bow your head and repeat after me. My God—"

"My God . . ."

"I am sorry for my sins with all my heart."

"I am sorry for my sins with all my heart."

"In choosing to do wrong and failing to do good . . ."

"In choosing to do wrong and failing to do good . . ."

"I have sinned against You whom I should love above all things."

"I have sinned against You whom I should love above all things."

After this prayer of contrition, the pastor told me that, before I left, I was to pray five Our Fathers and ten Hail Marys, and all my sins would be forgiven. I thanked him and returned to my spot in the pews, and dutifully recited my prayers to myself. At the back of the church, you and Nanay watched me learn how to be pious. I think I made you proud.

As the Catholic sequence goes, once I learned how to tell a robed stranger the truth, I could finally learn how to *receive* it, in the form of a dehydrated medallion of wheat flour, which had been transformed into a sliver of Jesus Christ's own body. In the spring months after Easter, on the day of my First Communion, for which I dressed to the nines—a freshly starched shirt and trouser combo, a crisp black blazer, and a tie you lent me from your IFIC-appropriate collection—I readied myself to taste Jesus's actual flesh. At home, I bit into my arm and tasted my own skin to prepare myself for the moment that the off-white biscuit changed into sinew and musculature in my mouth. But when the priest placed the host upon my tongue, all I tasted was a stale cracker.

When we got home, I asked you if I was finally ready to become an altar boy. You wiped your lips with the paper towel, swallowed the morsel in your mouth, and cleared your throat.

"Let's see how your report card looks like at the end of the year."

AT THE TURN of the century (or the millennium, depending on whom you ask), the intersection of Markham and Lawrence bustled like an improvised public square. There were no plazas except the strip malls, nor parkettes with benches to feed birds on, only asphalted lots and a smattering of establishments: Soon Lee Supermarket, the pharmacy, a movie theater that looked like a monolith à la Stanley Kubrick, a sari emporium, and a big-box combination Canadian Tire–Zellers–Toys"R"Us that announced another pocket of pseudo-public space, Cedarbrae Mall. Today, as an empty shell of its dazzling late twentieth-century self, Cedarbrae still boasts the same reputation it had back then, as an indoor extension of the ghetto that surrounded the area. I envied the kids who defied the security guards (and your judgment) and rode their bikes between the vendor booths or popped wheelies outside the Zellers diner while the aunties swatted at them with their long umbrellas. Outside, in the parking lot, would-be shoppers competed with BMX bikes and scooters and clandestine salespeople pushing mangoes and tape cassettes from the backs of their minivans.

It was at this intersection that you inadvertently nourished my love for *Pokémon*. At home, when I could sneak in some cartoons before you returned, I would occasionally include the anime in my regular rotation of programs, in between the future gym rat's supernatural fantasy (*Dragon Ball Z*) and the hopeless romantic's bible (*Inuyasha*). It was around that time when my friends at school started to show up with plastic rectangular handheld consoles, in the primary and secondary colors, boasting a pixelated screen without backlight, a directional pad, and some other buttons for actions and menu selection. Historians of popular culture would diagnose this era as a major wave of Japanese influence in North America, packaged not only in the Nintendo Game Boy but in its most popular game, in which the player endlessly accumulates non-human slaves to solve crimes and do battle on their behalf. I didn't own a Game Boy but was entranced by all the kids at recess who staged battles of their own between their devices, linked together by a neon-green cable. At home, I supplemented what I knew as a secondhand Pokémon Trainer with the franchise's anime, which moralized animal capture by evoking the power of friendship.

Sensing my infatuation with the franchise, you kept our Cedarbrae visits short and direct, unlike our trips to Scarborough Town Centre, where our family could wander and spend an entire afternoon just for fun. The expanse of the Toys"R"Us was adjacent to the manly jungle of the Canadian Tire, and while you strolled through the lights section, I tried to sneak away to the toy store to catch a glimpse of the video game section, then just a small selection of handheld consoles, a Nintendo 64 and the occasional Sega Genesis. "We have video games at home," you'd remind me, and hauled out your own prized possession, a Super Nintendo. You had bought this system in Saudi Arabia to keep you company, and with it, you kept a single game cartridge, an anthology of classic arcade games like *Super Mario Brothers*, *Duck Hunt*, and *Donkey Kong*. Still, the SNES didn't have *Pokémon*, so I begged you to let me gawk at the Game Boys the next time we went to the mall.

At the Cedarbrae theaters, you took me on a father-son date to watch a cinematic masterpiece called *Pokémon: The First Movie—Mewtwo Strikes Back*. An elderly man, Mr. Loader, dutifully tore our ticket stubs and in a measured cadence announced: "*Pokémon*, Theater Four, to your left." The movie elaborated on a foundational lore of the video games, the DNA splicing of a primordial creature called Mew to develop a humanoid clone aptly named Mewtwo. Under the brutal experimentation of Team Rocket, the Pokémon world's national crime syndicate, Mewtwo gained sentience and rebelled against his captors by breaking out of his prison. Like my literary hero, Edmond Dantès, Mewtwo fled to a remote island to plot his revenge against the world, in which he would clone every species of Pokémon in his own image. In a moving climactic scene, the protagonist, Ash Ketchum, was petrified into rock as he tried to intervene in a psychic collision between Mewtwo and Mew. He was revived by the tears of Pikachu, his lightning-aspected mouse companion, and Mewtwo was so moved by the boy's sacrifice that he turned back time to undo the cataclysm he had ushered into the world. *Mewtwo Strikes Back* was, at its core, a parable against biological determinism, preaching the virtues of a devoted love to one another and undying faith in the potential of great and small. In other words, it was a great Christian movie.

In the wake of our movie night, you and Nanay had saved up enough to grant me my wish. I had been a good kid recently, you said, with good grades on recent tests and swift progress in my piano lessons. After church, you drove *BEAST!* southward to Markham and Lawrence. I had surmised that we'd be doing weekly groceries at Soon Lee, or another shopping trip at Canadian Tire. Instead, you parked in front of the Toys"R"Us and told us to wait for you. In short order, you walked out with a small shopping bag and handed it to me. Inside was a brand-new Game Boy, in pistachio green, and a *Pokémon Red Version* cartridge.

Thanks to Balong, I didn't get to enjoy my new game for long. I lay down on the living room rug, holding my Game Boy inches above my face, squinting at a pixelated urban landscape. My sprite was in Cerulean City, a riverside town whose gym leader specialized in water types. Balong crawled over and rolled beside me, flailing his arms and legs in the air. My eyes were heavy from the strain, so I put my game down, holding it in my right hand, and fell asleep. I woke up to a warmth, like a lukewarm heat pack, spreading across my right hand. It felt wet. I rolled over and found the culprit: in his slumber, Balong had vomited all over my Game Boy. I jolted awake, tried to wipe it off with a moist paper towel, and flipped the on switch. The Game Boy didn't turn on. Nanay picked Balong up and cleaned his mouth, then placed him back in the crib. Because I suppressed my own anguish, you bought me a replacement later that week, with a fresh copy of *Pokémon Yellow*, a special edition that featured Pikachu as a companion sprite. To this day, when I feel like picking on Balong, I text him while he's at work to ask if he has saved up enough to replace my Game Boy he hurled all over as a baby.

The following year, on Christmas Eve, *Pokémon* would enrich my life yet again. We had spent all week getting ready for the festivities, with Nanay and Lola Pet on Noche Buena duty, with a baked salmon as the centerpiece, along with an assortment of casserole dishes from the Campbell's cookbook. You and I were on tree duty, a plastic one we bought from the Cedarbrae Canadian Tire, in a white box that, to this day, is still stashed somewhere in your garage, even when we could afford a nicer one. Balong was dutifully cheering from his crib, bouncing up and down, clapping at our efforts to assemble the tree. On the morning of Christmas Eve, Nanay hung up two red stockings on the window, pressing them into the glass with suction cups. Not wanting to miss out, I stuffed them with leftover wrapping paper from school that I had pocketed before we went on break. Your own contribution was a bag of mini candy canes from work, and to augment their aesthetic effect, I left a few dangling from the tops of the stockings.

That night, after we exchanged presents and sang carols, you noticed something peculiar about the stockings. One of them seemed chunkier than usual.

"Anak!" you teased. "Go check the stocking at the window. I think something's happening to it."

I wedged the stocking open with two paper clips, afraid that something inside would jump out to bite my hand. A gilded box peeked out, wrapped in plastic and adorned with a falcon whose feathers glistened in all the colors of the rainbow. A copy of the newest title in my favorite franchise, *Pokémon Gold Version*.

"It must have been Santa Claus!" Nanay exclaimed. You beamed at me from the couch. I leaped for joy, and thanked St. Nicholas, God's patron saint of children and repentant thieves.

ON THE FIRST DAY of the fourth grade, my new classroom felt like a different world. Not only were we seated at individual desks (as opposed to shared round tables) but we had to climb two flights of stairs to go to where the big kids were, the second floor. The usual suspects—the two Josephs, the Serbian twins, Beloved Disciple—no longer sat with me. We had become diasporic to each other, scattered along the linoleum floor, a community stretched as far as our seams would allow, the threads ready to snap at any moment. Sour Cream, my closest friend, had left for another school. Except for a spontaneous Instagram search in college, I never saw her again.

Robbed of our round tables and in-class congregations, we gathered at recess more frequently. The twins invited me to their house to play *Counter-Strike*, an invitation which I had to decline, because I wanted to be home to help Lola Pet take care of Balong. Egyptian Joseph introduced me to holographic Pokémon cards, and Tamil Joseph guided me into the wonderful world of Sri Lankan pastries.

On the second week of September, Tamil Joseph gave me a gift, one of the extra mutton rolls that his mom had packed him for school, a crispy golden-brown dough wrapped around minced meat and spices. I took a bite, and my mouth burst into flame. "How is it?" Tamil Joseph asked, while Egyptian Joseph looked on expectantly. Through involuntary tears, I assured him that it was delicious, but my benefactor wasn't convinced. I looked around for an authority figure to ask for permission to leave the room, but none were to be found. I excused myself to drink some water at the fountain. Outside, while I ducked my head and brought the water to my tongue, the teachers gathered around a TV, the same kind that they'd usually wheel into class whenever they didn't want to make a lesson plan for the day. But the TV stayed outside, in the hallway, two teachers transfixed to the screen, then a small crowd gathering, cross-armed, the still shock of death. I washed my burning mouth, bent over the water fountain, praying the capsaicin would slide off my tongue. When the flame lingered, I bit my tongue and scraped it against my teeth, begging God Almighty to spare me from the searing heat.

In the gaps between their heads, I spotted a live feed of two steel-and-glass monoliths in the New York skyline, their summits aflame and enveloped in thick smoke. Mrs. Frigidaire, my first-grade teacher, gasped and covered her mouth. A commercial plane soared across the blue sky, right into the towers. Another teacher, one I didn't recognize, spotted me and told me to get back into the classroom.

We were dismissed for the rest of the day. The same teacher I didn't know peeked his head into the class and told us that "tourists" attacked the United States, the world's most powerful country, in the heart of its biggest city. Toronto, he warned, was Canada's biggest city, and like the World Trade Center in New York, the CN Tower might be the next target. The country was on lockdown, and schools were in grave danger, the teacher said, flashing a glance at the

Josephs. On my end, I didn't understand why "tourists" would attack our suburb, since Scarborough was so uninteresting.

"I *hate* terrorists!" Ube Cake bellowed to no one in particular. His twin nodded, his face flush red. "I *hate hate HATE* terrorists!" Ube Cake glanced over at me, searching for a response.

"I hate tourists, too!" I blurted out. The twins turned away.

You and Nanay had called ahead that you'd come to pick me up and made your way back to Scarborough, speeding *BEAST!* into the pickup area at the front door.

When we were allowed to go back to school a week later, the classroom was half empty. The South Asian kids sat apart from everyone else, and everyone else gave them a wide berth, even the teachers. The two Josephs sat at the back corner of the classroom, their heads on their desks, wordless except for a few grunts when I tried to approach them. I learned later that the parents from Eastern and Southern Europe and Newfoundland had pulled their kids out of the school, and we were left with the immigrant kids from Africa, the Caribbean, and Asia. Ube Cake and his twin stopped coming to class altogether. From the teachers, I overheard that their family had moved further out into the suburbs, outside of the 416 area code, to a town called Whitby, where the schoolkids looked more like them.

Within a couple of weeks, you decided, too, that it was time to go. Joined by two new members, our family had outgrown Silver Springs at last. Nanay was going steady with her indiscernible government job, and you had just landed an even better position yourself, a downtown career just a few blocks from her, at the Law Society of Upper Canada. With the savings from your new jobs, you qualified for your first mortgage and bought a townhouse in a new construction project all the way to the south, further south than our first basement apartment, down the street from another Scarborough hospital, along the Eglinton Avenue throughfare, in a new subdivision conveniently built across from a No Frills supermarket, a bowling alley, and a neon-lighted establishment called Caddy's, its sign adorned with a decommissioned Cadillac painted over with pictures of two scantily clad women.

"Welcome home," you said proudly. A home all our own.

GREAT POWER

IN A POLISHED beige Oldsmobile, a silver-haired man drives his rebellious high schooler nephew to a museum. When they arrive, the teenager, a self-motivated and secretive nerd, begins to unbuckle his seatbelt, but his uncle stretches his arm across the back of the passenger seat. The man hasn't spoken to his ward in so long, he remarks, that the boy feels like a stranger, even though they live under the same roof.

"You shirk your chores, you have all those weird experiments in your room, you start fights at school—"

"I didn't start that fight, I told you that!" the nephew protests. One of his bullies, Flash Thompson, had been sitting behind him in the cafeteria when the teenager's uncontrollable new power—a weblike substance involuntarily oozing from his arm—accidentally caught a tray full of food. He flung the tray behind him, and the cafeteria lunch splattered all over Flash's shoulder. As the teenager briskly walked away, trying to avoid making a scene, Flash followed him out into the hallway and swung his fists at the boy who had dirtied up his polo shirt.

"Peter," the elderly man says to his nephew, decelerating the cadence of his voice, "these are the years when a man changes into the man he's going to become for the rest of his life . . . This guy, Flash Thompson, he probably deserved what happened."

Peter furrows his brow, recalling the hallway fight. His Uncle Ben has interpreted this as adolescent hormones, but Peter's own puberty is further inconvenienced by the fact that a radioactive spider has bitten him, granting him arachnid-like extrasensory perception. He made quick work of Flash Thompson, dodging the assailant's punches at breakneck speed and somersaulting into the air to avoid a second attacker, who then fled the scene, terrified at Peter's superhuman abilities. Flash swung at Peter once again, with sluggish and inefficient hook punches, and Peter caught his wrist and twisted his arm before landing his own reverse punch directly into the bully's sternum, pummeling him across the room.

"Just because you *can* beat him up," Uncle Ben continues, "doesn't give you the right to."

Frustrated with his uncle's car-seat homily, Peter leers at his driver with disdain.

"Remember," the elder opines, "with great power comes great responsibility."

Until Tobey Maguire's masterful 2002 performance in *Spider-Man*, I don't think I really had a favorite superhero. The protagonists from my favorite animes, like the half-alien Goku in *Dragon Ball Z*, I didn't really consider to be superheroes because they never seemed to account for any social burden beyond their own personal growth. Even though Maguire clearly looked way too old to play a high school nerd, there was something exquisitely vulnerable about his Peter Parker, something that captured the experience of a kid flailing about in a body he could never reconcile with, in an environment that—in his view—was always out to get him.

Together, you and I watched *Spider-Man* on opening weekend, that first year (that only year) we lived across from the bowling alley and the strip club, in a townhouse subdivision that developers quaintly named Neighbourhood Place. And when the movie was finally available on DVD, we brought it home and I spent afternoons in the living room watching it on repeat. When Balong was able to speak, he, too, adopted Spider-Man as his favorite superhero, a fandom that you supported for both of us, even though your own preferred fantasy character of choice was Superman.

Superman, like Goku, and like you, was a physically gifted immigrant from a ravaged homeland. What destroyed Krypton was the planet's natural death, leaving Kal-El (Superman's birth name) as the only survivor, hurtling across the universe and crash-landing into Earth. Goku's own story, written by the great manga artist Akira Toriyama, was based on Kal-El's tale, but what destroyed his home planet was the wrath of a genocidal warlord named Frieza. Your homeland's destruction wasn't a single catastrophe but the sediment of its own history, Bataan's remarkable survival across multiple apocalypses: the Spanish occupation, the American wars, the forced death marches under the Japanese Empire, and then the slow death of the peninsula's land and water once the country was free. Still, I think Superman resonated with you because, unlike my superhero of choice, who grew into his powers, Kal-El was born into his and spent his adult life hiding behind an alter ego, masking his refugee origins and his devastating strength behind the pious meekness of Clark Kent.

But unlike you, and unlike our favorite superheroes, I had no special talent. When we lived in Silver Springs, I ate voraciously of the instant mashed potatoes you brought home from our grocery trips. At Neighbourhood Place, this enthusiasm grew into an addiction, and on Saturdays at the gym, I felt my body atrophy as the potato-filled weight of my stomach impeded my ability to move. I think I wanted you to be my own Uncle Ben, a compassionate compass who could awaken me out of my self-imposed slumber and tell me that it was okay to stop picking at the tight fabric around my expanding belly. Instead, you told me that I needed to behave and be an example to all the other kids around me. Yet by the fourth grade, I was a fat kid who couldn't even defend himself in the mock fights of a martial arts class and on weekdays was paralyzed by an inability to hold a conversation. What, then, was the responsibility of the unpowerful?

THE INTERSECTION OF Eglinton and Danforth had no high-rises, no boysenberry orchards to gift me with morsels on the way home. You warned me never to cross the street south, and to avoid the establishment with the Cadillac above the door. After school, I made sure to stay north of Eglinton, a street which, like Finch Avenue near Silver Springs, was a multilane death trap. Our own block was safe enough and as expansive as any other concretized slice of Scarborough land. North of the complex was the school bus stop. It was my first time taking the yellow vehicle with other kids, since we lived too far for me to walk to my new school and too close to seek out any other options. Along the Danforth edge was the Mecca of the neighborhood kids, the 5 & Dime convenience store, which boasted massive glass jars of candies at—you guessed it—five cents a pop.

On weekends, and sometimes on weeknights, we did the bigger grocery trips at the No Frills, far less wondrous than Soon Lee but with cheaper bulk items and abundant discounts on frozen meats. On special occasions, we partook of the Chinese buffet at $9.99 per head, for bottomless plates of sumptuous orange chicken, bland chop suey, and jellied cubes that tasted like polyurethane and congealed Kool-Aid.

In the neighborhood, we called the local Catholic school the Santa Claus School, because it was named after St. Nicholas. For church, we still trekked up north to St. Aidan, because Santa Claus didn't have an eponymous parish around it. But like St. Aidan the school, Santa Claus was a nondescript brown box, surrounded with a scattering portable classrooms added when the original building could no longer sustain the area's population boom. What it lacked in classroom space it made up for in its track-and-field oval and a robust athletics program.

My homeroom teacher was an Italian man in his late twenties, Mr. Cognoscenti. He bore an uncanny resemblance to Bing from kuntaw, the Filipino simulacrum of Lance Bass, complete with front-spiked hair and a squinting smile equal parts charming and restrained. He wore a thick musk, something between Lysol, Old Spice, and the odor of a martial arts tournament, a cocktail that saturated the portable classroom in which we spent the day. It wasn't off-putting, nor enticing in any way, except to Ms. Chiacchiera, the fifth-grade teacher, armed with a thick keyring on a Volkswagen Beetle keychain, who popped in every day to ask for markers and always lingered too long. Mr. Cognoscenti was a charming man. You must have thought so, too. One morning, you recounted the dream you had, that Mr. Cognoscenti showed up at our front door and made us dinner. You brought this up several times, always pausing on how much Dream Nanay giggled and tossed her hair whenever she received him into the Dream House.

When I joined Mr. Cognoscenti's class, it was a month into September, in a school already filled to capacity, so he sat me at an empty seat that belonged to someone who was away with an illness. The desks were arranged perpendicular to one another in groups of four, forming a set of pinwheels. These had been segregated by gender, but as a newcomer I was seated with a group of three girls. None of them set out to ignore me, but they seldom acknowledged my presence. I made to lift my desk to see its contents. Across me, Jellyfish, a Filipina and Portuguese girl with wavy hair, gave me a stern look. "She's not gonna like you snooping through her stuff," Jellyfish warned. I shut the lid and laid out my books on the desktop.

After the first week, the seat's original owner, a Filipina girl with jet-black bangs and a handbag, came back from her illness. Mr. Cognoscenti asked us to share the desk until he was able to get me one for myself. I introduced myself to the girl, who ignored me. "Come on, Prada," Mr. Cognoscenti said. "Be nice."

"You smell," she snarled at me. I tugged at my collar, wrapped it above my nose, and inhaled. I divined a blend of your morning coffee, Bounce dryer sheets, and my L'Oréal Kids shampoo—nothing offensive. Prada scooched her chair away, making sure to accentuate the scraping of the chair legs against the linoleum floor.

Mr. Cognoscenti must have picked up on Prada's disdain for me, because the next day he rearranged the classroom so that all the desks faced the front in a perfect grid. He managed to swing an extra desk from Ms. Chiacchiera, who hauled it into the classroom that morning. Prada was seated at the front right of the room, farthest away from the windows, and I had the center left, in my teacher's direct line of sight.

Despite that social hiccup, it was easy to make friends at school. Thanks to my Game Boy, I gathered around myself a group of boys who loved *Pokémon* like I did: Juggernaut, a freakishly tall Jamaican whom the girls fawned over for his overflowing confidence; Mountain Man, a Haitian boy who lived around the corner at Neighbourhood Place; Tyler, one of the few white kids at the school; and Krillin and Yami Yugi, two short Filipinos who traded cards with me. We all took the same school bus home, a path that snaked around identical bungalows and high-rises before dropping us off at the last stop, right in front of a tall white-and-blue building, a ten-minute walk away from our townhouse complex.

Yami Yugi and Mountain Man walked in the same direction, Yami Yugi joining us halfway before splitting off to the north, so we made a habit of separating at the 5 & Dime. At the back of the store, we discovered a vending machine for trading cards at a dollar each, the kind where you put four quarters in metal grooves, push the coin slot in, and out pops a card that's too shiny and poorly aligned to be legitimate.

In one of the most prescient decisions you made in our relationship, you rewarded my new social life with a gift: a green link cable that connected two Game Boys together, so players could battle or trade Pokémon between each other. With your and Nanay's new jobs, we were suddenly flush with money, and I didn't have to perform my yearning for a link cable for you to come home and surprise me with one. With the link cable, it was so much easier to make friends in the neighborhood, where everyone seemed to own a Game Boy. When I figured out how to exploit a glitch in *Pokémon Gold Version* and duplicate the rare Pokémon I owned, I cloned them for the kids on the bus, who gathered around my group of friends at the back to receive their gift. If Mewtwo were real, I thought, I doubt he would have been happy that I was splicing his virtual DNA to pawn off at school.

IF YOU COULD IGNORE the rattling bass from Caddy's at 2:00 a.m., or the swaying and incoherent crowds tumbling out of the bowling alley, Neighbourhood Place might have been the coziest area we'd ever lived. We were, at last, homeowners among homeowners, first-time homeowners among first-time homeowners, a congregation of '90s immigrants who'd finally made it, single-family properties be damned. Every resident took pride in grooming and resodding the sliver of grass that lined their driveway, trimming the slim rectangular lawns in their fenced-in backyards, and keeping pristine the bricks of their house. These were dark brown or pale beige, the brickwork alternating from house to house for a sense of variety between each nearly identical unit.

The developers had made maximum use of the land by slicing it into minuscule parcels, so each townhouse was tall and every flight of stairs boasted no fewer than ten steps, each of which I counted diligently so that I could end the climb on my right foot. Eleven steps up from the sidewalk—twelve if you count the threshold—into the open-concept kitchen and dining and living room, a narrow expanse that Nanay tastefully segmented off with a white floor-to-ceiling Ikea Expedit, a four-by-four grid of open shelves, upon which she arranged family portraits and asymmetrical vases with willow branches. Adjacent to the living room was a door out into the backyard, a wooden patio with twelve rickety steps down to the grass. And up top, to the third story, fourteen carpeted steps to our three bedrooms, and Lola Pet and Balong undertook their first of many forays as roommates. I had my own room, with two windows that faced out into the front street and a door that swung smoothly so I could leave it cracked open when you were sleeping, afraid to get locked inside.

If I were to enter from the garage, as you often did when you came home, it was to a lightless unfinished basement, sixteen steps underneath the living room. At night, our basement was the stuff of nightmares. The single lightbulb hanging down from the center of the ceiling managed to both blind me with its glare and obscure most of the room in shadow. What made the darkness worse was our semifunctional washer and dryer, which spun and rumbled in irregular intervals, an hour and a half per cycle, before wailing an onomatopoeia into our personal crypt: *DONNNNNNE.* To allay my fear of the basement, you surmised that it would make a perfect replacement for the L'Amoreaux parking lot, a place to train kicks now that we had the luxury of domestic space. From a wooden beam on the ceiling, you dangled some twine and tied it to the neck of a water bottle, the way you'd done across that park, from *BEAST!*'s back hatch, leaving enough slack in the twine to adjust the bottle's height. Together, we pushed our unpacked boxes to the walls, leaving enough of a radius for me to spin into a biakid as fast as I could.

When the weather was nice, you brought out the kicking pads, both the rectangular ones for straight kicks and the clappers for spinning and roundhouse kicks, and we moved our training to the backyard, where the sod could cushion my falls. Once, you suggested that we practice after the autumn rains. When I protested, you told me that it would help me experience how the original sikaranistas, the rice farmers from Central Luzon, developed the martial art as a pastime for their villages. There were two circumstances in which farmers could play sikaran in the rice paddies. The first was right after the floods from the Lingayen Gulf to the northwest, which would irrigate the fields with brackish water filtered fresh from Pangasinan's delta. The second was right after the rice harvest, when stalks were cut down with sharp curved bolos and bales of rice carried to the village to be washed and processed. The runoffs from the Cordillera mountains to the north would keep the paddies moist, with the spongy texture our lawn took up in a Toronto fall. When it was time to play, fighters tied ropes around their waists and looped another rope between themselves, affixed to their hemp belts, so that they couldn't run away without the weight of the opponent impeding them. The ropes were loose enough for each fighter to biakid endlessly but kept the players close enough so that any misstep that didn't result in someone smacked down to the ground would bring *both* fighters down. It was from this game that sikaran developed its signature move, the biakid, which was most effective from point-blank range. Fortunately, we never did any of these exercises in the backyard, thanks to Nanay's emphatic veto.

As it turns out, Nanay had her own schemes for making the basement more hospitable and less of a dingy gray prison. She decided to throw me a birthday party down there, on a date made more auspicious because it was also the opening night of *Harry Potter and the Philosopher's Stone*. She had gifted me a copy of the book from a catalog that the school sent us home with, filled with collector's sets and new releases through the children's publisher Scholastic. It was only thanks to the lack of good video game adaptations that Harry Potter didn't gentrify Pokémon out of my nerdy areas of interest. When the first novel enraptured me, and you complained that I spent too much time with my face in the books and banned me from bringing *Harry Potter* to the dinner table, Nanay openly nurtured my fandom instead.

The Harry Potter birthday party was a stroke of genius. Nanay reached out to the parents of my friends from St. Aidan and Santa Claus, as well as the younger students from the gym. It was a costume party and a makeshift movie premiere all at once. Egyptian Joseph (who still called me Maree, to my embarrassment) wore a purple robe adorned with stars, and Beloved Disciple wore a wizard's hat to complement his demure all-black sorcerer look. You made me a wand out of a wooden dowel from the hardware store, the same wood you used for arnis sticks. After an evening of prizes, you and Beloved Disciple's dad drove us to the Cedarbrae theater in your minivans, where we filled half a row of seats close to the front. With the exception of Beloved Disciple, whose family ended up studying with you at the gym, that party was the last time I saw those St. Aidan friends.

SCARBOROUGH, WHICH WAS my entire world, stretched into a concerto after our move to Neighbourhood Place. By contrast, Silver Springs was a short sequence of pieces, maybe a prelude and fugue, the apartment complex as the opening theme that unfolded into the fixed counterpoint of home, school, church, and piano. From Neighbourhood Place, our commutes to church became longer and more onerous, and so I was able to learn the cadence of the city: the undulations in the concrete above buried rivers, the crescendos of car honks near the Scarborough Town Centre interchange, the sulfur accenting Midland Station, the monotonous legato of the identical midcity bungalows, the arpeggiating wires and scaffolds of the hydro fields, the ornamental cracks in the asphalt near Bridlewood Mall.

As much as possible, we tried to keep the same touchpoints of our Silver Springs life. We still went to St. Aidan and ate lunch at the Zellers diner or the Cantonese bakery in Bridlewood Mall, saw the same overburdened family doctor on Victoria Park Avenue. But the same commitment couldn't be made for my music lessons. West of Neighbourhood Place, toward a smaller and soggier Soon Lee location, was a strip mall dotted with signage for Sri Lankan garment stores, sandwiching a white-and-red declaration that simply read PIANO. We combed through the storefronts for a music store, like the one near Silver Springs, but instead found a flyer taped to the front window of a stairwell. Up the steps was a hallway of medical specialists, both Chinese and Western, and at the farthest room to the east, a glass entrance into a waiting room, behind which was another glass wall that looked into a single piano next to a tiny window. After work, you and Nanay took me in for an assessment with Mrs. Christakos, a Greek woman with a Lady Diana haircut, a thick accent, and an undying grin. At first, I scrunched my nose at the office's perennial odor, of stale cigarettes. You must have disliked it, too, because you volunteered to wait in the car while Nanay sat in the waiting room chatting with Mrs. Christakos, and I sat at the piano, a short upright with heavy keys, heavier than those at Mrs. Chu's classroom.

"It takes some time to get used to them," a voice behind me said. Mrs. Christakos soundlessly stepped through the room, while Nanay took her place in the cushioned chair outside, looking into the window.

"Why are the keys so heavy?" I wondered aloud, my shoulders curling in to help my hands push into the ivory.

"They'll help make your fingers strong. Here, why don't you try out some scales?" She placed a Xerox printout of an F major scale on the stand.

There is a subtle trial when a pianist first encounters an F major scale. With most of the other major scales—those that sound happy when you play them—you can get away with rehearsing the same finger pattern as you glide up the ivory. On the right hand, you push the bass note with your thumb, the following two with your index and middle fingers, respectively, then pivot your thumb under your palm to hit the fourth note, after which the final four notes of the upward octave correspond to each finger you have left. The bass note's higher counterpart is struck by your pinky, and the reverse motion guides you downward to your original note. The parallel motion with the left hand begins with the pinky, and walks up the full range of fingers before the middle finger pivots over the thumb at the sixth note, ending once again on the thumb. Played together, an octave apart, these comprise the foundational exercises that every pianist practices, at every level.

But for the F major, this rule doesn't apply. The first three notes, an F then a G and then an A, are played on white keys. But the fourth—where you'd usually pivot your thumb—is elevated on a black key, the B flat above the A, physically impossible for a thumb pivot. Instead, for this scale, you play out the B flat with your ring finger and with a little extra jimmy pivot the thumb underneath, pushing out the right wrist to make space for the maneuver. The top of the octave ends on the ring finger, an awkward position without the closure of a pinky at the apex of the scale.

"How many octaves up?" I asked Mrs. Christakos.

"Three. Both hands, parallel, two octaves apart."

I placed my palms over the first range of notes, the tips of my right thumb and left pinky atop two F notes sixteen whole tones apart. I inhaled, mentally rehearsed the awkward pivot, but Mrs. Christakos raised her hand to stop me.

"Crescendo upward, diminuendo down," she added, and leaned back, folding her fingers on her lap. At home, I was still practicing on the Yamaha that you and Nanay had surprised me with. The Yamaha without the volume control. My palms clammed up, and I wiped the chilly sweat on my pants and brought my fingers back to their original position. Beside me, Mrs. Christakos shuffled in her seat.

After the first lesson, I hung my head in shame. My technique was far from perfect, Mrs. Christakos remarked. My wrists were either stiff or jerky, no happy medium, no natural grace befitting a virtuoso. Despite that, my pivots were smooth, and to my surprise, my scale gradually swelled to a fortissimo at the apex, before gliding back down to a whisper. Every week, we spent half the time working on scales—despite my internal protests, because I had wanted to play some cool stuff. "Patience, anak," you'd remind me when I would bang the Yamaha keyboard after my finger position slipped up, or when my wrist ached because I pushed it to the side for better mobility. What I didn't want to tell you was that I blamed my poor performance on kuntaw, a weekly activity that demanded I pummel my hands into the texture of a burlap sack.

To push me out of my comfort zone, Mrs. Christakos assigned me a new piece, an abridged piano arrangement of the most famous aria from Georges Bizet's scandalous opera *Carmen*. Instead of trying to discipline me out of my unruly style, she found a piece that maximized its aesthetic value. In the aria, the titular character sings in a descending chromatic scale, in a staccato, over an orchestration that plods at a low and resonant D, then leaps up two octaves to a staccato that meets the start of Carmen's every phrase. Mrs. Christakos assigned me a deadline for this piece: a local music festival where other students performed, which would take place in February.

At home, I practiced the aria obsessively until I could play it with my eyes closed. To help my progress, you relieved me from dishwashing duty if I practiced right after dinner for at least two hours. "It's just like a tournament," you'd soothe me, when I started to grow nervous the closer the days crept to February. And on the day of the festival, we made a family event out of it, and Nanay bought me a kid-sized suit. Before we climbed into the van, you took one of your oversized ties, popped my collar, and carefully wrapped the tie around my neck.

The week after the recital, we drove out to Mrs. Christakos's class. I remembered her promise to use the performance as an evaluation for Level Three. I raced you and Nanay up the stairs, but you made light work of our impromptu track-and-field event, skipping every other step to beat me to the top. "No running," you teased when we got to the hallway, so I cheated and jogged instead. At the last unit, through the two glass walls, Mrs. Christakos sat at the piano and beamed at me, holding up the Level Four repertoire.

AS YOUR CHURCH participation at St. Aidan reduced to a weekly occurrence—the church was too far away for us to commit beyond that—you delved into a fuller life with Couples for Christ. With a townhouse under our belt, and a living space that stretched wide enough to host full parties, you and Nanay took on more responsibilities for the community and volunteered to be parent coordinators for the local chapter of the youth auxiliary group, aptly named Youth for Christ. It wasn't until I was a professor that I came to appreciate the impact of your work. Unlike Couples for Christ and the corresponding children's group, YFC was designed to recruit Filipino teenagers from underprivileged or difficult backgrounds: the kids out of juvie, the petty criminals, the young men and women shaped by hardship. Of course, the adolescent children of CFC families were also encouraged to join YFC, but the energies were directed at bringing other young people into the fold. Years later, during the Covid-19 pandemic, something gnawed at me to begin studying Filipino migrant youth culture. I put out a survey on Twitter and quickly received a hundred responses from Filipinos who grew up in North America. Nearly half of them had been members of YFC.

As parent coordinators, you were exempt from most of the household meetings that we had attended in Silver Springs. Instead of the awkward children in the basement, listening to our parents sing hymns and play guitar upstairs, you hosted youth leaders at home and held your own worship services, and checked in on how they were faring in their own events. I could learn from their example, you suggested, and figure out how to be an upstanding young Filipino man.

I recognized a couple of the attendees. Shane and Past-Life Pastor, the demure older boys from kuntaw, were frequent attendees at the townhouse meetings. I tried playing with them the way we had at the gym, but at home they were laser focused on their religious charism. All business, Shane would say, and no martial arts—"Or your dad might get mad at us," he winked. Others whom I didn't know—and whom you failed to recruit to the gym—also arrived as regular fixtures. The two I loved the most were Kuya Fresh Fade, always in a short-shaven head and a fitted hat, and Ate Smize, who wore long earrings and squinted when she smiled. Unlike Shane and Past-Life Pastor, Kuya patted my head whenever he saw me. He smelled like all of the Filipino teens did, covered in Axe body spray and the tang of sage and butane.

"Learn from your kuyas' and ates' example," you reminded me, and then set an example in turn. This became the mantra at home, to comport myself outside in a way that could help the kids around me grow better, while being an upstanding representative of our family. Following their example, then, I tried to be more charismatic at school. I brought my Game Boy and link cable and amassed a small crowd around me and my friends during breaks, kids from other grades who grew curious about our Pokémon battles. In time, we added a whole smorgasbord of other games to entertain us at recess and after school: Yu-Gi-Oh!, the trading card game based on ancient Egyptian gods; Beyblade, the glorified spinning tops that you could customize ad nauseam; and Pokémon trading card games, which never beat the Game Boy version for me.

At the 5 & Dime, we concocted new ways to maximize our vending machine purchases and build the best trading card decks. The machine only took quarters, which were among the most difficult coins to procure, behind loonies and toonies (which only the rich kids at school had on hand), so Yami Yugi suggested that we try beefing up some nickels with Play-Doh, wrapping and flattening them until they were the size of quarters, and then drying them out so they firmed up into coins. The owners must have caught wind of our exploits, because they changed the machine slots to take only full dollars, or loonies, the Mercedes of Canadian coins.

To build my collection, I started asking Lola Pet for loonies. She was happy to give them to me, collected from the spare change that she gathered from her daily coffee trips to Tim Hortons. But instead of spending them at the 5 & Dime, I stored them in a green piggy bank from TD Canada Trust, one of the pieces of free swag that Nanay brought home from work. Quickly, coin collecting replaced any ambition I had of building a better Yu-Gi-Oh! deck. I scrounged the couches after your YFC meetings for spare coins that people might have dropped, and the neighborhood streets, where there were sure to be a few pennies and nickels littered around. Eventually the piggy bank was filled to the brim, so you and Nanay bought me a ten-gallon jar with a lid on top, into which you carved a slit for my coins. Any spare change you could find you dropped into the jar, to supplement my own scrappy earnings.

In time, the big jar was full of coins, so full that you and I had to work together to roll it into the van. At the No Frills, there was a machine that converted loose change into cash credit at the store, so we drove across the street and lugged the jar there. You helped me hoist the jar above my shoulder—the safe way to carry big loads, you taught me—and tip it over the receptacle. The coins cascaded out of the plastic and into the metal tray, which I tipped over so that the monies poured into the machine. The big number on the LED screen grew the more I tipped over. We must have been there for an hour, since the No Frills traffic was dwindling, and all the cashiers were staring at us pouring the change into the clanging steel. At last, we scooped the last of the coins into the machine, which printed a voucher for seventy-five dollars. We walked over to the last cashier, who was closing out her station, and she gave us the cash equivalent. "Congratulations," she muttered, her eyes weary from a long shift.

With my money, I wanted to buy myself a new scooter. That spring, as the winter ice thawed out, a few kids at Neighbourhood Place wheeled around in their new vehicles, inefficient alternatives to bikes but much more portable in tight spaces. Mountain Man's parents had gotten him one, too, and he liked to show off by kicking donuts on our driveway. The weekend after we exchanged the coins, we drove up to the Toys"R"Us at Cedarbrae Mall. Next to the bicycle section, the clerks had lined up the scooters to fill the corner, tall and polished and tempting. To my disappointment, the cheapest model was a hundred dollars. I was twenty-five short.

"Pick one," you said. "I'll make up the difference."

I chose a silver model with red wheels and a pronounced heel brake for the back foot. I proudly presented my seventy-five dollars to the cashier. From your wallet, you produced another fifty, to cover the difference and tax, and to buy an extra pair of wheels. As the cashier rang us up, I hugged you tight.

At the next YFC meeting, right before everyone left, the boys lingered for a while to chat with you. I came over to say goodbye, and you boasted about all the money I had saved and the scooter I bought with it. Not once did you mention that you made up for the missing amount.

"That's amazing!" Kuya Fresh Fade exclaimed, patting my head and scruffing up my hair. "You deserve it."

WITH MY NEW SCOOTER, Mountain Man and I could cruise down the mean streets of Neighbourhood Place. Along the cul-de-sacs, the winter snow had been piled high, and it melted gradually, leaving only the uneven ice sheets on the asphalt. In another life, Mountain Man might have been a Bear Grylls type, intrepid and daring—he turned the melting snow into a ramp and scooted down along the ice, wobbling skillfully, then drifted his wheels onto dry land. "You try!" he nodded to me as he climbed back up—but knew to never pressure me, because I was sure to say no. After our scooter escapades, we retreated to Mountain Man's unit, where his parents left us a cold plate of orange chicken and noodles, a combination I'd never had before. Mountain Man fixed us up some plates and suggested that I forego reheating the dish in the microwave and try it cold. The chicken was less of a tangy fruit and more like savory citrus candy, crunchy against the soft bite of the yaki udon. "Yeah, eh?" he grinned when I asked for seconds.

At our house, while Lola Pet watched her shows, I taught Mountain Man how to make fried eggs. Thanks to your mother-in-law's mentorship, I had gotten quite good at the dish, and could cook an after-school breakfast on my own. Lola Pet's method, basting the yolk with the hot pan grease, differed from the method I had learned from Mountain Man's parents, who flipped the egg over medium. Neither Mountain Man nor I were confident enough in the flip, so we settled on Lola Pet's approach and ate the eggs with white rice and ketchup. He grew fond of the Filipino kind of ketchup—the superior alternative, really—which an ingenious Filipina scientist once made with bananas and bright red food coloring.

As the temperature swelled and the humidity replaced the dry winter air, we didn't always feel like scooting around the block, so I took Mountain Man to our garage and opened the door. On the back of the garage was your dartboard, a game that you came to love—and, true to your spirit, competitively play—in Saudi Arabia. Until I hit my growth spurt in later years, I was atrocious at darts. The proper technique, an upper arm parallel to the ground and the elbow a fulcrum for the swing of the forearm, demanded a stillness and upper-body strength that I had yet to develop; my throws arced down to the bottom of the board, and the dart wobbled from a shallow impact.

"Why don't you just whip the dart at the circle?" Mountain Man suggested. He took his position, more accurately a Bruce Lee–like stance, and sized up the dartboard. I stood six feet behind him, waiting to see what he would concoct. Like a baseball pitcher, he cocked his arm back, the dart between his fingers. "Destructo Disc—*engage*!" he screamed, in the manner of a *Dragon Ball Z* side character, and emphatically threw the dart at the board. Unsurprisingly, it struck out of bounds to the bottom left. We approached the board to see the results. The needle was completely submerged into the cork, and the metal chassis had pushed its way onto the board, too.

I wanted to try the technique. The anime battle cry was mandatory, Mountain Man reminded me. I took my position in front of the board, a ready stance, shoulder width apart, and closed my eyes. I imagined the *Yu-Gi-Oh!* anime, early in the series, when the protagonist's grandfather gifted him five cards, each corresponding to the five body parts of an invincible monster named Exodia. I cocked my arm back and leaned to the right, and flung the dart at the board. "*Obliterate*!"

"That's sick!" Mountain Man exclaimed as I pulled the needle out of the black cork underneath the curl of the number 2. "I want to Exodia, too. Here, give me the darts." I handed them over, and he walked out of the garage. I waited for him inside and thought he was just psyching himself up for a strong throw.

"Dude, what are you doing? Get out here, you might get hit!"

As it turned out, he was going to Exodia the darts from the driveway. Too petrified and too amazed to stop him, I watched him wind his arm back as before. This time, his right foot followed, stretching into a remarkably accurate left forward stance. He inhaled sharply.

"*Exoooooooodiaaaaaa* . . ." he droned in a prepubescent baritone. With full force, he hurled his arm forward, and chucked the dart to the board. "*OOOOOBLITERATE*!!!"

The dart launched itself way to the left of the board and thudded against the garage wall. We ran over to retrieve it. The needle had completely pierced the drywall. It took a little effort to yank it out. For the rest of the afternoon, until Mountain Man had to run home for early dinner, we whipped the darts against the wall, occasionally landing on the cork, with increasingly ridiculous battle cries to match.

"Did you play darts?" you asked when you came home.

"Um . . . *opo*," I answered with the affirmative honorific.

You grunted, assessing my partial honesty. "You need a lot of practice, anak."

THE APRIL SHOWERS that year yielded to a May heat wave, inconveniently the exact temperature and humidity thresholds that made the capillaries in my nose burst. In that early summer heat, recess was intolerable. The teachers kept us indoors only in the case of rain or snow but never on a sunny day, even when my face was covered with blood. The first time my nose bled, I sprinted to the washroom, but a teacher I didn't recognize—a tall and muscular Irish lady—stopped me before I could get to the door.

"You have to ask for permission first," she scolded me. I dropped my hands, covered in scarlet, my face drenched with the same. She looked horrified. "Never mind—get in there!"

In the washroom mirror, I imagined that my face was half of a Spider-Man's, dripping in red, and I was in my secret air-conditioned lair, safe from the evil forces of the humidity outdoors. There, I could collect myself and bide my time before I was ready to swing back into the battle. Inside the washroom, a long hallway of urinals and toilets and a semicircle group sink with a pedal, the air conditioning blew strong. I sat under the vent to cool myself down. By the end of recess, my nostrils, which I had stuffed with rough brown paper towels, stopped bleeding.

On the second washroom visit to clean my face, Krillin was the first of my friends to check in on me. He was worried that I had run off from our game of manhunt, a variation of tag where no one hides and getting caught doesn't mean you're out—it means that you become the predator. All the boys in our class ran a game of manhunt that day, and instead of running across the field, I sprinted straight into the building. He followed me inside and yelped in horror. I wiped my face, the paper towel drenched dark.

Eventually, the rest of my friends followed suit. Krillin and I had told them about the wonders of air conditioning, a better alternative to running around outside drenched in sweat, and for me, certainly a superior option to bleeding my brains out. During the heat wave, we made a habit of sneaking to the washroom. When the Irish lady tried to stop us from going in together, we split up into teams, one or two at a time, and skulked into the building.

In the absence of a spacious field, we created games for ourselves to pass the time. First, in the tradition of young boys everywhere, we held contests to see who could piss into the urinals from farthest away. This was Mountain Man's idea, inspired by our dart games in the garage. Intrepid as ever, he chalked up a three-game winning streak. I could only manage to aim from a couple of feet away. When we got tired of that game, we climbed along the toilet stalls, doing our best impressions of Spider-Man. Yami Yugi was the nimblest of us and figured out the most efficient technique to scale the wall and climb up to the high window ledge, hang off of it, and cling onto the top of the stall, where he could hoist himself up and sit on the top. I never managed any higher than standing on a toilet bowl and slinging my torso over the top.

The third game we came up with was a shitting contest. The goal wasn't to excrete the highest-quality turd but rather to produce the most resonant strain. One didn't even have to actually take a shit to win at the game. It was, in short, to create putrid music.

Frustrated with not winning any of the previous games, Krillin readied himself for a surefire victory in this one. He took his place at the stall closest to the door, sat down at the toilet, and strained until his voice resonated across the room. The rest of us climbed over the stall, eager audiences for his performance. Krillin had so thoroughly devoted himself to the contest that his face swelled to a red hue, his veins popping out of his forehead.

"WHAT'S GOING ON HERE?"

The janitor, an elderly Italian man, burst through the door.

"Oh, *SHIT*!" Juggernaut cried. He and Yami Yugi bolted for the door, but the janitor blocked the way. He peered out the door and hollered for the nearest teacher.

At home, I prepared myself for another beating. In your bedroom, you hardly had to tell me to lie prone before I had crouched over to take my position. The first whip. Across my waist. I forgot to wear extra layers to protect myself. The second whip. The third. The fourth. The fifth. The sixth. The seventh. All on the same strip across my ass. The eighth, against my upper thigh. Tell me what really happened. The ninth. Tell me the truth. The tenth. The eleventh. The fifteenth. I lost count.

The next morning. A group of parents in front of the counselor's door. Two by two, parents only, in Dr. Doomsday's office. The bathroom brothers, on stools, hanging their heads in shame. After half an hour, you and Nanay stepped out of the office, Dr. Doomsday behind you, peering at me, a sneer. You glared at me, and wore that Filipino smile, the contextual one, the ambiguous weapon, the machete.

"You're suspended."

ON THE MORNING AFTER my suspension—a single day, in which I locked myself in my room—Mr. Cognoscenti pulled me aside while everyone else read their copies of the Catholic school health books on their own, snickering at the page with the genitalia. To my delight, no one stared at me or expressed any scorn, save for Prada, who hated me anyway. We sat by his desk, and while everyone cackled away at the anatomically accurate penises, Mr. Cognoscenti launched into a speech. I only remember excerpts, because in those moments, he sounded exactly like you.

"You're not like the other kids."

Beat.

"Don't forget that when you're in this class, you're setting the tone for how everyone else behaves."

Beat.

"Remember what Uncle Ben said in the *Spider-Man* movie?"

Beat.

"With great power—"

Beat.

"—comes great responsibility."

When I took my seat, Tyler nodded at me. He was never sent home for a suspension, and instead Dr. Doomsday gave him a proper scolding. "The scariest half an hour of my life," he lamented. The next day, Yami Yugi returned to school, and two weeks after that, Krillin made his grand reintroduction. A month later, in the beginning of June, Juggernaut and Mountain Man came back, and we greeted them with a round of applause. The teachers, predictably, began to regard them with disgust, including Mr. Cognoscenti, who had thought very little of them in the first place. They were not among his strongest students—I was—and before I left for the day, he asked me to linger behind, saying nothing in particular, so that everyone else could leave and I could head out alone, his only exception.

For a little while, Dr. Doomsday's punishment was a bonding experience. At the end of each day, we checked in on each other at the bus stop and, as before, gathered around my link cable and staged some Pokémon battles. But at recess, under the scrutiny of Dr. Doomsday, who took to monitoring break periods herself, we drifted apart. Yami Yugi and I played with our Pokémon cards at the portable classrooms' stoops. Krillin sat in the corner of the schoolyard, watching the girls play double dutch, nodding his head to the rhythm. Juggernaut, the tallest among us, clung close to the basketball net. Mountain Man, whose attendance worsened over the last four weeks of school, meandered around the field, a vectorless path, until the bell called us back inside.

MOUNTAIN MAN NEVER came out to play that summer. His parents, who still lived in Neighbourhood Place, avoided us and kept to their corner of the complex. Shortly thereafter, they put their house up for sale. And hardly a year after we'd moved into the neighborhood, you put our unit up on the market, too.

After spending all summer touring properties, we found a house, a real one, far to the east, a single-family property on a massive corner lot, near our old neighborhood on Morningside, a "side split bungalow," which meant that most of the house was a single story, except for four steps upstairs that took you to four bedrooms and a bathroom, and eight steps downstairs into the laundry room and the basement, and a bedroom adjoined to the crawl space door. The backyard was twice the size of the one we'd had at Neighbourhood Place and came with a shed and some rudimentary garden plots, and a high fence so that Nanay could have her privacy while she worked the land.

Years later, when we declared bankruptcy, you blamed me for you and Nanay having taken on a mortgage for a bigger house. Whenever I forgot to mow the lawn or shovel the snow, you printed out your bank account statement, always in the single digits. "You wanted this," you'd scream. "We wouldn't have moved into this house if it wasn't for you." To this day, I don't think I ever wanted a house that big. Nor, even then, did I think it was fair to blame a schoolkid for major financial decisions.

Like all deflections, there were other stories, less exciting ones than the easy excuse you held over my head. Neighborhood Place, despite the developers' temptations, was not where you wanted to raise your kids. We would quickly run out of space when Balong was old enough to want his own room. And even though I was never privy to the conversation you had with Dr. Doomsday, I learned years later—from Jellyfish, whom I got to know in college—that all the parents came to our defense. It was clear, even to a group of immigrants trained to keep their heads down, that the good doctor triaged her punishments according to race.

The local school, the same one where I pissed my pants as a kindergarten student, offered an extended French program for fifth graders. You had always wanted me to learn French, occasionally punishing my misbehavior with mandated francophone television. Now, at the new school, I'd have no choice but to be more Canadian than the Canadians.

There was another reason why we moved. One summer weekend when we were all home, we heard sixteen thuds down the stairs, too swift to sound like sensible steps. I was in my room. Outside the door, a painful groan. At the bottom of the stairs, in the living room, Lola Pet was flat on her back. She had slid down the steep flight, and you needed to take her to the hospital. At the new house, you declared, we could each have our own room, and Lola Pet could conduct her nightly hijinks with as few safety hazards as possible. And until Balong needed his own room, you looked forward to using the spare bedroom for future visitors and family who needed your hospitality. If the townhouse was a point of pride, the new bungalow was an act of care. In those difficult decades that followed, you and Nanay stretched that care as far as it could go, to needy neighbors across the street, to kin across the ocean. You stretched it so much that its center softened and flayed—and eventually, from the force of your own generosity, completely broke apart.

GIFTED

BEFORE WE LEFT the neighborhood, Mr. Cognoscenti left us one last present. As the year ended, and Neighbourhood Place no longer felt like home, he recommended me for an assessment with a psychologist at the school board. What you named my chronic laziness he obliquely called "productive boredom." It wasn't that his class was too boring for me. In our year together, Mr. Cognoscenti had kept tabs on my complete lack of interest in whatever we were talking about. Yet even though I seemed to be more invested in trading card games and doodling in my notebook, I still managed to ace every test.

"This style of learning simply isn't working for you," he'd say, calling me up to the front for our chats, always reassuring me that, no, Adrian, you're not in trouble. That word choice, I now realize, was an act of mercy. I could coast through any evaluation he threw at me without studying at all but rarely submitted any of my homework on time. In his early report cards, Mr. Cognoscenti marked the "Takes Initiative" criterion with an *N—Needs Improvement*. I peeked at the report card when he handed me the envelope. All subject grades were the acceptable minimum you expected, an array of A's with the occasional A-plus. Any less, and I was doubling up on undergarments, stiffening my ass, lying prone, steeling myself against your leather.

A *Needs Improvement* was worse—far worse—than any dip under an A. It was an F, a spiritual one, even if it didn't count for my grade point average but instead spoke to the poverty of my character. After that report card, my throat strangled itself, and I sat at the back of the bus, breathing in triplicate, and swung my heavy legs home as sluggishly as possible, preparing for atonement.

The good Italian must have noticed my fright. At the end of the year, you let slip that you and Nanay had been considering transferring me to a French-language school come September. To keep you off my case, I pretended to be more proficient than I actually was. To test my skills, you printed government documents in Canada's second official language for me to peruse and fill out for you, as if bureaucratic English wasn't hard enough, and you promised the whip if I couldn't navigate your francophone texts after roughly five years living in this country. "Figure it out," you encouraged, "or I'll send you back to the Philippines," as if our homeland was a penal colony.

In the middle of the summer, we received a packet in the mail from the school board's gifted-program office, announcing that Mr. Cognoscenti had nominated me for admission and I had to come in for that psychological assessment. "Parang doktor, no?" Lola Pet remarked over the dining table, when you explained how I should present myself to the examiner. I asked if there was a study guide included in the envelope. Nothing except for an information slip and directions to St. Richard, a school I'd never heard about, where the evaluation was to take place. *Of course* I had to pass it, you'd repeat as my preparatory mantra. *Of course* I had to pass the test, "Because you are my son."

While we still lived in Neighbourhood Place, the route to the test center was simple enough: a single bus from the stop in front of Caddy's, the 16, get off at Brimorton Drive, walk east until I hit Bellamy Road, turn left, head into the school. To help me navigate, Nanay printed out the directions on MapQuest.

Once I arrived at the school, a balding man in a collared shirt ushered me into his office. I unzipped my backpack and started to take out my pencils. "You won't be needing those," the man said, a bead of sweat glistening in the clinical light. "This is a different kind of test. Just sit back and relax."

The assessment was an all-day affair, five hours with the balding man in an empty school, in an even emptier office, a placeholder room, scant little as decorations save for the notes he took as he watched me squint over an endless stream of picture cards. Inkblots first. Words for me to associate with other words. Then cartoons, animals, and plants, then scenes from everyday life, kids in the park, workplace politics, all with something offbeat about them that I had to identify: a see-saw with an off-center fulcrum, a blue oak tree, a man with two neckties, a crow with three eyes. With eidetic clarity, there is one picture card I can still see in my mind, a cartoon of a woman pushing a shopping cart filled with groceries.

"What's out of place?"

The other cards were a breeze; it took no longer than ten seconds for me to point out the abnormality. This picture was an exception. Every strip of metal on the cart accounted for. The lady wore a red collared shirt, the same hue as Nanay's favorite top. The grocery aisle, lined with canned goods, showed nothing out of the ordinary: cream of mushroom soup, fava beans, syruped fruit. My face dipped lower, two inches from the image, scouring every detail, for something like fifteen minutes. Two of those fifteen minutes I spent poring over the cartoon, the other thirteen dreading what would happen if I failed.

"Let's move on to the next one," the balding man said, pulling me back into the present. He snatched the card from under my nose. I scrunched my face in frustration.

"*Nothing* is an acceptable answer, too," he winked.

IN THAT LAST MONTH at Neighbourhood Place, other homeowners followed your lead. At least two real estate brokerage lawn signs popped up on every strip of townhouse, and U-Haul trucks became a regular fixture of the neighborhood. The great subdivision experiment, it seemed, had ended. You prided yourself on being a trendsetter, the proverbial Moses to the tyrannical Egypt of shoddily built skinny homes. But when September came around, the new house wasn't ready yet. You had finalized the sale, but the previous owners left in a hurry. They took their belongings but left heaps of garbage in their wake, hastily stuffed into bags that were now our responsibility. It was an older house, within the blast radius of a nuclear power plant, and I suppose I couldn't expect the polish of a newly built townhouse.

As you and Nanay got to work on the new place, I would slowly become acquainted with a different bus, the 116, which ran from Kennedy Station—a strange chrome trapezoid surrounded by a bus and train terminal—to a spooky bridge in the northeast hinterlands. My stretch of 116 would teach me the heights and troughs of Scarborough's undulation. From the stop in front of the bowling alley, I paid my fare, and the diesel bus wheezed eastward, hacking its smoky brown cough, crawling along a river of strip malls whose shores were lined with bounties I'd never appreciated until then: halal pizza joints beside Afghan kebabs, silk dealers and MoneyGrams, car mechanics with attached driving schools, a community garden with an apple-shaped sign, bakeries peddling carefully wrapped samosas, the thumping of tawas for fresh roti, and at Markham Road, the Dominion grocery store, where elderly couples wheeled their personal carts to buy their daily fare.

After Markham Road, Eglinton Avenue's eastern terminus is an abrupt bend, and the plazas yield to gray postwar apartments and the Eglinton traffic spouts into Kingston Road, a former regional highway paved over during Scarborough's suburbanization. Kingston Road, I later learned, was not just a major artery but a palimpsest of paltry fantasies. The British settlers, true to their uncreative energies, audaciously thought that they could carve into a landscape already lined with a transportation network—rivers and canoes, trading villages for voyagers, portages from the sea into the inland lakes to the north. The earliest attempts were buried in marshlands, and when a permanent road was finally in place, very few settlers were swindled into trying to build on barely dry riverbeds. In the end, it took a global war, punctuated with a genocide and two nuclear bombs, for Kingston Road to finally take hold; white families with affordable vehicles could travel along the highway to take vacations out of the city, and to cash in on the new market, intrepid businessmen erected motels with grand old parking lots and affordable rooms lined with floral fabric. Scarborough, it seemed, was determined to be a major tourist attraction.

As the 116 turned left onto Kingston, those fantasies still clung onto the roadsides: motels in faded red paint, half-assembled lettering that charged BY THE HO R, gravel parking lots, potholes underneath the owners' car tires. Elsewhere, retirement homes and British pubs with discounted pints symbiotically lived together, while some upstart strip malls tried to introduce some color into the area: a takeout Chinese restaurant, a Jamaican patty shop, minuscule beside the wide asphalt. And that bus route, I liked to imagine, was its own fantasy, too. Before Kingston Road could touch Lawrence Avenue, and the dying Anglo-Saxonry of the street gave way to the rest of the world, the 116 abruptly turned right, down a steep winding path, surrounded by thick bush and gated communities, the kinds of neighborhoods that'd call themselves "outside of Toronto" when they were technically "still Scarborough." That idyllic road, Guildwood Parkway, carved gently through cottagelike properties and lakeside mansions, and in deference, the bus slowed down, its stoner's cough quieting down to an *ahem*.

In the easternmost stretches of Guildwood, those dead dreams of a different Scarborough gathered into a mausoleum, a dilapidated mansion and a stage with Greek columns along the front lawn, an old artists' colony and hotel, many times abandoned, certainly left behind until I grew up, even when Drake filmed the "Headlines" music video there. Until the city finally reorganized the land into an event space, I came to know the Guild Inn as a haunted house, ripe for midnight raids and games of manhunt, discreet blowjobs and cruises for the grown-ups, and Sunday strolls and picnics for the families, at least where there weren't any stray syringes or used condoms in the grass, the kind of place that meant whatever we wanted it to mean.

Past the Guild Inn, my throat tightened. It still does, whenever I visit home and take the bus. On the right side of the bus, the curbs transformed into thick corrugated railings, separating the overgrown grass from the street, and another high fence with a door cracked open into a path in a ravine. The corrugated railing, slightly bent out of shape, in front of the gate, was the same one that had sliced my knee open a few years before. The thick bush continued for another few minutes, and I'd trace the winding path down the cliff as the bus crawled east, until the woods cleared, a green field, freshly mowed and railed in, over the cerulean expanse of the sea. If you had the misfortune of being on this bus, you'd get only a couple of seconds to see the water before you'd lurch sharply to the right, as the bus veered northward up Morningside Avenue and the vehicle roared in its phlegmatic voice again and sped toward the railroad, barely stopping to check both sides, rattling everyone inside, as if the driver didn't really want to be there. A road continued east of Morningside, but no bus was allowed in, and even if there were no signs that said otherwise, it was clear that none of us could really enter, either.

A metallic gash bisects Morningside. South of the cut, mansions demurely shy away from the main road, hiding their faces in the trees, and tell their friends that they live just at the border of Pickering, the next town to the east of the shoreline. Up north, the houses cram in together, duplexes, triplexes, x-plexes sharing a single yard, adorned with the same faded brown bricks, and in the interior streets, single-story bungalows like ours, each home a capsule for immigrant secrets. And further up, townhouses and mid-rises along Danzig Street, where we first rented a basement, spiritually fenced in by wandering cop cars, and at the Lawrence Avenue intersection, St. Martin, school and church both, a package deal shuddering toward Kingston Road's northeastern reaches, away from the rabble of the rest of the neighborhood.

LIKE MORNINGSIDE, St. Martin was cleaved in two. From the fifth to the eighth grade, the student body splits into the regular curriculum and the Extended French program, in which half of our classes were in the target language. Each program had a different set of homerooms, a different set of teachers, who derived great sadistic pleasure in pitting the two colonial subjects against each other. Frenchies, we were called, and our modus operandi was to hate on the English. This premise was the reason you took pride in sending me to this school, so that I could live chaque demi-journée en français. But between the brick walls, this premise was why every day in that place was a civil war.

My homeroom teacher was Monsieur Khoury, an older Moroccan man who only revealed that he was Arab two years into my time with him. Every morning we began with the daily ritual, delivered in the official language of Her Majesty's separatist nation, which begins avec l'anthème, quelque fois en français, puis une prière à la Mère de Dieu, in a catchy lyrical meter that established a habit I never rid myself of, long after I left the Catholic Church: *je VOUS saLUE MaRIE . . . PLEIN de GRÂCE . . . LE SeigNEUR . . .* You loved how I would recite Christian prayers in both official languages, like a good Canadian, and for nightly prayers at home, I eagerly flexed my francophone muscles, emphasizing each accent and fricative. As I recited Hail Mary in emphatic French, I had hoped that Nanay would learn the language one day, too, so we could upgrade our *zhu-zhu-zhus* into real speech, a secret language that we could speak within your earshot, beyond your understanding.

What I couldn't reveal was that, as far as Monsieur Khoury was concerned, only two things were necessary to become a bona fide francophone in class: recite all prayers in French, and listen to him reprimand you in French. This second requirement was the most important of the two, because if he had to switch to English to scream into your face, you knew that you were bound to be sent to the principal's office, complete with a stern phone call to your parents after school, who were guaranteed to pick you up and beat your ass. Fortunately, even then, I knew that Monsieur Khoury held special favor for me, despite my newness to the school, and for no particular reason other than the fact that, every Monday, I was excused from class to attend the gifted program.

I can't remember a thing about my gifted program. I knew that it was every Monday, and so after the weekend, I'd commute to St. Rose, a rival elementary school with a smaller building and a larger attached church than St. Martin, and we'd spend recesses indoors, to keep us apart from the "regular kids," as the teachers unironically called them. The other thing I remember was that, on Tuesdays, everyone in class would glare at me, probably because they had to suffer the Monday morning version of Monsieur Khoury, who—as I would learn the following year, when I stopped going to gifted classes—was extra grumpy on Mondays, and his classrooms would suffer the collateral damage.

Besides me, who never spoke in class, Monsieur Khoury always treated our two white people well, Valentina and Elena, two Spanish girls whose parents, like him, hated having to spend all that time in the neighborhood. This shared struggle was obvious in Monsieur's homilies about his goal to sell his Scarborough house and retire in France, because he loved the old culture of Europe so much, and glanced knowingly at Valentina and Elena, who kept their heads down.

To show his goodwill to his three favorite students, Monsieur Khoury recommended us as our school's designated ambassadors for an important British visitor, who had marked Toronto as a major stop on her anniversary tour. Monsieur handed us permission slips excusing us from class that Wednesday, and instead, we would meet with one of his colleagues, a short bearded man who taught the first graders, and be chaperoned by him to the Canadian National Exhibition building downtown. You and Nanay understood the gravity of this event—*a great honor, anak!*—and dressed me in a suit and clip-on tie, one appropriate for my small neck, and sprayed me with your best cologne, in a slender plastic bottle, the same fragrance you wore to work. In the back of the unknown teacher's car, Valentina and Elena murmured to each other, casting glances at me, and their whispers sharpened into hisses. I smelled my armpit to check if the cologne was still working.

At the exhibition, the masses were dressed to the nines, while the Great Hall smelled like shit. Behind metal fences, exhibitors kept herds of cows and sheep in makeshift stables to showcase the agricultural bounties of Ontario. The animals were given more space than the people, who were shoulder-to-shoulder between the live exhibits, or in my case, shoulder-to-waist with all the tall adults who had gathered to celebrate the British woman's anniversary. Sometime in the evening, an announcement on the loudspeakers gathered us toward a red carpet. A bull groaned at the echo, and his bovine companions mooed in response. The crowd had collected itself around the carpet, and I was still by the cows, Valentina and Elena and the bearded teacher nowhere to be seen. I cautiously approached the crowd, which had erupted in applause, not quite drowning out the moos, in harmony with the blaring of a bagpipe chorus, and snaked my way between a forest of legs. I pushed ahead, spotting a clearing on the other side, winding my way past the sturdy trunks and the spindly saplings, and spilled out onto the red carpet, tripping over my Oxford shoes, stumbling to my knees. None of the trees seemed to notice, as their attention was fixed several yards away, to an approaching group of black suits flanking an old white woman in a long pink coat, the shade of Pepto Bismol, her silver hair in a tight bob, removing her black gloves to shake hands with her adoring subjects. Transfixed, I waited for the posse to approach me, so I could have a chance to shake hands with the fancy lady.

"Hey, kid! *Hey, kid*!"

A man in black tugged at my arm and pulled me up, and tossed me back into the forest. Mercifully, the trees cleared out, though none of the canopies looked down at me to help me stand. Bent on all fours, I collected myself, my head facing away into the woods. I craned my neck down and peered under my body, and my ass was turned straight toward the pink lady, who leaned in my direction to shake someone's hand. When I stood myself up, she was gone, leaving the bagpipe chorus in her wake, their tartans pressing into the crowd, their elbows pressed in close, exhausting the last of the air in their bellows.

"You're a true Canadian!" you exclaimed when I came home. To Nanay's annoyance, my knees were still dusty from the exhibition floor, and she slapped the ashy marks away, while you proclaimed your patriotism over the dinner table. "You saw our Queen with your own eyes—I hope you never forget today!"

ST. MARTIN WAS a hard place to make friends. In those years, it was difficult not to be both resentful and jealous of the cooler kids, who were always on the latest trends: Phat Farm for the guys and Baby Phat for the girls; the short-lived K-Swisses that we all thought would give Adidas a run for its money; the springy Shox that promised dunking prowess (and in my stupidity, I had once asked you to buy me the less bouncy Shaqs, because I thought they were the same thing); and eventually, the Air Force 1s that had everyone in a chokehold but were out of our price range. But if you were a boy, the economy of coolness, so to speak, was quite easy. The secret sauce was that you had to be good at a team sport—specifically, basketball. The best players among us cut their teeth playing on the roughshod half courts in the schoolyard, meshless nets bolted ten feet in the air, and faded three-point lines in graying paint. There was Iverson, a short Filipino in the English class, a tumbling and crouching embodiment of every cheat code in the *NBA Street* video game series. Iverson's Filipino facsimile, Muggsy, had less finesse with his handles, but much more audacity and talent for comic relief, which allowed him to get away with travels. Kobe and The Truth, their families from St. Vincent and Goa, respectively, were an inseparable one-two punch, except that their shooting form—an emphatic push from the chest—was quite janky. Alonzo, probably the only boy in class who was more uncool than me, had an inconsistent but deadly long-range shot, his jump form so perfect and his body so needle-straight that his baggy pants always slid off. Then there was Scottie, already boasting an insane growth spurt in the fifth grade, who was an energetic high jumper in the schoolyard courts, notorious for his merciless blocks. And finally there was Kareem from Colombia, whose hook shot was sniper-caliber and earned him first or second pick in virtually every pickup game.

There was good reason for the basketball hype. Until the We The North era of the late 2010s, the early 2000s were the best time to be a Toronto Raptors fan. The franchise was founded in 1995, the heyday of dinosaur fever, and in their wisdom, the founding fathers named the team after *Jurassic Park*. After playing some floundering rosters in its first three years, the team struck gold in the 1998 draft, trading its fourth pick for the Golden State Warriors' fifth, and signed a Floridian who had led the Tar Heels to two consecutive Final Four appearances. That man, Vince Carter, became our neighborhood idol. The purple Raptors jersey and the fitted hat, adorned with the grinning dinosaur, was the de facto uniform on Morningside. Only two other team colors rivaled the Raptors': the gold and purple of the Los Angeles Lakers, and the red and white of the Chicago Bulls. Scottie, the prodigious defender, appropriately wore his dad's Pippen jersey.

Not wanting to catch yourself in the Raptors hype, you revealed that your personal favorite team was the Boston Celtics, the winningest team in the NBA. And to top it off, your favorite player was Larry Bird, a Midwestern man who would become the league's most historic trash talker. Because of you, I started following Celtics games and found myself gravitating toward Paul Pierce, who in a decade would himself become the Raptors' Public Enemy Number One. At Scarborough Town Centre, the area's biggest mall, Nanay bought me my first fitted hat, a green-and-black Celtics one, in the biggest size they had, so that my curly hair wouldn't press against the edges.

Armed with official NBA merch, I tried out for the intermediate-grade basketball team. Not that I was any good—my fingers, soft and lotioned for piano and bent out of shape from kuntaw, were the least-suited topography for good dribbling and shooting. In fact, my shooting was rather subpar, and until Lasagna finally taught me to shoot properly one summer (*flicka da wrist!*), I swung the ball a little too far from above my head. To improve my form, I started to wake up early to get some shots in the morning. Noting my poor but improving form, Iverson bestowed upon me my first street name, STBG, short for Soon To Be Gangster.

"You'll be real gangster if you can shoot over Scottie," Iverson said, joining me in the morning.

"How do I do that?" Scottie had a whole foot over me, and despite Iverson's quickness, not even he could consistently lay the ball up past the freakishly tall defender.

"Here, pass me the rock. Try to guard me how Scottie does." Iverson walked over to the top of the key, the apex of the three-point line directly facing the net. I threw him the ball and crouched down, my left hand in front of his face, my right arm extended away from my body. Iverson nodded down to my legs, which were spread wide in a horse stance. As the most skilled street baller among us, Iverson could weaponize the gap between the knees and weave the ball through them, blowing past the defender straight to the net. I readjusted my legs, my right foot forward. "Stay on me," he warned, and faked to the right. I didn't budge. He jabbed right again, and swept left, nearly crossing me over, but I recovered and ran after him toward the net, my arms up high so that he couldn't shoot over me. In the span of a second, he caught the ball with his other hand and readied himself to shoot. I jumped as high as I could. But it was a pump fake, and I had taken the bait, and stumbled behind Iverson as he pivoted toward the net. Two points.

At last, the day of the tryouts came. It was tough to find opportunities to practice my new move against Scottie. I had a few inches over most of the boys in school, so it wasn't productive to pump fake over boys shorter than me. As expected, I flunked the dribbling drills and kept bouncing the ball over the pylons. Offensively, I was middling, my shot still hoisted above my head. But defensively, I was monstrous. When his usual clowning was neutralized, Muggsy's game relied on layups, and he couldn't get past my long arms. Frustrated, Muggsy hoisted the ball in a fadeaway, leaning back to try to make space for a clean shot. I smacked the ball to the ground, but instead of hitting my open palm, the ball pressed against the tip of my ring finger. The knuckle swelled; bending it was painful.

You noticed my finger almost immediately. The dinner after my tryouts, I couldn't nail the scales on the piano in the way I normally could; my ring finger, which had been perfectly agile, throbbed on the B flat of the F major scale.

"See?" you warned. "This is what basketball does to you. You'll ruin your future." In school, you yourself were a hopeful basketball player but injured your ankle in practice. Not wishing the same fate upon me, you banned me from any further basketball games. There was no arguing with you. I resigned, even though the basketball coach had told me that I'd made the team.

After I broke the news to the coach, Shippuden, a Grenadian kid from the English class, hollered at me outside the gym. Like me, Shippuden wore a nonpurple fitted hat, a Houston Rockets one, because his favorite player was Yao Ming, the freakishly tall draftee from China, "and I'd be that tall, too, if my big boy self just stretched out!" he chortled. We sat together on the wooden steps to a portable classroom, a ritual we held for the next couple of years, until the seventh grade. He introduced me to his favorite works of literature, the weekly subscription of *Shōnen Jump* his mom got him, replete with proto-animes, which he told me were called manga, or Japanese comics.

"Like the word for mango in my language," I offered.

"What a coinkidink!" Shippuden said. "You should teach me more Tag-along."

I had just the text to bring for him. Back then, years before some young folks tried to jump her in the street, Lola Pet was the consummate intrepid diasporic subject, and she wandered around Scarborough plenty enough to get herself plugged into the community in no time. From some of her fellow senior citizens at Tim Hortons, she received a weekly Tagalog-language paper, *Taliba*, simultaneously a pun on the word for "news" and an arcane word for "sentinel," because Filipinos in Scarborough evidently liked to watch each other suspiciously. At the back of the paper was a humor section with a handful of Manileño jokes, sometimes in English and sometimes in Tagalog. Shippuden always made an effort to pronounce my tricky, agglutinative native language, and in return, he taught me some of the ninja hand signs from his favorite manga, *Naruto*.

Alonzo, with the beautiful shot and the beltless pants, started to hang out with Shippuden and me. He, too, had tried out for the basketball team, but his buckets were too inconsistent for him to get over the top. He lived on the other side of Morningside, and as the weather grew colder, he encouraged me to take the school bus home with him. It was a longer commute than my walk home would have been, even though our intersection wasn't that far from St. Martin. But the bus was a fun time, he said, and there were some delightful rituals I was missing out on.

"You've never jumped over the tracks before?"

"Like . . . leapfrogging over the rails?"

"No, stupid. You'll see."

Unlike the classroom, the school bus had a refreshing anarchy about it. There was no social order to determine whom you sat with, no segregation between the Frenchies and the English. The walls of the bus were a gallery for its passengers to tape up their drawings, Xerox sheets of pencil crayon illustrations about anything that came to mind, landscapes in green pastels and spiky yellow suns, portraits with eyebrowless faces and smiles drawn as sideways Ds.

The bus route carved into the lushest parts of the neighborhood. West toward Galloway Road, the bright graffiti tags and murals peeked out from behind the deciduous autumn, orange oaks and scarlet maples against the neon-green paints. To the south, corner stores seemed to pop out from nowhere, in between bungalows dug out from stubborn forests. In the distance, as the bisecting railroad approached, Alonzo nudged me out of my seat.

"Get up, it's time!"

I followed him to the back of the bus, where the older kids were gathering. They stood in the aisle and gripped the backs of the seats. I mimicked them, and we faced forward. The bus lurched to a stop in front of the tracks, and the driver opened the doors to check for oncoming trains. When the coast was clear, the doors shut, and the bus rumbled over the tracks, and the chassis shook. We jumped like trout, flying into the air. Leaping again. The bus lifting us into the sky. Weightless.

THE FOLLOWING YEAR, in my pursuit of being cool, I stopped going to the gifted program. You were surprisingly accepting of this decision; I argued that the program was taking away from my French acquisition. It was a good move. Once I could spend the entire week at St. Martin, my social circles widened, and to consolidate these new friendships, we added each other on MSN Messenger, which I suppose was our proto-version of Facebook Messenger, except that we could customize our name fonts and write statuses synced to our music players. Iverson, whose streetball was flashy, kept his plain default name he registered with, perfectly capitalized, no embellishments and no emojis. Alonzo, in trying to coin a street name for himself, made a very unfortunate and very un-Christian innuendo in his email, and I had to let him know exactly why our peers gave him weird looks when he tried to give his address out. Careful to avoid his mistake, I wanted a name that evoked some terrifying and omnipotent aura, from one of the edgiest cultural texts I knew, the *Lord of the Rings* franchise. The screen name I chose was "I Am Lord Sauron."

Here, online, more than in class, I could get to know everyone's inner idiosyncrasies. Sweater Weather, my Peruvian neighbor down the street, used to show off her Usher playlists online, until she came back from a summer in juvie, and then only played Juelz Santana, whose lyrics she would spit every Monday in class. Sweater Weather and I kept to our respective friend groups at school, but in the neighborhood, we would walk home together and promptly log into MSN, when she'd let loose about how Usher's "Throwback" really resonated with her. On the other hand, Curlz, the Guyanese girl everyone crushed on, was remarkably consistent in her branding: on and offline, Ciara and Christina Milian were her muses, as were any lines from the movie *Love and Basketball.*

The internet in the 2000s was an unruly place, not just because you were always one click away from credit card and identity theft but because it didn't have the finesse that today's platforms do. You considered it to be a dangerous place, and whenever some study about children's misuses of the internet came up on CablePulse24, you'd call me over to watch it with you, then lecture about how sinful and detrimental being on the computer was, and ban me from using it, until I told you that I had to use Microsoft Office for my assignments. Half the time, this was a lie, and I developed a rhythm of when to use it on you and when to enjoy the computer outside of your supervision. The internet was the kind of freedom I wanted, a chance to reinvent myself away from the vicissitudes of my language and body, and the kind of kinship I had gleaned at Santa Claus, with my link cable and my Game Boy. On MSN, I could extend the sociality of recess into something that felt like a social life, even if I wasn't getting invited to the games and mall trips after school. During your Couples for Christ meetings, I'd exchange my contact information with the other kids, and we could finally find a place to talk to each other outside the context of our parents pulling us along for their worship services. I added only a couple of people from kuntaw, because most everyone else was older than me.

If MSN expanded my local world, online games opened for me a multiverse. At home, I started playing a game called *RuneScape*, which one of the kids at the Couples for Christ meetings introduced me to. *RuneScape* was a medieval landscape in poorly rendered polygons where you quested your way to saving the world from cataclysmic dragons and demonic resurrections. Or, if you were a player like me, you'd spend your time outside of the in-game banks and buy cheap valuable goods, then move to another bank or server and sell for higher. This merchant enterprise made me a *RuneScape* millionaire (though this merchantry never translated to actual financial literacy), but it instilled in me an even more useful real-world skill. Outside of the bank, if you wanted to sell your wares, you had to type out your advertisement, which would appear over your sprite's head and fade away after ten seconds. This time crunch meant that I could become a master typist, hammering SELLING RUNE SCIMITAR FOR 25K onto the keyboard at 120 words per minute.

But as quickly as I latched onto my new virtual obsession, a new gaming website, Newgrounds, had kids my age in a stranglehold. At the Couples for Christ meetings, where the kids would hide out in the basements or bedrooms, we orbited around the computer to entertain ourselves. One of the older kids put on Newgrounds, and we trawled through the home-brewed Flash games that creative minds put together with a healthy dose of 2000s sexual humor. There was a dress-up game with ridiculous animalesque outfits, where you could literally strip down your sprite until it was ass-naked. In another game, *Stick Death*, modeled after the *Matrix* movies, your stick figure could perform bullet-time maneuvers to leap over enemies and shoot them in the head until their brains exploded out of their one-dimensional skulls.

Newgrounds was also a repository of early Flash videos. Today, my friends and I look back at those short films with a mixture of nostalgia and biting self-disgust for how poorly that content has aged in the post-Obama years. One of the most famous videos was an anthem for diasporic Asianness, one that my scholarly self is half-tempted to study, a music video for a rap song called "Got Rice?," which begins with "It's the A-Z-N, n****, fuck the rest. Dallas to New York, n****—we the best." During the CFC meetings, we came to chant this song like it was our national anthem. Other videos, animated with stick figures, boasted catchy hooks like "I don't want to talk to you, I just want, *bang bang bang*!" and "I know . . . how to count . . . all the way to *schfifty-five*."

One night, we screamed out the *bang bang bang* song a little too loud. You came down to the basement to let me know that it was almost time to leave. When you opened the door, the stick figures on the screen, at maximum brightness, were fucking each other's brains out, while we screamed *I JUST WANT BANG BANG BANG!* into the dimly lit room. Someone tapped me on the shoulder, and I turned around and met your steely gaze. Someone else shut off the computer, and we obediently marched out of the room and returned to our families without saying goodbye to each other. You didn't say a word, but we knew that we had disappointed you.

What irked you the most, however, wasn't the content of the website but that I didn't stop the other kids from going down a sinful road. The homeward drive was silent, save for the loud sighs you'd expel, and the piercing glances you'd give me through the rearview mirror. Once we got home, I wrapped my waist and buttocks with extra layers of underwear again, to prepare myself for the consequences.

You know you can't look at those things. Beat. Why are you doing hanky-panky. Beat. You know better. Beat. The other kids don't know better. Beat. You're my son. Beat.

You're my son.

Beat.

FOR THREE DAYS, you and Nanay didn't come home. She told me that you were just at the hospital for a regular procedure, a minor surgery that needed only a touch of recovery time. "Take care of your brother and Lola," she said every morning.

"Is Tatay okay?" I asked over the din of hospital noise behind her.

"Just a procedure, anak."

The hint of a tremble in her voice over the receiver.

To entertain myself, I played *RuneScape*, while Lola Pet and Balong watched *Wheel of Fortune* in the basement. After the Newgrounds incident, you banned me from using the computer for an indefinite amount of time and locked down my account with a password. To get around your restrictions, I taught myself how to turn on Windows XP in safe mode, a low-intensity boot-up that IT guys use to sweep for viruses and diagnose for user issues. With safe mode, I could get around the password lock, since it created a default administrator account, and I'd be able to use the internet to my heart's content without a trace.

Three days later, you and Nanay came home. You were dressed in loose clothes, and your cheeks were sunken. Nanay held onto your arm as you walked inside, ready to topple over at any moment. I joined Nanay and gripped onto your other arm, and we steadied your body as you teetered down the hallway to the bedroom, your head to the pillow. You fell asleep immediately. Nanay told me to ask Lola to make some food. Her hair, usually a thick black mane, was tangled up. In your slumber, your own hair looked thinner than I had ever seen it. Between Nanay's knots and your wisps, I spotted new streaks of gray.

RUN AWAY

AT THE FRONT of the class, in your freshly starched gi, you began with a question.

"What is the best kind of self-defense?"

I was finally tall enough to be your demonstration partner. Once the shortest kid in my class, I had spurted upward in the early years after we moved back to Morningside. Our lease at the fish market basement was done, and with your same karate master friends, we all moved to a new location on Birchmount Avenue, the north-and-south to Scarborough's west, the main thoroughfare of our Silver Springs apartment. It was just as big as the fish market basement but was on the ground floor, full of mirrors and bright windows so light poured inside. Upstairs was a dance studio, and our Saturday classes corresponded with beginner Irish jig lessons. As the students upstairs stomped, the ceilings bent downward at every beat.

Again. "What is the best kind of self-defense?" A few seconds of confused silence until a student raised her hand.

"Is it to disarm your opponent in as few moves as possible?"

You smirked and beckoned me over. "Anak, come." I walked to the front of the class and stood next to you. "Any hold or lock you want." I positioned myself behind you and wrapped my right arm around your neck, locking it in place with my left hand—a "sleeper hold." I knew the choreography: chin down, wedged into my elbow, to give yourself room to breathe.

"Sure, let's do it in two moves." My arm muffled your voice.

"One—" You grabbed hold of my elbow joint and my left hand and stepped to the left. You swayed your waist left and locked your right hip behind my left. I stumbled forward, and my arm was no longer wrapped around your neck.

"Two!" With a flick of your hip and a heave over the shoulder, you disarmed me and dragged me along the ground. All of a sudden, my body was supine and I faced the ceiling as my right arm was caught in your pressing lock. A sharp pain in my right shoulder. I tapped the floor with my left hand for release. You let me go and helped me up. We caught our breath.

"Good, but that's not quite it."

At the behest of the students, we demonstrated other locks: bear hugs and other wrestling moves, maneuvers with knives, swinging sticks. When I grew tired, you brought forward other volunteers: burlier men who towered over your five-foot-seven frame. After several attempts and through heaving breaths, you finally stopped and addressed the class.

"Those are all good moves. But there's one technique that none of you have talked about yet." You beckoned me over again. I hid a grin, because I knew where this was going. "Come at me with the same technique you did first," you said. I lunged forward, ready to subdue you in a sleeper hold.

You sprinted away.

The class broke out into an uproar. The younger students rolled on the floor, laughing and wheezing. You turned around and made your way back to the front of the class.

"Running away," you said through heaving breaths. At the back of the class, Nanay scrunched her face, upset that you had exerted yourself too hard. "That's the best self-defense." A few students nodded as your lesson clicked into place. "Or, better yet, do everything you can to not be in that situation in the first place. If you find yourself in these sorts of situations, avoid fighting entirely. If you don't have to fight, don't. Only as a last resort."

Your lessons in self-defense answered a theological question for me. Why is it that Jesus Christ, who spent his brief public life under intense scrutiny and persecution, never kicked the Romans' and Pharisees' ass, when they clearly deserved it and when the son of God Himself could have subdued them to devastation? How were we supposed to follow in the good Palestinian's pacifist example, when the world he left behind would become far worse than the one he had lived in? I figured that we were only human, imperfect beings, theologically freed from the Original Sin but dirtied from the millions of sins afterward. But God was always going to forgive us, you'd remind me, if we asked for forgiveness, even if we hurt others, even if it wasn't in self-defense.

AFTER YOU CAME HOME from the hospital and you had rested plenty and felt cogent again, you checked in on me to see if I was worried. I didn't know how to respond. Neither of you had told me what had happened, beyond the fact that you'd had a procedure done, the nature of which was still a mystery to me. I nodded, and your brow furrowed, perplexed at the lack of any reaction.

To emphasize what had happened, you sat me down at the dining table and produced a Xerox paper and a pencil.

"In the heart," you muttered, tracing the organ's four chambers, leaving tube-shaped holes around and between them as valves, with other arteries webbing out, "each of these passages needs to be as open as possible to keep pumping blood. And here," you continued, drawing an X over one of the valves, "is where mine clogged up. They had to put something inside to keep it open."

You drew a tube in one of the valves, cross-hatching it for added effect.

"Then it expands to let my blood flow in properly."

I nodded.

"Any questions?"

I had a thousand questions in my mind, all wanting to burst forth at once, and two thousand more visceral reactions to each of them. So . . . you had a heart attack? Why didn't you tell me first? Why did you want to protect me from the truth? Why did Nanay lie to me? Why did you lie to me?

And then a deluge of darker and intrusive thoughts. Would you have to stay home while you recovered? Did this mean that I couldn't log in to the computer without your permission? Would you be watching my every move?

Darker still: Would you beat me more? Would you use your heart attack as an excuse to kick my ass? Would I have to defend myself? Would I be forced to endure?

Are you going to be okay?

I resented you at the same moment that I feared for your life.

SHORTLY AFTER I started the seventh grade, I got into my first schoolyard fight. It was the first time that neither my French nor English homeroom was taught by a white teacher. Madame Ingabire, a no-nonsense middle-aged Rwandan lady, was far less volatile than Monsieur Khoury before her, but in exchange, her outbursts were muted and precise, and her gaze could immediately shut down an entire classroom conversation. Ms. Jimenez, my first Filipina teacher, new to the school, was the exact opposite. She glowed with the energy of a pinay older sister, an ate, especially because in parent-teacher interviews she called you tito. Both Madame Ingabire and Ms. Jimenez endeavored to dissolve the French/English linguistic wall that had hardened into a bitter war. But by then, the damage had been done. In that first week alone, two fights broke out between the classes, one between two younger boys in the grass, and the other between two girls in the church parking lot. Except on the basketball court—structured warfare—there would be no intermingling between the two postcolonies.

Something about that summer seemed to transform something about each of us students. Sweater Weather had just gotten out of juvie, and her entire demeanor had changed. She was once a bit of a teacher's pet and was now trying to square up against almost anyone, even the more popular girls, who clearly only kept her in the friend group out of fear of retribution. The rest of that group had gotten meaner as well, as had the guys, who spent every class break screaming at each other. Curlz, who was a foot and a half too short, tried to punch The Truth in the face, and in return, The Truth called her ugly. "Say that to my face," Curlz snarled, and The Truth walked over to the trash bin, leaned over, and screamed, "*YOU'RE UGLY*!"

Another game had started to rival basketball as the schoolyard sport of choice, something that we called Red A in front of the teachers, and by its real name—Red Ass—to each other. We would face a wall and throw a tennis ball against the brick as hard as we could. If your thrown ball was caught by someone else without a bounce, you had to book it to touch the wall before the person who caught it whipped the ball at your body. And because a bunch of us had hit growth spurts over the summer, with a handful having started to work out, those whips often yielded black eyes or bruised necks. To prepare myself for this new game, I developed my tennis ball throw and chucked it as hard as I could against the wall, but Muggsy and the others conspired to catch everything I threw, and because I wasn't at all a fast runner, they gleefully whipped the ball at my head.

That year, my hands started to drum up their lifelong twitch. At first, it was a shiver, an unsteady hand that I attributed to kuntaw strain, except for the fact that playing piano always managed to calm me down. So I started to bite my fingers as hard as I could, and when you noticed the teeth-shaped bruises on my knuckles, I reduced my activities to biting my hangnails, which would bleed profusely for a few seconds until I sucked the capillaries dry. At the gym, to try to treat the twitch, I practiced my punches against the kicking bag, in groups of three first, and then up to five and ten, switching the count and the pace, always straight jabs, because hook punches would never land in real life.

Kidd, a new student from St. Kitts and Nevis, who always wore fur jackets even in the warmer months, learned this the hard way. Until our scrap, we had never had a conversation with each other, because he was an English kid and I was a Frenchie. After one game of Red Ass, when Muggsy and Kobe predictably chucked tennis balls at my stomach, Kidd scrambled for a turn. He threw the ball against the brick, a high and soft bounce, and a gentle landing a foot away from me. I caught the ball before it touched the ground.

Ooh . . .

The players waited in anticipation to see if I'd whip the ball at Kidd. He looked at me with a snarl and told me that I'd never land a hit on him, because I threw like a pussy.

"Say that again," I blurted out, before I could catch myself.

"You throw like a *fucking pussy*." The last labial stop exploded, his spit flying as shrapnel.

I cocked my arm back. When he noticed my murderous intent, he booked it toward the wall. I pitched the *shit* out of that tennis ball. The neon yellow slipped from my fingers at the release, a fluorescent bullet, outpacing the running Kidd, clocking him square in the nose. He covered his face, but before he could completely obscure it with his coat, I saw that his nostrils were bleeding. He wiped the blood across his arm and, pushing through the crowd that was spacing out into a circle, he charged straight at me.

I wanted the fight to be more interesting, I really did. I wanted to be the guy to put this cocky bastard in his place and make him bleed even more. I wanted to wail on him and be one of the guys who go down in school legend for their brutal and prolonged fights, or to be forcibly pulled away by the teachers and thrown to the concrete, and suspended again, or worse. I wanted Kidd to try to kill me. And I wanted him—and all of them who thought it'd be fun to whip me every recess—to suffer for their audacity.

But you trained me well. My response to Kidd's aggression wasn't pacifist but clinical. For every punch that he threw, he tucked in his chin, exposing the top of his head, as if the extra motion would give his strikes more power. He also threw hook punches, strong only because of the momentum his swings were building, but sluggish and predictable from their lack of restraint. I stepped back a few times, once per swing, and then to the left, just after a right hook, and pushed him down and stepped on the back of his knee. He lunged forward into the brick wall and fell to the ground. By the time he got the chance try to stand up, the teachers had already separated us and dispersed the crowd. The fight was over.

In the principal's office, neither of us could explain exactly why we started fighting. I muttered something like "*wewillneverdoitagain*," and Kidd nodded, gazing at the ground, his face covered by the fur lining of his hood. We walked out of the office together, our classes down the hall from each other, and without a word, we separated at the top of the stairs, and never spoke again, all the way through eighth grade graduation.

That weekend was sparring day at the gym. Kneecap, one of the junior students a few years older than me, was assigned to be my fight partner. By then, I had reached blue belt, two below black, advanced enough to fight without a padded vest, a privilege reserved for students ranked green belt and above. Kneecap had just reached his green belt, and I would be the first opponent he would fight without the same protection. At the ring, we bowed to each other and faced each other. "Ready . . ." you said, the *dee* sound dropping to a vocal fry. "*Fight*!"

For a second, his face looked like Muggsy's, then Kidd's. Then yours. I threw a roundhouse kick to his face, the bony top of my foot landing right on his chin. He fell to the floor. I turned around and kneeled while you tended to him. Later that night, you returned the favor and smacked me in the jaw.

AFTER THAT SUMMER, no one jumped at the back of the bus anymore. Alonzo and I had become regular bus buddies but, sensing the stratifying social economy of our classroom, didn't ever want to get caught flopping about like dorks. A rumor had been going around that the school principal caught wind of rowdy kids on the bus and would punish anyone standing up when it was unsafe. Going home became a somber affair, a seated vigil, and we the parishioners rumbled along the asphalt on our rigid pews. That year, two white kids joined our cast of characters: Chestnut, a grade below me, and his younger brother, Peanut, both from Newfoundland, at a time when a lot of Newfies still considered Scarborough a home away from home. They sat together at the front of the bus, well apart from everyone else, greeted by their grandmother at the bus stop.

To make up for the churchlike environment of the bus, Alonzo and I began to visit each other's places. His family's house was to the east, at the membrane between residential and industrial blocks, just a brief bike ride from ours. He was a plant enthusiast and, in his basement bedroom, introduced me to a whole array of new species, sticky buds that he crushed between his fingers, yanking the stems out in the process, and rolled between thin paper. With one of his dad's business cards, he tore a strip off at the white space above the real estate brokerage logo, and folded it into a cylinder with a Zig-Zag between it, and slid the work of origami at the end of the joint. He cracked open the small window near the ceiling, under which he had placed a stool.

"You've never smoked before, have you?"

I shook my head. To demonstrate his technique, he climbed on top of the stool and produced a lighter from his pocket. He held the joint at the threshold of the window, his face level with the garden soil in his family's front yard. He wrapped his lips around the filtered end, lit the other side of the joint, and inhaled sharply. The joint dropped on the dirt. He crouched over the window and hacked out a phlegmatic cough. I watched him from the edge of the bed, wondering if this was part of a sound technique, too.

When Alonzo's coughing fit subsided, he handed me the joint, still covered in dirt and the filtered end moist with his spit. We switched places, and when he wasn't looking, I wiped the joint clean on my shirt. I brought it to my mouth, but folded my lips in, because the end was still wet. I lit the joint, but couldn't pull.

"Come on, stupid, don't be a pussy."

I tried again, and inhaled sharply. The smoke punched against my tonsils, and I retched it out. Like Alonzo, I crouched over the window and hacked out a wheezing cough. Alonzo shook his head.

"Let me try something," Alonzo said, and took the joint from me. I climbed down to make room for him. He wrapped his wet lips around the end and pulled again, and held his breath. "Mmh!" He made a motion over his pursed mouth, pinching his fingers together and spreading them open, a gesture for me to keep my lips apart. He approached my face, his mouth an inch away from mine, and slowly blew into my mouth. I inhaled the smoke, much gentler this time, but tinged with his stale breath, and held my breath, before blowing it back in his face. Alonzo hit me in the head.

"Stupid!" Alonzo was still looking at me, his eyes holding my gaze, wisps of smoke seeping from between his teeth. "Blow it outside the window!"

I cleared my throat and composed myself. "Can we try again?"

"Fine. Don't waste the goods this time." He repeated the process, and pulled smoke from the joint, but this time, he cupped his hand around the back of my head, pressed our foreheads together, his lips half an inch from mine, and he blew into my mouth. His bottom lip, plump and cracked, grazed mine. I inhaled as much of his breath as I could, as much as I could without pressing my lips against his, because I was afraid of getting smacked in the head again. I closed my mouth and he pulled away, and I climbed on the stool and stuck my head outside the window, and blew the smoke into the garden plot, the wall pressing against the stiffness behind my upper jeans.

THAT WINTER WAS ROUGH. Almost at once, right when school broke for holidays, the snow furiously pressed itself against the lawn. Overnight, the driveway was covered in a foot of it, as was the pathway to our front door, the concrete blocks that cut through the grass. You and Nanay still had work, and you reminded me that I was still grounded from the computer, and that I should watch French-language programs to keep my skills fresh over the holidays, and "Don't forget to shovel the snow before we get home, anak." Instead, I stayed home and played *RuneScape* all day. And for my disobedience, you smacked my face.

I called Alonzo the next day to tell him what had happened. "Fuck winter," he said, "and fuck your dad. Just come over instead." Lola Pet always did me a solid and never ratted me out to you, and neither did Balong, who spent most of the day sleeping and watching television with her, the same ritual that I had participated in when I was younger. I wrapped myself in a jacket and a scarf and slid my boots on, and sprinted east to see Alonzo, where we indulged in our favorite ritual in his basement, though we kept our coats on because it was cold outside but found sufficient enough warmth against each other's faces that we could leave our scarves off.

Three days into my minor rebellion, you called me into the living room and showed me a receipt of a cash withdrawal you had made earlier that day. You pointed to the balance on the slip—$32.68—and asked if I knew what it was. I shook my head.

"That's how much money we have left in our bank account." You reminded me that you went to work every day to support my brother and me, and that if it wasn't for me begging you and Nanay for a bigger house, we wouldn't have left Neighbourhood Place to begin with, where you could probably have enough money to be lazy at home, instead of paying down the mortgage. The least I could do—and you delivered this midslap, of course—was shovel the fucking driveway.

The week before Christmas, I forgot to shovel the snow again. I only realized this when, mid-*RuneScape*, I heard the doorbell ring, and it was already 6:30 p.m. The day had sped past, and in the lightless basement, I hadn't realized that the sun had gone down, because in the ageless world of *RuneScape*, the sun never sets. I quickly turned off the computer and ran to the couch.

Nanay stormed down the basement and slapped my head. "Your father is killing himself because of you." She slapped me again.

I ran up the stairs. You were outside shoveling the driveway, knee-deep in the snow, covered with blizzard, and crouching over to catch your breath.

I opened the door and called out to you to ask if you wanted me to take over. You ignored me and continued to work. I waited on the living room couch, too guilty to move. When you came in, I approached you at the doorway to take the back of your hand and press it against my forehead. You shoved my face back.

"Go finish it," you concluded, after yelling expletives at me and repeating, "*Do you want me to die? Do you want me to get a heart attack again and die?*" until you stormed back into your bedroom.

"Fuck you," I muttered to myself, covered in my winter gear, scraping the shovel against the driveway, hoisting mounds of snow to the side of the yard fence, "and fuck this house," a mantra under my breath, "and fuck winter," each *fuck* paired with a sharp dig into the gash on my hangnail.

AFTER WINTER BREAK, the war between the Frenchies and the English reached a ceasefire. Over the holidays, it seemed like everyone around me had discovered a new social media platform to join. Some early internet entrepreneurs, working from the frugality of their college apartment, discovered that Asian people in North America might want their own social media platform completely separate from MySpace, where they considered themselves practically invisible. It was a clone of the model website, a profile picture with basic information about yourself, and space to post blogs and updates on your life and add one another as friends, a proto-Facebook just for Asians. Back then, the Black kids had their own website,

Black Planet, but it was Asian Avenue that spread like wildfire, so that by the end of winter, almost everybody in class had an account.

Thanks to you, I had the skills necessary to build my own Asian Avenue page from scratch, straight from the HTML code. You had asked me to design an early draft of a website for our gym, and I quickly threw something together based on web design tutorials on Google. It was a rudimentary enough project—a basic homepage, a side menu for instructors' profile pages and philosophy statements about the different martial arts we offered, and a contact information form to fill out. Today, a later version of the page still stands, and while it looks ugly compared to the luxuries of today's Squarespace sites, it's a veritable work of art coming from a twelve-year-old in the early internet.

I modeled my Asian Avenue page after the kuntaw website, with the exception of the color scheme, which I tried to make black and gray, matching the color scheme of my favorite boy band, G-Unit. My name, on the banner up top, was in Lucida Sans Handwriting, the closest approximation of 50 Cent's group-branded T-shirts. Once it was ready, I shared the link to my Asian Avenue on my MSN Messenger and accumulated a follower circle of about thirty people. I looked through my classmates' friend lists and followed some other pages I liked, too. The coolest ones used their sites to write about their sports and music takes, and Curlz explored the inner workings of Ciara's hairstyles, while The Truth and Kobe composed pieces about their favorite video game, *America's Army*. Down below, I gave myself space to write out my own thoughts based on my least nerdy interests—back then, an amalgamation of yearning for reciprocated crushes and meanderings on my favorite Bible verses. Asian Avenue allowed me to reimagine myself as a bona fide writer, even if no one cared enough to read what I wrote.

Alonzo, on the other hand, became something of a local internet star. His Asian Avenue page was tastefully maximalist, smattered with album covers and adorned with blaring background music, an underground track called "Purgatory Gangsta." He liked to share links to new games on Newgrounds and videos of people who fell over on their face in painful ways. And because he was consistent, he amassed a following of over a hundred online friends. Like a jealous lover, I kept track of his friend count and sent requests to a handful of his fanbase, a lot of whom were in other local Catholic schools around Scarborough.

What I didn't anticipate was how much Alonzo hated how much I kept tabs on him. He stopped sitting beside me on the bus and ignored my calls. I tried to sit next to him once, but he looked out the window and pretended that I didn't exist. Early that spring, I finally confronted him about it at recess, and he shoved me to the ground.

"Why are you so obsessed with me?" he spit at me. "You fucking gay, bro? You a faggot?"

I collected myself and stood up. A crowd had gathered around us, hollering and pressing us enough to fight. Alonzo swung at me, a hook punch. "Fucking faggot." Instead of leaning away to dodge it, I grabbed his arm and stepped inside, and punched him in the eye. Before he could try to swing at me again, I grabbed his hair and pulled it down, and wrapped my arm around his neck in a chokehold, his head squeezed tight underneath my armpit. "Call me—a faggot—again—" I gasped in between swings at the side of his body. He dug an uppercut into my gut, but my belly absorbed the impact.

Behind the crowd, I spotted Ms. Jimenez in a panic, waving down two of the taller teachers to break us apart. I let Alonzo go, and we caught our breath. He extended his hand and shook mine.

"I don't believe in war," he said, his left eye blackened from my knuckles. He repeated this—"I don't believe in war"—until I took his hand and grasped it, and repeated it to himself as the teachers yanked us away from each other.

After recess, Ms. Jimenez mercifully sat us on opposite sides of the room. She had convinced the teachers not to rat us out to the principal or send us home for the day. I was seated right in front of her, and Alonzo at the back corner closest to the door. When the final bell rang, I turned around to see if he was still there, or if I could follow him to the bus stop and talk things through. He had already left class. On the bus home, we passed him walking home, his hands in his pockets. At the stoplight, our eyes briefly met, and I understood that we would never smoke together in his basement again.

ON A MONDAY MORNING that spring, before I could step through the front doors, two kids spit on my face. Inside, a group of fifth graders I had never met jeered at me. A taller eighth grader in the French class, Muggsy's older brother, brushed his shoulder against me. Under his breath, I heard him say, "Hater."

In class, just as I sat down, Curlz threw her pencil case at the back of my neck.

"Pick it up, hater," Muggsy sneered. He kicked the pencils from his seat and they scattered across the floor.

Madame Ingabire tapped my desk. "Ramasse-les! Qu'est-ce que t'as fait?"

Behind me, the class snickered. I crouched on the floor and collected Curlz's pencils and gathered them into the case, and walked over to Curlz to return them. "Don't touch them, hater." At the back of the class, Alonzo kept his head down, looking only at his notebook.

After school, I spotted Shippuden walking back home across the church parking lot. He was on his way to McDonald's, so I asked if I could join him. At the McDonald's, over a box of chicken nuggets, Shippuden told me what he had heard. He didn't have an Asian Avenue account, so he didn't know how it all worked, but someone in his class had shown him something that looked like it was my page, with the same URL but all of my blog posts gone, and in its place a list of names from the Frenchie and English classes labeled I HATE YOU ALL.

"But I didn't put that up," I pleaded. "It wasn't me."

"I'm sure it wasn't . . ." His voice trailed off, and he ate another chicken nugget. I figured that he didn't believe me.

When I got home, I saw that Shippuden was right. My Asian Avenue page was wiped out except for a list of people. I racked my memory to see if I had done something this foolish. All I'd done over that weekend was play *RuneScape*. I opened the site management page and tried to log into my account. It didn't work. I entered my email to recover my password, and went back and refreshed the homepage. It was back to normal. I tried to log into my account again, and the password worked.

Someone had had access to my account and, I surmised, would modify the page and regularly change it back right after school before I could get home. I changed all of my passwords to the first word I could think of—DILDO—for no particular reason, except that it was a word I had learned from the porn videos we used to watch at the Couples for Christ meetings.

The next day, Ms. Jimenez realized that something was wrong. She pulled me aside at recess and asked to speak with me alone in class. I told her however much I could manage, even though half of the time I was a snotty mess, my head on her desk. She patted me on the back.

"I don't think you did it," she said softly. No dishonesty lingered in her voice. She really believed me. I sniffed and she handed me a Kleenex for me to blow my nose.

"Thursday's parent-teacher interview day. Madame Ingabire and I talked it over, and we'll try to work out a solution to help you out. Just don't do anything until then, okay?"

I didn't want her to tell you and Nanay what had happened, but I couldn't tell her exactly why, because as far as I knew, she loved considering you her very own tito and tita.

That night, I didn't show up for dinner and locked myself in the bathroom. I periodically flushed the toilet while you were all eating, pretending to take a terrible shit, until dinner was done. When you were asleep, I wanted to talk to Alonzo, the old Alonzo that I knew before the fight—or anyone, really, who could listen to me. I dialed 911 and cried to the operator, who kindly waited until I had gathered myself to remind me that this wasn't the right way to use an emergency hotline. Before she hung up, I momentarily considered telling her that you had hit me, which wasn't a lie, and according to the movies, they would send someone to take me away from home to a better place. But before I could even fathom the consequences, the line clicked shut.

THE THURSDAY AFTER the Asian Avenue incident, the night of parent-teacher interviews at the school, my teachers told you what had happened that week. The hatred I got walking into class on Monday. The cyberbullying. The hacked profile page, the hate list. The head on the desk. The crying. The accusations. The classroom intervention.

With sympathy, Ms. Jimenez assured you that she and the other teachers would take care of me. They'd do their best to speak to the other students, to get them off of my back. They'd consult with the administrators and the local authorities to see what could be done. Cyberbullying was completely new terrain for the school board, and they did not have the procedures yet to deal with it properly. But, Madame Ingabire opined, the school would make it all better.

You heard none of that. When we got home, hardly two steps past the threshold you said: "Basement, now."

You told me to log into all of my social media websites so you could trawl through them. Then you told me to write down my password, which I intentionally misspelled at first. Then you asked me to write it out properly and slapped me when you realized what I had written. On my Asian Avenue page, you read blog posts out loud, my thoughts on Christianity and finding love as a young person. Then you told me to write down all of my passwords, including the ones into my MSN, so that you could see the conversations I was having. It was the same word, and you winced in disgust. You highlighted my status message, a quote from Usher's "Burn," the one about the speaker mourning an ex-lover he had cheated on.

Then you slapped me across the face, your palms striking my thick cheek. You grabbed my hair and slapped me again, lower this time, hitting my right jaw.

As you positioned in front of me, energized from a fit of rage and honed by decades of craft, your combat stance was flawless. Back leg anchored firmly to the ground, front knee raised, and in a swift motion, leg extended at a right angle. Toes up, so that the ball of the foot strikes its target like a blunt hammer. Retracted back to bent knee, delicate landing to the ground. The target crumples onto the wooden floor of his childhood home.

That first time you kicked me in the stomach, I admired the perfection of your form.

In the safety of our gym, you had landed many of those kicks before. As a child, for my protection, you would dress me in a padded vest before our sparring matches. It was an intimate ritual: I raised my arms, and you elaborately tied the strings through the loops and tightened it around my body. The vest was musky with the stale sweat of other students' sparring matches. Once I got accustomed to the rigid cylinder holding my torso in place, I backed up into a fighting stance.

At practice, you raised your knee slowly—*Anticipate the kick, anak*—and, as you stretched your leg out, I blocked it in one of two ways. If we were practicing our "hard style," I would close my fist and strike the ankle to deflect the blow, meeting a hammering kick with a rigid hand. Followed by a direct punch to the opponent's gut or face. If we were working on the "soft style," my hands would open up and my breathing would ease. In a fluid circular motion, I would scoop the ankle in my open hand, clearing space for a counterattack. I would catch the lower leg with my arm, step inside, and deliver my strike to the jaw or the throat.

By twelve years old, I knew the more complex defenses by heart. Unlike its rotating variations, a frontal kick has a single line of attack, straight ahead, from the fighter to the target. The foot can only reach as far as the leg extends. You were a mere five feet and seven inches tall, by then already an inch shorter than me, so your gait left me two options. First, a step-back into an agile cat stance with my left palm striking down at your foot, then lunge forward to punch your face. With enough force, a disorientation, a loosened grip—enough time to escape. Second, a diagonal step to the right of the line of attack, and with my left arm, scoop your extended leg and sweep the anchoring foot with my right leg. You would fall sharply onto the ground, and I would finish by breaking your knee and delivering a blow to the head.

Despite years of training, my body couldn't defend itself. My eyes crossed from a ringing in my skull: my head had bounced off the floor. In the fog, I grasped around me to find steady ground. A wheezing filled the room, an animalistic hiss that, seconds after impact, I realized was coming out of my throat. Your heel had landed right on my solar plexus, the small area in front of the aorta whose dense nerve endings connect directly to the gut.

Your own flesh and blood, bludgeoned by your exquisite kick.

EAGLE-SPREAD ON THE basement floor, I came to. As you stomped back to your bedroom, the house's old wood creaked. I listened and recognized the patterns. Up the eight steps from the basement to the living room, then four more to the hallway of bedrooms. Heavy steps down the hallway, to the room perpendicular to mine at the end of the house. The door slammed shut, and the bed creaked. Then lighter steps followed, Nanay's, a slow opening of the rusted door hinges. A lamp crashing onto the floor. A fist against the wall. And another. And another.

I got myself up, still short of breath, still tense along my abdominal muscles. My face stung, and my gums pulsed from the impact of your palm. Like a rat, I scurried upstairs, on tiptoe, as quietly as I could, to run into my room. I didn't turn on the light.

My room wasn't sanctuary enough. I kept the lights off but wanted to disappear into the abyss. My closet door stuck to the frame. With two hands, I pulled on the knob as hard as I could, stepped inside, and closed myself in.

In the movies, the suicide attempt always seemed like a premeditated and squarely middle-class affair. Always the convenient rope lying around, and a sturdy enough pipe on the ceiling to hang oneself from. Or the sharp knife, dramatically across the artery, in bloody fashion, then the neck. Or the abundant painkillers in the bathroom cupboard, the hunching over the toilet, retching out the last acidic drips of life, before fading to black. Or asphyxiation in the garage, in a luxury car, windows down, the oxygen slowly draining from the air, then the lungs. Or off of some infrastructure, always some landmark like the Golden Gate Bridge or the top of the Empire State Building, police and alarmed crowds trying to convince you not to jump. Don't do this; you have a long life ahead of you.

I had none of those things. In the darkness of my closet, I could dig the end of a clothes hanger across my face or across my wrist.

Or I could punch myself until I internally bled to death, or wrap my hands around myself until I couldn't breathe anymore. Without many creative options available to me, I bludgeoned my face. Beat. A hook punch as close as possible to my right ear, then my right jaw, where you had already struck me. Beat. Another, and another, and another, even after I collapsed against my laundry basket, my head against a shelf, my knees on the ground. Beat. My head against a shelf, against a shelf, harder, harder, at the painted wood's edge, a clean line on my forehead, the sparkling of light, beat, my corneas, beat, my ear, beat, my cheek, my jaw my jaw my jaw

PART THREE

SON

~~2005–2010~~

~~1898–2023~~

~~1898–1935, 1945–1986~~

~~2005–2010, 2020, 2024~~

historic filipinotown, los angeles, 2020s

From a soft leather armchair in Marina del Rey, Steve wanted to try something new.

"Bilateral stimulation," he announced. He had just completed a certificate in some new therapeutic methods for patients with trauma and anxiety. These somatic methods promised the practitioner a variety of creative ways to help their clients connect with their bodies. "BLS for short."

"BTS?" I jokingly asked, wondering if he got my reference to the Korean boy band. He guffawed.

I knew Steve could ask this only because of our level of trust. And I think he knew that, for all intents and purposes, he was not what I had envisioned as the ideal therapist, given my Very Ethnic Problems. He, a silver-haired white Angeleno with a penchant for Hawaiian shirts, was the only therapist available at my employer's understaffed in-house mental health office, and I, coming out of the last throes of a terrible graduate program and a worse series of relationships, needed to see someone—anyone—as soon as I could. Steve and I first worked together in his office for a handful of sessions, and moved our appointments online after he left the company to start his own private practice. By the time he wanted to try these new techniques, we had built a digitally mediated relationship, and for an hour each week, my laptop and dining table transformed into a therapist's clinic.

"For sixty seconds," Steve explained, "you're going to hear something like a heartbeat in your headphones. As you're in that space, close your eyes and grasp the first scene that comes to mind. After a minute, we'll come back and I'll ask you what you felt. Sound good?"

"What do people usually see when they're under?"

"Good question. It really depends on the client. It might be wishes and aspirations, or daydreams you've never let yourself have. Or it could just be a feeling, a really intense one that you want to explore. Or, as I suspect, you might replay old memories, including those repressed ones that you might not realize you remember."

It's worth a try, I thought. After thirty months of sessions with Steve, during which we had waded through so much already, I wondered what else our conversations might have unlocked, and if I still needed therapy at all. But a gut feeling told me that I should stick it out, that the real labor was yet to come.

"Let's do it."

I closed my eyes.

Da-dum.

Da-dum.

Beat.

A scene pulls into view. I'm in my Manila neighborhood. My mother's family, living in both sturdy and shanty homes, surrounds me. My toddler arms feel soft and plump, untainted yet by the acne of Toronto air. Beneath my soft feet, a stream of red dots marches in single file out of a hole in the concrete. I poke at them with my fingernail. One climbs atop my big toe. After tracing circles near my cuticle, it punctures my skin.

My foot burns as if there's an ember against my skin. The pain builds slowly first, then spreads unbearably across my foot. I look around for help but find only the narrow alleyway of our complex. With no one around, I inhale and ready myself for tears. Before I can cry from the ant bite, a *psst* behind me. "Don't cry."

The burning on my toe quickly fades and gives way to a lurching stomach. Each *da-dum* of my headphones grows louder, less of a pulse and more like dreaded footsteps pounding, until the head of a man with a military comb-over comes into view, hauling luggage upstairs. With each stomp, my belly gurgles. I want to double over and release.

"Okay, let's come back," Steve said gently. I inhaled sharply, and I was back in my bedroom. My teeth gritted against one another. I felt nauseous.

"Where do you feel?"

I caught my breath and accounted for my body. I couldn't feel the fire ants, but my stomach still churned uncontrollably.

"I feel like shit."

"No—*where* do you feel?"

My upper stomach still ached. "Right here," I pointed out. He nodded.

"Hang on to that feeling, in your gut." I closed my eyes, and the thumping began again.

The next visions were blurrier. Falling in the mud of a soccer field. Puking as I prepared myself to confront a school that hated me. Clutching my abdomen in the cool darkness of my closet. But nothing clear—except for the tumbling of my insides. When the thumping stopped, I caught my breath. Steve nodded.

"Pull into focus that exact feeling, the lurching you get in your stomach—can you do one more?" he asked. I was almost there. I could do this one more time. Inhale, exhale. Still.

Beat.

As my left ear pulsed, a blunt force struck my solar plexus. A beat against my right ear, and I nearly retched onto my keyboard. In the haze, I could make out an off-white popcorn ceiling, the sloppily painted browns of the wall details. Standing above me is the outline of man with a comb-over. Speckled face contorted into a sneer. I try to stand up, but his foot pins me to the floor. My throat is raw from coughing, my back rigid between the man's weight and the laminated wood.

You're stupid, he mouths.

He lifts his foot from my chest and storms off upstairs. Crumpled against the floor, I turn to my side and hack my lungs out.

Get up, a woman's voice commands. Her outline, one yard behind where the man stood, blurs into an impression. I shut my eyes, denying myself the closure of seeing who it is.

GET UP.

VERSE

a young me, another me, freckle-faced, sun-kissed but still pale at the neck, a tank top and shorts and flip-flops

runs into the sugarcane field

a clearing, just past the brush, after where the rows of cane digress into unwieldy stalk

young me steps into the muddy soil, soft and spongy after the summer rains

he trips

knee scratches against stone
invisible in the brown soil and the slender leaves along the ground

young me hoists himself up and shakes off the impact

cough, cough again

at the clearing: a tall, muscular man

hair just barely silver, wisps of black and maroon,
in the afternoon sun
tall man is shirtless, his torso already gleaming with sweat
two rattan sticks tied to his right hip, and a crescent scabbard
on the left

in his right hand, a machete

the boy watches the man swing the blade at the overgrown cane,
a figure eight, high-right to low-left, then high-left to low-right,
to cut down the tops of the stalks, another figure eight, lower this
time, to hack at the next layer down, then two strikes lengthwise,
with more force, the thicker cane, at the base, two reverse figure
eights, low to high, with an extra heave upward to slice through
the woody plant, then a downward cleave with both hands, a stab
through the heart

Little

                    the man beckons

I hope you're watching, you'll give this a try

Little is in a different tank top now, a white one, a sando. Barefoot. He is running. The cane delicately shudders at each of his light, fugitive steps. He dives into the brush, where the wilder sugar, the stalks at the precipice of overgrowth, strangled each other's roots in a fight for water. They still grow, grow in spite of the cramped plot, grow from the nourishment of the roaring river nearby.

"TATAGAAN KITA."

Taga, for cleave in two. Taga, for sunder apart. Taga, for slaughter.

I'm going to slaughter you.

A familiar voice cries out from the muted silence of the brush. A guttural, heaving scream. The boy shallows his breath, reins his panting into himself until he is barely whispering. He wants to cough. His trachea fills with phlegm, a wheezing exhale, the wake of a bout of bronchitis. He gulps. Not now, he mutters under his breath, choking on a cough that is trying to claw out from inside him. *Not now.*

watch and learn, anak:

if you can't cut him down
    pound the spiders into the steel
    and the dagger slaughters later

if the house rots in the bagyo
    tabi-tabi po into the forest
    and they'll build you a mansion

if the ilog crumples into mud
    follow the river's throat
    and cast your line at its lips

if the mountain rages
    pray to the mother sea
    its tears will scald the earth

if the japs smoke you out
    run and scale the foggy slope
    in the sky you'll be free

lolo was a forest man

in the trees
where the GIs dared not go
his father found peace
so the americans chopped them down
and the filipinos followed

his father's father's fathers
from a distant peninsula
razed the forest first
the blood sweetened the earth
the ashes nourished new cane

to break the curse
lolo climbed the trees
learned their limbs
the bends that held him
the bones that broke him

to fall in love
lolo climbed nanay's balcony
up the typhoon chipped wood
skipped the kundiman the ligaw
straight to the shotgun's mouth

death march
to a home enrubbled—

at gunpoint, brother soldier prods
the forest man's spine

march, his rifle groans,
while tatay, the forest man

scrawls freedom dreams
in a childhood cave,

brother will kamikaze
before his war is done—

forward, forest man's feet slosh
in the bomb crater

in the mud, his toes brush
young rice shoots

the americans march with us, too
their names to be engraved

in iron; *our own will nourish*
the nameless earth

this land will adorn the streets
of the liberators

who freed us
from themselves—

before the soldier gunned
forest man's sunburnt neck

before these rivers drench
the history page

before his bullet skipped
across bataan's blood

did his fingers ever shrivel
in the embrace

of the mother sea?

lola, or *a triptych of peninsulas*

iberia
her blood
and birth-
rightly razed
the pope
~~the moors~~
armadas
her face
launched
a battered
escape

bikol
begrudged
homeland
the chilies
smoldered
first
the cane
to finish
her exodus
the mountain's
blood

bataan
enchanted black
they scorched
the forest
in the ash
they etched
old plots
and fenced
her home
between
the cane

tatay is gone, she says—too were the workers—

the cane overgrew into a wilderness, then started to wither, then flake away, retreating into the earth as the river's waters faded into a trickle

a land scarred

        a peninsula

kanin and ketchup
is a feast
if you allow your gut
to dream

tatagaan kita (masculine)

tatagaan kita (feminine)

the mothers found him
where the mother left him

the mothers beat him
where the mother forgot

the mothers raised him
when the mother couldn't

when does a boy become diaspora?

is it past the gate
an aperture in the fence
incarcerating
a vibrant soil
force fed the roots
it once called home?

is it outside the town
at the back of the river's tongue
once more toward its teeth
where the boy leapt to its depths
and the leeches
jumped on his skin?

is it beyond the province
along the carved delta
above the paddies
where the jeepney's
orange wheeze
transfigures the sky?

is it beyond the capital
in the corrugated membrane
between the crypts
and the manicured vines
where his pummels
draw their first blood?

is it past the shoreline
into the island's sinew
once its own archipelago
now an expanse
exhumed
from the coral's corpse?

is it outside the palace
where millions meld
a battering ram
in secret barracks
where he steals away
a final stand?

is it in his namelessness
where he rips
from his innards
an exalted name
and crawls along
his earthen love?

is it the desert
where ancient bones
burn like him
to nourish
his shanty
family?

or is it in time
salted and peppered
eroded into the forehead
a topography
a throat flayed
from the poltergeist
a little boy of his own?

when the dragons
launched their hoard
into the clouds

you saw him one more time

over dinner, you say it had been eons
since you shunned his genuflection
to the envenomed altar

of his flesh and blood

in some versions you hold his hand
left palms cupped in one
fingers laced in another

your right taps the table

in another rendering
you linger at the threshold
wait for him to cross

at the passage

he rues his skeletal state
his sinews long drained
a guerrilla's shade

he claws for you

gnarled around the hilt
of a bolo that spoke in
spiders, cane, and flesh

tagalog has no word for sorry

did he ask instead for patience
or strike a bargain for his debts
or wail the remorseful village scream?

he smiled, you said, when he slept at last—

was that story
a blueprint
for the bridge

you'll abandon me

where your rattling
breath begs me
to forgive you?

you wanted to systematize a new martial art, something you'd dreamed of since you were a kid, you said, the style that you had inherited from your own father, Ingkong of the village, great master, whose techniques were developed in the thick of war. the kicking bag is a stalk of cane. you swing at the top, the temples, as in the original twelve strikes you taught me, the sugar's spindly tops, and then the shoulders, where the wispy branches converge, the waist where the phloem stands like bone, the cane's tortoise thighs, up to the neck, to cleave the plant's esophagus, the crown, where the leaves gather, and then the heart, where if you squeeze it tight enough, you can sell its blood in delicious cups. nanay and I workshopped different names for you, different systems, derivatives of kuntaw, of sikaran, of our okinawan and korean kin, wondering if we could invent a family tradition of our own. we already had a tradition, you reminded us, a proud lineage your tatay entrusted to you with his dying breath. you flinched at the wind of his swing, in the brush of bataan, blowing against you one more time. we will call this new martial art by the name it deserves. ~~ta~~tagaan ~~kita~~. tagaan arnis.

historic filipinotown, los angeles, 2020s

"That wasn't me."

I blinked myself back into the present. Outside my window, two patriarchs, the ones who always bicker about the homeowners' association policies around motorcycle noise, argued over the malfunctioning parking gate. It was the fourth week into our bilateral stimulation exercises, and we had built a ritual of our own; I'd sit myself down as comfortably as possible on the dining bench that Nanay bought me as my housewarming gift, and Steve donned his usual aloha shirts but also glasses without rims, and typed up notes on the side. A Californian shrink.

"What do you mean it wasn't you?"

I cupped my temples and tugged on my hair. "Sometimes, it was like I was in my dad's body, a younger him. And then it was his father, or his mother, or someone else entirely, like some barely visible ghost against the wall."

Steve took off his glasses and leaned back, and transformed into his usual talk therapist self. "That's so interesting. I read somewhere—it might have been in one of your suggestions—about something called postmemory."

"Yeah, that's kind of it," I said, impressed that he had actually read my Marianne Hirsch recommendation. Postmemory, the literary critic once wrote, was the way that difficult and traumatic events marked the experience of the generation after those who experienced them. "They weren't my memories, but they felt inherited."

For the rest of the session, I recounted to him all the scenes that flashed from a different life, and I found myself contextualizing them in everything I knew from years of studying our country. Like two historians, we pieced together a remarkably robust picture of what I imagined to be your family's life in Bataan: the plantation that aggrandized the clan's wealth, the sugar crash, your father's flight and prodigal return, your mother's tough love, your struggles in Manila. Out of these postmemories, we assembled a family archive.

HARD AND SOFT

LATE AUTUMN, A frigid morning. Oak and maple leaves hanging on to their slender branches by the knuckle. Sidewalks as bleached as birch. The valleys, natural wind tunnels, gasping and wheezing onto the lakeshore. The Pickering nuclear plant a hazy gray in the cloudy November skyline. We had just turned right from four-lane Kingston Road to three-lane Eglinton Avenue, an endless array of dreary strip malls in Toronto's east end.

You had volunteered to drive me to my science enrichment camp downtown. After a few hours in the laboratory, I would commute back east for kuntaw. It was a carefully scheduled weekend to maximize my individual academic success and our family's precious time together.

I sat shotgun, my middle finger tracing 愛 along the frosted window, over and over again, until the dew on the glass dripped all over my palm. A chasm between me and the driver. Your hand, habitually hovering over the stick, reached across the gulf. I recoiled.

"I love you so much, anak," you murmured softly. Your words diffused in the stale minivan air. They clung near my face like pungent smoke. I leaned harder against the door.

THE NIGHT BEFORE, after a long day at work, you came home with at least ten bags of groceries. I brought the canned goods inside, Campbell's soup cans and Spam tins bulging out from underneath the flimsy plastic. I hoisted them onto the kitchen counter and arranged them by shape, to make them easier to put away. Wedged between the corned beef and the sardines, I found a printout of an email, hosted on Yahoo.com. Sent from a Philippine address, .ph, from someone named Marlo. Most of it was in colloquial shorthand

Tagalog, turns of phrase that my rudimentary comprehension could not decipher.

My eyes darted across the email again. I couldn't understand it word for word, but there was a warmth, a knowing kinship, a familiarity, in the tone.

"Nanay," I called out to her, "who's this from?"

When Nanay saw what piece of paper I held in my hand, her face went pale. "Don't worry about that," she snapped, and snatched the email from me.

"Is it someone I know?"

"Just keep unpacking the groceries, anak. Don't ask questions."

"Okay, but—"

"*No questions.*"

I thought nothing of the email until the next morning. You knocked on my door, offering to drive me downtown. I agreed, even though I relished the alone time that a bus and two trains gifted me on Saturdays. You started the car, a mid-2000s Dodge Caravan, and it groaned to life. The local soft rock station, 97.3 *I Love EZ Rock!*, mumbled a staticky rendition of "Big Yellow Taxi" by Counting Crows. We slowly crawled out of the driveway, past the broken cedar railing, vandalized several times since we moved into the neighborhood, and took two left turns to a subartery street. At the red light, you turned the radio off.

"Nanay told me that you saw an email in the grocery bag last night."

I nodded, half-listening, looking ahead past the intersection. Around the bend, west of Morningside Avenue, was the house of the first boy I ever loved. To my right, Joe's Convenience nourished the local kids with diluted sugar water and (if we could manage to pay off an elder) cheap cigarettes. A fifteen-minute walk north of the intersection was my elementary school, half dilapidated brownstone, half temporary portable classrooms. Beside that was the church where I volunteered as an altar boy every Sunday. The neighborhood felt small on foot, more expansive by school bus, and now but a blip of a larger geography in a minivan.

"You're *not listening*," you snapped. I jumped. You sighed.

The light turned green, and you pulled ahead. Westward along Eglinton Avenue, past the South Indian takeout stores and the faded yellow No Frills groceries, beyond the community center and over the rickety railroad, toward the cloverleaf to the Don Valley Parkway.

Your next words, a revelation I never asked for. I heard you, but I didn't want to listen, because I didn't want to believe.

Leslie (2013, 2018)

On Sundays, Daddy used to drive us down
To let Ikea start our day. A tank
Of gas would cost us more than eggs and meat.
Potatoes, too! Those golden wedges meant
To make us feel deliciously at home,
But neither Mom nor Dad would dare to cook
Potatoes without beef and lard from cans
Or big ol' helpings from the tube
Of Tex-Mex (or whatever else the South
Could grind and clobber in memoriam
Of Alamo). Hmm. Maybe home is one
Of those weird Swedish names they stick on chairs
And lightbulbs, cushions, blankets, even meals.
To stretch that tank of gas, we'd spend a whole
Day after Catholic mass to stuff our plates
And faces with those "home fries," eggs, and bacon.
I think that home was in those fries. We stayed
So long at times that even janitors
Would get to know our names and stuffed faces.
The chairs, the beds, the showrooms: our playground.
The setting sun, it darkened Scarborough first—
Ikea candles, rays of light, burned brightly.

union station, cheap marijuana, spicy lucky strikes, 2020s

"What did you do for your birthday?"

"Nothing, man. I'm still not used to it."

A man in a hoodie asks us for a cigarette. I offer him a spare. Balong flicks the lighter on. I cup my hands around the man's mouth. His damp breath coats my palm. The smoke folds itself between my fingers. He nods and walks away.

"You too, huh?"

"Just never bothered to celebrate. It's just another day."

"Or we couldn't afford it."

"Yeah, that."

"Do you remember my Leslie poem?"

"Dude, that's my favorite. The meatball one, right?"

"Yeah."

"Shit made me cry, man. I thought I was the only one who picked up on it."

"Those meatballs were fire, still."

"Fucking gas."

At the intersection, a cab splashes across a puddle and drenches two toddlers. Their mother screams at the driver, who snakes his car between them in spite.

"So what did you end up doing?"

"Nothing, man. Just *Call of Duty*. I'm pretty good at it now. It's all your fault."

"I'll take the blame for that."

"For the downfall of my academic career?"

We cackle. Balong hacks and spits on the ground. I light another joint.

"I don't think I ever asked you . . ."

"Uh huh."

"How did Tatay tell you?"

"About *that*?"

"Yeah. *That*."

Balong wipes the ashes on his white *Dragon Ball Z* shirt. His thumb knocks against Bulma's blue hair and traces a black vertical smudge on her forehead. I complete the horizontal cross with my finger.

"He just told me one day, out of nowhere. I think it was at the dinner table, when it was just the two of us, and you were—where were you again?"

"I don't know."

"Same. Probably Hawai'i or something. Or downtown. Actually, we might have been driving."

"Where were you going?"

"I don't know. You know how Tatay just likes to go on drives to clear his mind."

"And you go with him?"

"Yeah, he asks me to come, when he wants to talk shit."

"For real?! You just casually drive around with him?"

"Uh huh."

"The fuck—"

"He's different now!"

"With you, at least."

I clear two puffs and pass Balong the joint. The cherry at the end dies out. He tries to light it again, but his Bic can only manage sparks. I rummage through my tote bag and hand him a spare lighter.

"Usually it's when he needs to complain about the rest of the family, or when he's beefing with Lola Pet. We went on a bunch of these that one time after we tried to bring Lola to the hospital at four in the morning, but she wanted to get dressed and put her makeup on first, even though she was literally screaming in pain."

"Wait—she wanted to get dressed first? Before going to the hospital?"

"Uh huh."

"That's crazy. That's commitment to swag, dawg. I get it."

We cackle again. He roaches the joint and tosses it into a puddle, where it sinks away.

"Okay, hold up. So how did you react to the thing?"

"I just thought it was cool. It kinda shocked me at first, but it's nice to know now."

"Damn, you reacted better than I did."

"I know. You literally shut him down that one time."

"Oh shit. You remember that?"

"Even I could tell that you hated it."

"I didn't—I *don't* hate it. I just never want to think about it."

"Well, I do. But my Tagalog is trash."

"I didn't hate it, not even then. I just hated how much Tatay tried to use it against me."

"What do you mean?"

"I told Tatay that I wanted to drop out of high school and become a chef."

"Ayo . . . I bet they *hated* that."

"They weren't having it, for sure. But tell me how that fuckface tried to force me to be a doctor, because—."

"Oh, right. That's why you told him to stop bringing it up."

"Never brought them up again."

"Aren't you technically a doctor?"

"Hey—I'm *actually* a doctor. Except I can't prescribe drugs. Only reading lists."

Under the canopy, against the wall, safe from the light drizzle and the blaring rush hour, a teenage couple grinds against each other. Their faces meld together at the mouth.

"I won't tell you that you overreacted, but we definitely had different reactions."

"Sometimes I think we have different dads."

"Uh huh. And different moms."

"I get along with her better than you do."

"Still, they tried to pit me against you. Especially when my report cards were shit, or when I'd stop showing up to class. I swear the only reason why we're good is that you told me you almost failed school."

"Nah, there's more to it than that. Remember my breakup in my senior year? And you tossed out the shirts that she gave you?"

"That's true. But unlike you, I *actually* dropped out of school."

"That must have been crazy. I'm glad Tatay ended up supporting you."

"Nanay hated it. But Tatay, I think, was more scared than upset. He was worried that I'd get jealous of my boys when they all graduate before me."

"That's his stuff."

"He was genuinely surprised when I told him I didn't care. He left me alone after that and even offered to look at my résumé."

"It took a few tries, but I think he finally got fatherhood right."

I open my pack and hand him a Lucky Strike.

"Where did you get these?"

"Smuggled them over the border."

"You can't even get these up here anymore."

I cup my hands over his mouth while he lights his cigarette. He hands the lighter back to me.

"Nah, keep it."

"Thanks."

"Watchu saying after this?"

"Nothing. Probably go home and play *Call of Duty*. I already closed up the café."

"I'm only in the city for the night."

"You tryna eat?"

"I'm marved, still. Kinda craving dim sum. Come through. I'm seeing Lasagna and them for bubble tea after."

JESUS CAMP

IN THE MID-2000S, a couple of years before the housing market collapsed, Scarborough began to seep into the farmland. Just forty-five minutes north of the city, the bungalows broke open into cut-and-paste subdivisions, the three-story homes where immigrant families fled when they could afford to leave Scarborough. Twenty minutes past that, and the rooftops yielded to spindly husks, ribbed yellow heads peeking from the green, all crowded together, shoving each other out of the way, swaying to the humid air. I'm told that this is what the city used to look like before the war, a quilt of cornfields and orchards for export into the city and across the country, Toronto's very own Orange County.

One autumn day, as we drove north through this landscape, we passed a blue Ontario sign declared the new municipality—Queensville—and turned right onto a gravel road that led to a thick and nearly impenetrable ravine, save for the path carved into the trees, and in the distance, a gray clearing, the parking lot for a Catholic retreat center called Regina Mundi, named for Mary, the Christian queen consort.

You reminded me that I had been here once when I was a little kid, a weekend Christian camp I could barely conjure in my head, save for a wild Filipino kid named Italia demanding everyone's attention when I just wanted to play *Pokémon*, and a camp monitor teaching me that the word *industrious* meant hardworking, which meant that it was a virtue that God would love and that I should work as hard as possible to get into the kingdom of heaven.

Most of the Regina Mundi compound was a gravel parking lot surrounded by single-story cabins, including an extra-long one for the main retreat center, where a priest could hold mass if the seats were arranged into pews, or where a camp counselor could sit some young people in a circle and teach them about repentance.

This was the reason for us coming here. I had long asked you when

I would be allowed to join Youth for Christ. I had wanted to be like Kuya Fresh Fade, from your household meetings at our Neighbourhood Place townhouse, who beamed fluently and cocked his hat at a slight angle, just enough to show off his barber's sharp lineup but not enough to look stupid. Unlike a lot of the teenagers in YFC, you said, Kuya Fresh Fade grew up in a warm and loving household and could set a good example for most of the other members, who came from rougher backgrounds. When the boydem shot at him, supposedly for brandishing a knife (he was empty-handed), and the local news kept spitting out the police propaganda, they stole more than his life. They robbed me, too, I thought, of the chance to make him proud and conquer my stage fright, and testify fearlessly about how he felt God's love in his everyday life, and sing my heart out at every worship session like he did.

We turned into an empty parking spot. As we pulled up, the wheels agitated the gravel, and I opened the door to a cloud of dust. I sneezed my way to the conference center, but not before I could adjust my hat a little to the side, the fabric just barely covering my right ear. You handed me my duffel bag and hugged me goodbye. When I tried to pull away, you lingered. You'd never embraced me this tightly on my first days of school, not even the first time you left me at St. Martin, our first day of school in our new country. When you finally let go, I thought I spotted a misty eye in you.

In the retreat center, they had arranged the chairs in rows, like a church, except that there was no priest in the front, and instead two microphone stands for the worship leaders and a full band behind them. The leaders called themselves counterparts, male and female, like they were about to board Noah's Ark and multiply, except that in Youth for Christ, the first thing we learned was that we were bound by a chastity rule. "No hanky-panky," the parents on the sides would say, whenever a boy and a girl would get too cozy with each other. At the front, the camp leaders, Ate and Kuya, kept a respectful two inches away from each other, occasionally brushing fingers.

The program for Jesus Camp consisted of five sessions over three days. During the first two sessions, "God's Love and His Plan for Us" and "Who Is Jesus Christ to Me," I completely tuned out. It was all lazy theology, I scoffed, as if my osmosis of your lectures were enough to school me in all Catholic thought. It was frustratingly simple—he died for our sins, which absolved us of all of our sins, so that our default destination wasn't hell but heaven. I doodled in my notebook, cross-hatched figures from *Archie* comics or fluid strands of hair for anime characters. One of the parent coordinators told me to take off my hat, which I had worked to angle perfectly. After that, I didn't want to talk to anyone, and sat in the corner, waiting for the weekend to pass.

Something I couldn't ignore, however, was the band. For a group of teenagers, their synchronization was crisp. The lead guitarist, who sported wispy bangs over his forehead, played a Squier Stratocaster and hung the strap low, just over his crotch, like an entry-level Slash, but without the top hat. His backup guitarist, rotund with a shaved head, strummed and harmonized backup vocals for faster songs, and stepped into the spotlight for slower meditative pieces, guiding the band through the verses with his finger plucking. The bassist, a pixie-haired older teenager, who had brought a long blue acoustic bass, sat nonchalantly on top of the amp, and she nodded along to every track, looking at no one else except the drummer, whose stool creaked under the weight of his wide body and his enthusiastic bouncing. And the lead singer was a tall young woman with a bob, wearing red flannel and tight black jeans, whose face I could have sworn I'd seen before.

Together, the band performed at worships so well that I struggled to focus on the word of God when the guitarists were unleashing their most fire licks. For every worship session, however, the coordinators had carefully chosen the most charismatic young man to hype up the crowd and raise his hands in evangelical abandon when the band repeated the chorus of the Hillsong adaptation of "Here I Am to Worship." As the worship leader tightly closed his eyes and spread his arms wide, his open bomber jacket swaying around like a cape, I imagined Kuya Fresh Fade in his place, singing the same songs, his hat barely clinging on, dangling on his forehead from the back of its brim, pointing to the sky, where God might hear our prayers. At that point, I couldn't help but close my own eyes, left hand on my chest, my right hand open and held just above my shoulder. I cracked open one of my eyes to see if anyone was watching me. Without exception, all of us in our seats had our eyes closed or were engaged in some other form of personal worship, even the most gangster of us, who respectfully kept their heads down and entered into their own meditative space. I caught a glance of the band. They were in the zone, repeating the progression between B major, C sharp minor, and A major, eyes closed, caught in a prayerful trance, except for the lead singer, who was looking straight at me.

Talk Three was YFC's secret weapon. The first two talks of Jesus Camp were a redundant drag, and I had resigned myself to playing along and admiring the performances. I'd go to several Jesus Camps in the four years after that, and there was a very specific formula to Talk Three, which was called "Repentance, Faith, Healing, and Forgiveness." In some iterations, it was held during the day, and the course of the events took place in a windowless room, with the lights dimmed at the emotional climax. Talk Three began with a carefully chosen speaker, always someone who had, by Catholic standards, hitherto been leading a deviant life: a drug addict whose new fixation was Jesus Christ, a former juvie repeat offender who had found the light, a disobedient son who ran away to become a teenage father, a daughter who had gotten pregnant and become a teenage mother. And always, for these selected speakers, there was a drastic pivot—a volta—in which the prodigal child had come back to God and His emissaries on Earth, their parents. Unlike the previous speakers, this one was given very few theological guidelines; instead, they were afforded the opportunity to craft a gut-wrenching tale, an hour-long testimony of their journey to hell and back. And most importantly, they were allowed—*encouraged*, even—to cry.

While the speaker was delivering his testimony, the sun outside had turned in for the night, the autumn light pouring through the windows, setting the room ablaze. At the end of the talk, our sniffles periodically punctuated the room, and the last of the sun was barely visible beyond the trees. The parent coordinators handed out slips of paper and pens, and we were asked to write down any and all sins that we wanted to repent for. This wasn't the Sacrament of Confession, the speaker reminded us, but it was a way to teach us to apply remorse and seek forgiveness where it mattered the most: our families. On the slip of paper, I hesitated at first, wondering how I might word my own transgressions. *I don't listen to my parents.* Too generic, I thought. At the corner of the room, the bassist and the lead singer opted to participate in the exercise, and as they wrote down their own sins, they held each other, sobbing into each other's shoulders. I turned back to my own slip of paper, and mustered up the courage to jot down the things that made my hands tremble to write:

I hate Tatay.
I hate that I hate Tatay.
I hate that it's a sin to hate my father.

Each statement, written in bullet points, grew smaller, to squeeze it all into the page, and sloppier, because it was hard to write when my eyes were stinging. And then, with the last slivers of space on the paper,

I deserved it every time he hit me.
I deserved the kick.
I deserved the

To augment the emotional experience, the YFC coordinators made full use of the Regina Mundi landscape. Beyond the dormitory cabins and the retreat center was a brief meadow, enough rolling hills to give the grassy expanse character, but not enough to feel like a hike. In the area behind the retreat center, on top of a small undulation, was a plain brown crucifix, just barely visible in the autumn twilight, a geometric outline against a backdrop of indigo and navy blue. The architects had left a gap between the long cabin and the smaller dorms, enough to remind all visitors that, no matter how you might use the space, this was still a holy place, though no one ever told us why the church deemed it so.

During my first Jesus Camp, Talk Three took the fullest advantage of this manufactured sacredness. When the sky had descended into its twilight navy blue, the speaker asked us to file out of the room into the gravel parking lot. Outside, the camp coordinators lit a bonfire and ushered us into a circle around it. From the band, the acoustic guitarist and the lead singer squeezed into the circle, and the guitarist strummed an open D major chord pianissimo, as softly as possible. The speaker approached the bonfire and held up his own slip of paper. Against the light of the fire, shadows flickered across his face. He called on us to throw our slips into the fire when we were ready—"when the Spirit moves you"—and tossed his in. The sniffles around the fire grew into light sobs. Then more people trickled to the fire and threw theirs in. The sobs swelled into bawling.

At this point, the guitar's strummed D major crescendoed into an opening riff. The singer bowed her head. At the cadence, in a descending cascade, she implored the Lord Jesus, personified as a metallurgist, to render her heart down into "pure gold" and "precious silver." I had heard this song before, "Refiner's Fire," in your household meetings, at the point of your worship sessions when all the parents went around and talked about their transgressions. It was a central part of the Couples for Christ musical canon, collectively sung in the living room, swelling into the chorus, before fading into a meditative quiet of submission: *Ready to do your will.*

After the bonfire, I finally started talking to the other attendees. We had all been through the symbolic catharsis of Christ's forgiveness, and for a few hours, the emergent cliques stretched open into a welcoming embrace. Over dinner, the band played a set of songs, secular ones, acoustic covers of hits that I now call the Filipino American canon—Extreme's "More Than Words," Usher's "Superstar," Tamia's "So into You," Destiny's Child's "Cater 2 U"—and an array of songs that I hadn't heard before but some attendees recognized as recent original compositions from Asians on the internet, young men like Gabe Bondoc and A. J. Rafael. I made a note to myself to look them up later.

One of the girls remarked on the quality of the band, and I agreed. They were really fantastic, a blend of natural Filipino musical talent and a synergy one could only achieve with many hours of collective practice.

"I never knew that Shrimp Chips sang this good!" she said. "And we go to the same school!"

"What was her name?"

"Shrimp Chips. Why?"

I looked at the singer again, who was crooning a one-hit wonder I only marginally knew from the radio, while the rest of the band harmonized around her. For a split second, we made eye contact, and I remembered those evenings watching *Passions* at Lola Aling's Silver Springs apartment. I looked away and avoided the band for the rest of the retreat.

On the final day, at the end of the last session, a lecture on the proselytizing mission of Youth for Christ, you arrived right on time. At the end of the lecture, the camp coordinators revealed that our parents had written us letters, and they were here to deliver them. Across the room, you waved to me and handed me the letter, which I pocketed, and we embraced again. I wish I could tell you that I remember what you wrote, and I'm sure it was something about following a Christlike life, with the love and support of you and Nanay, my parents.

On our drive home, I rummaged through my bag to finally read what you had written. It was nowhere to be found, maybe left behind at the retreat center, or perhaps under my bed, or in some other fire, burned away to a crisp.

WHEN I CAME HOME, I asked if I could finally learn guitar. You lent me yours, a massive dreadnought you had picked up at the music store, the one you used for household meetings for Couples for Christ. It was a cheap and well-loved instrument, the metal fret lines dented from your grip against the strings, worn down by the same four-chord progressions notated across the songbook. And even though I had shot up in height, the guitar felt gigantic, and I struggled to curl over the body and reach the end of the fretboard.

That summer, my first one after the ninth grade, or the eighth grade, I can't really remember which, you gave me permission to use the computer to my heart's content, so long as I used it to learn guitar. A new website, YouTube, had recently been bought out by Google, and its offerings exploded for anyone with any kind of interest. Instead of paying for more music lessons, you would let YouTube be my guitar teacher. Over the summer, I taught myself how to read chord charts and tablature, and practiced for hours until my fingers bled.

A month into learning guitar, I started to trawl through the website to find those songs they played at Jesus Camp. What I found instead was an entire subculture of Asian Americans online. There were vloggers like Ryan Higa from Hawai'i and KevJumba from Texas, and Timothy DeLaGhetto from California, who attracted millions of views with day-to-day confessionals about what it was like to grow up Asian in the United States. And then there were the musicians, like David Choi, a skinny Korean guy with a visor and spiky hair, whose raspy voice crooned for an ex-lover, and Urban-Germany, a Japanese dude from Berlin whose sultry voice cooed over lyrics about being a homewrecker. I promptly learned these songs, figuring that they'd come in handy one day.

Back then, the Filipinos were the undisputed monarchs of YouTube. There was HappySlip, a comedian from Virginia Beach whose sketches articulated the young Filipina woman's experience. But the superstars were the musicians from California, luminaries like Gabe Bondoc, A. J. Rafael, and Jeremy Passion, who got their starts on early streaming sites before migrating to the video format. They played with that kind of swagger that Filipino Americans seemed fluent in from birth, the kind that we were all trying to emulate in Youth for Christ, with a musicality that was decades more mature than their teenage selves.

That summer, and in the years that followed, I devoted myself to studying their work. As I emulated their techniques, their influences clarified, a blend of John Mayer's virtuous thumbs, and the lingering crunchy chords of a long tradition of soul songs from Luther Vandross and Maxwell, and the vocal runs of Alicia Keys and Whitney Houston, clearly practiced at family karaoke parties and Christian youth group jam sessions. In time, as I navigated my way through their copious use of bar chords and jazz licks, my fingers stopped bleeding.

By the following June, I had become a consummate Filipino YouTube fan. At the monthly YFC assemblies, which were minuscule versions of Jesus Camp, I mustered up the courage to join in on the band's jam sessions during break and borrowed their guitars to practice my take on Jeremy Passion's "Lemonade." The first chord, I learned, was nothing less than a call to ritual. It was an A minor 7, not played in the traditional way with open strings but as a single motion, all your fingers pressed against the fifth fret as hard as you can, plucked into a muted impression of the actual chord.

Later that summer, Toronto hosted the national YFC conference. Chapters from all over Canada gathered at a technical college in north Scarborough for something like a Jesus Camp on steroids. The audiences for the talks weren't fifty but five hundred, and the worship sessions were accompanied by entire concert bands, with multiple electric guitars and synthesizers, an audio engineer at the back, and a veritable choir of singers. Those worships introduced me to the ways that being Christian could be like a rock concert. They introduced us to a corpus of works from Hillsong, a new-age church in Australia whose services sold out arenas with numbers that rivaled the American music superstars. And as at every Jesus Camp, the conference band's set was perfectly choreographed. They knew exactly when to drop their intensity for a subtle interlude, and cultivate our cries to God, a chorus of sobs, swelling into full-blown panic attacks at each chorus. We convulsed uncontrollably on the ground, uttering nonsensical words that only the heavens would understand.

When I got home, I added Hillsong to my list of music I wanted to learn. I didn't want to be the devotee in the masses but a guitarist on the stage. The YFC's music ministry, as the bands were called, was a closed system, open only to those at a semiprofessional level who had either memorized the entire songbook or could sight-read the chord charts and lead a worship with little preparation. When I told you about my goal, we drove to Costco and picked up an electric guitar, black and white, in the shape of a Fender Stratocaster, and a tiny amp. We set up shop in the basement, and soon enough, we filled an entire corner with our guitars, both acoustic and electric, where I'd spend hours after school practicing. Eventually, you replaced my old electric keyboard—the one without touch sensitivity—with a professional synthesizer, and added a bass guitar to the collection. At the expense of my social life—and I had even abandoned my daily dose of *RuneScape* gaming by then—I would dedicate all my spare time to music.

MY CHOICE TO PURSUE music bestowed upon me an unexpected boon. At YFC and at school, I learned how to reinvent myself from a quiet and awkward nerd into a guitar-wielding Filipino fuckboy.

I wasn't good enough yet to audition for the music ministry, but in the meantime I began to carry a guitar with me to school every day. I hadn't gotten into Mary Ward, my high school of choice in the city's north, but because St. Martin was a feeder school, one of its terminal points, Pope John Paul II, a twenty-minute bus ride north of St. Martin, sent me an admissions letter with a spot reserved for me. And because you had wanted me, a former Frenchie, to be in the best possible program, you requested that I be admitted into the International Baccalaureate, a separate curriculum that was supposed to prepare students better for college.

Not wanting to be an uncool Frenchie again, I spent my lunches and breaks finding the musicians. In my religion class, which was offered irrespective of academic standing, I befriended Frusciante, a Filipino skater boy who lived across the street and also played guitar. Because religious education didn't really matter, and the teacher spent most of her time reading novels at her desk, we played hooky and practiced Red Hot Chili Peppers songs in his bedroom and snuck back into the classroom before period's end.

The following semester, Frusciante and I were in the same instrumental music class. Because piano and guitar weren't an option, I volunteered to play the bass, an instrument the orchestral program randomly had lying around. I was seated with Frusciante, who wanted to learn how to play the drums but had no sense of rhythm, and Gretzky, the Austrian French-horn player from my IB classes who seemed too cool to study but miraculously aced every test and would occasionally lend me his mp3 player packed with Guns N' Roses songs. Frusciante, Gretzky, and I made a habit of showing up to class as early as possible to put on jam sessions with our incommensurate instruments, and soon enough more of our class wanted to join in, like Pink, the Filipina and Vietnamese flautist who was also in our IB classes.

Mr. Folk, the music teacher, a tall Newfie who looked like Michael Bolton, was an endless fount of patience. We were a terrible band, and I was a middling bassist, interested in little more than learning Flea's lines. Mr. Folk's secret sauce was the piano in the corner, where he'd play the score lines and walk us through the exact dynamics he wanted. By then, I hadn't told anyone I was a pianist, because I wanted to reinvent myself as a wannabe rocker, but I wanted to impress him, so I turned my bass amp down low, because it was little more than a subwoofer in a room of horns and woodwinds.

To correct the clarinet line, Mr. Folk played out its melody, a tricky passage littered with accidentals and swift grace notes. He pressed the F key, just above middle C. It was slightly flat, too close to the E below it. Truthfully, it was grating my ears.

"I think the F is flat," I murmured to Gretzky.

"What did you say?" Mr. Folk said. He stepped away from the piano and turned toward me.

"I said the F is flat," I repeated meekly. I hoped that I hadn't offended him, in case he had tuned the piano himself.

"How did you know that this was an F?"

The class fell silent.

"Well, uh . . . it's an F . . . ?"

Mr. Folk played other notes and asked me to repeat them. I named them all immediately. And then the notes of melodies he played, and chords, like the ear-training tests that my piano teachers used to give me as a kid.

"Mr. G.!" he yelled in the direction of the office, a separate alcove at the back of the music department. "Get over here!"

A balding Italian man popped his head out of the office, wearing a scowl. "What do you want?"

"We've got a kid with perfect pitch in here!"

"What's perfect pitch?" I whispered to Gretzky.

He chuckled in his deep voice. "No idea, but apparently it means you."

At the piano, Mr. G. and Mr. Folk traded melodic lines, and I named all the notes in rapid-fire. The rest of the class had devolved into apathetic chatter, while I, in the corner with my bass, sat through this impromptu examination.

At home, I asked Balong to play me some pieces from his new book. You had sent him to piano lessons, per tradition, and he was picking up on the instrument quicker than I had at his age. I sat on the couch with my notebook and wrote down all the notes I could hear, then played them back on the ivory. Later that afternoon, I sat at the piano and closed my eyes, listening for the Jesus Camp songs in my mind.

When I blinked, it was 9:00 p.m. I had been reproducing Christian songs for hours and didn't hear you two come through the door.

You nodded behind me. "Very good."

WHEN I FINALLY was ready to audition for the YFC music ministry, the organization tore itself apart. You and Nanay decided to leave the CFC and join the splinter organization, the aptly named CFC-FFL, meaning Foundations for Family and Life. It was a return to basics, you said, a Christian mission closest to the original vision that God had laid out for us. When I didn't understand, you sat us down at the dinner table, and with your deft political analysis, you painted for me a picture of a community in crisis.

A schism had broken out between Couples for Christ's major leaders. Frank Padilla and Antonio Meloto, wealthy men both, diverged in their visions for the global congregation. Meloto wanted to expand Couples for Christ's worldwide conversion mission into the work of applied humanitarianism, and invested members' donations into purchasing unused land, where they would try to compete against Habitat for Humanity and build their own housing for the poor. This branch was called Gawad Kalinga, meaning "to give care," and through its subsidiary ANCOP—Answering the Cries of the Poor—Couples for Christ scooped up old shantytowns and drained rice paddies around Luzon. Missionaries from all over the world, including parents and teenagers from Scarborough, traveled to the Philippines and built these houses for free, and when Manila's urban poor were allowed to move in, these missionaries stayed on and cultivated in them the CFC's version of the Christian faith.

When the global tithes weren't enough to fund the new venture, Meloto transformed himself into a prodigious fundraiser. He tapped into his professional networks in the country's pharmaceutical companies, which bankrolled his ambitions. Frank Padilla, who was one of the organization's original founders, resented this new direction. He accused Meloto of being an apostate, someone who opened the doors for the evils of pro-choice politics to enter into a Christian mission. For Padilla, CFC had diverged from its first principles, laid out in the waning of the Marcos dictatorship, which sought to restore in the Filipino people a respect for God and the family. With his followers, which came to include our family, he defected and formed a new group tasked with becoming missionaries for preserving the sanctity of life.

You became the chapter head in Scarborough and worked with everyone who had defected to reorganize quickly into a facsimile group. And despite my inexperience, I wanted to follow in your footsteps and volunteered to become a founding leader of the new youth group. Moving for me was not difficult at all. I never felt that I could do anything more in YFC besides trying to audition for the band. In a new setup, I thought, maybe I could start all over again.

To my delight, the new youth group needed a music ministry. At your suggestion, the parent coordinators asked me to play guitar at the inaugural assembly, which we held at the St. Martin church hall. I borrowed your guitar and CFC songbook, took my place at the front, and selected some familiar songs to play, some of the ones you used for your household meetings. I think it landed on the wrong audience. To the teenage millennial Christian, they were dated and uncool, with none of the fancy chord work that the Hillsong band was famous for, and way too many verbatim Bible verses to sound current. It was hard to bring teenagers to worship with lines like "For You, Lord, are my sure foundation."

At the assembly, it became clear that we needed to recruit members, so the first order of business was to hold a Jesus Camp. I could be a good band leader, I offered, but there was a group of cousins in Hamilton, a city to the west, who were seasoned worship leaders and musicians. "No offense," one of the titos said, "but you've got a long way to go before you can lead a band." My time would have to wait.

The Jesus Camps were held at least twice a year, one in the spring and one in the fall. For the first two, I sat on the sidelines and helped arrange chairs and bring out the food for the meals. It was fulfilling work; as with the music ministry, I had never experienced the labor it took to organize these three-day events. By the third iteration, when more numbers had joined the organization's ranks and we could hold more Jesus Camps across specific regions, the parents had deemed me ready to take on new responsibilities. For that year's first Scarborough-wide Jesus Camp, I was to be its music ministry head.

To start the band, I put together a motley crew of semitrained musicians: Tumblr, a stylish girl with a beautiful soprano voice; Baron, who had just started learning guitar two months prior; Swagapino, who always seemed to date five girls at the same time and was a prodigious pianist; and Italia, the loud kid from the first time I ever went to Regina Mundi, whose family had also moved over to the new group. Tumblr and Swagapino were to be the bedrock of the band, since they had cut their teeth in their church's music ministry as backup singers and could bring their experience to the camp. Italia was to be our drummer, though not a very good one, because he was always distracted with trying to play the other instruments, even though he had been playing the drums since he was a kid. As for Baron, I would teach him myself how to play bass, starting with some basic lines I'd learned in Mr. Folk's class, single quarter notes at the root of every chord, to give our songs body.

Over the winter, we trekked to Italia's house in north Scarborough, east of Silver Springs, to practice. His parents generously cleared out the garage and converted it into a music studio so we could leave our instruments there instead of lugging them back home. Because your dreadnought didn't have an amp pickup, you bought me my very own acoustic guitar, an Epiphone with a cutaway at the neck, so I could reach the higher notes. Baron's parents bought him a bass, a black Yamaha with a hefty amp, which he insisted on bringing home every week so he could practice.

My self-study on YouTube translated remarkably to our new band. To start, we tackled one of Hillsong's most famous works, "Hosanna," because it would demand each of us at our best. The bass lines were simple enough for Baron to learn, but in time he started to add his own musicality, glissandos before every chorus to generate momentum for our future worshippers. On our first attempt, I tried to lead with an acoustic guitar, but "Hosanna" had an electric guitar solo, and I had never played one before. Italia, with a flair for the epic, insisted that I switch over to my Costco electric because "We gotta be better than those Hamilton dudes."

Our work paid off. At Jesus Camp, we set up shop at the front. The parent coordinators were skeptical at first, their standards already high from years of YFC bands performing above their weight. We began with a song called "Redeeming Love," which I led on my Epiphone. After three months of practice, my wrists strummed naturally and rapid-fire, the opening riff a series of three sliding open chords in the same E major shape, up and down the fretboard. During that first performance, I didn't look at anyone else except the band. The only thing that existed was my guitar and the crew we had put together. When the first sequence of songs had finished and the attendees dispersed for a break, we sighed in relief.

The camp coordinators, Timmy and Garbanzo, already in their early twenties, approached us after our performance. *You guys were so good! How much did you practice? Every week?! In the snow?! You were amazing.* The words almost slid off of me, until Italia let slip that I was the one who insisted that we spend all of our spare time to get good at this music ministry thing.

Over the course of the camp, I found myself growing less nervous, and even volunteered to sing backup vocals behind Tumblr whenever she called for harmony, though I kept my microphone levels low because I hated the sound of my voice. But in those three days, I came to treat my guitar less like an instrument and more like an extension of my body. Like an arnis stick, in a tightly woven dance with my dominant arm, the fretboard and strings and my fingertips moved in a choreography that learned to adapt to the emotional atmosphere of the camp.

On the guitar, I finally got past my childhood limitation of not being able to control my volume. After Talk Three, during which we burned our slips of paper in the parking lot of the community college dorm the coordinators had rented out, the speaker led the collective into worship. The centerpiece of this set was "Hosanna," the first song we had ever learned as a band, and we wanted to pull all the stops. Worship began with a few minutes of reflection, much needed while the sobbing still filled in the room, and the air had grown humid in a way that felt like the Holy Spirit surrounded us. I cued the band to play at pianissimo, and I plucked a pared-down version of the opening chords of the song, letting the strings resonate and the notes linger so that the audience could hang on to each one. During the exhortation, the moment in which the leader guides everyone into song, I strummed the guitar and we swelled into a crescendo, until he cued us in, and I played the opening riff. At the chorus, the room, barely coherent from their tears, sang together, *Hosanna in the highest*, as loud as they could.

When it was time to play my eight-bar solo, my body moved on its own, my eyes stung shut, my cheeks sticky; my fingers chanted on the fretboard with fluency, like God was commandeering me. I could hear Tumblr ad lib over the instruments, at a distance from her mic, and Baron escalating his line to eighth notes, and Swagapino pounding away, and Italia strengthening the steps on his bass pedal and crashing on the cymbals. We weren't a band anymore but vessels, and God had seized control, so much so that after my solo, we screamed the bridge at the top of our lungs, *heal my heart and make it clean*, microphones be damned, *open up my eyes to the things unseen*, shamelessly into the sky, *show me how to love like you have loved me*.

I wish you could have seen me play.

AFTER THE TALK THREE WORSHIP, everyone needed to wind down from the spiritual high. We had been completely taken over by the Spirit, our bodies buzzing and trembling, and we held on to each other, squeezing away every bit of guilt and shame we had sat with over the past three hours. While Tumblr, Baron, and Swagapino ate dinner, Italia played the drums. He nodded at me to pick up my Costco electric. My fingers throbbed from the set we had just played, and my hangnails were crusted red with blood. "Play a twelve-bar!" he shouted over his snare, and I did my best impression of John Mayer.

"Can you play 'Lemonade'?" asked one of the campers, a brunette I hadn't met before but recognized from the hallways at school.

"The Passion song?"

"That one—I *love* Passion!"

I replaced my electric on its stand and took out my Epiphone. I asked Tumblr if she knew the song. "Of course, I'm Filipino," she joked. The rest of the band nodded. We sat on the ground in a circle, and I mounted the guitar on my leg and played the first bar chord. I nodded Tumblr in, and she and Italia sang the opening verse. A small crowd gathered and sat around us. At the chorus, *she's soothing like an ocean rushing over sand*—a cheesy refrain penned by a Filipino teenager in San Francisco who went by the stage name Passion—twenty of us had become pining Californian boys. *She's so beautiful*—the *ful* in emphatic falsetto—and the song's infatuated speaker, pantomimed by us, the yearning teenagers, closes his eyes to savor the afterimage of his addressee's face.

It was time for the final session. We assembled ourselves around the instruments and ran through the set list for the last worship. Garbanzo rushed over to us. The guy who was supposed to lead worship had called in sick, she said, and Timmy could do it, but he was coordinating the arrival of the parents. Would you do it, she asked me. I said that I had never done one before, but I could do my best. "Let the Spirit move you," she encouraged me.

The Spirit did, indeed. For half an hour, the band was guitarless, and Swagapino masterfully took over with the keyboard, and I cued them in from the stage, and none of my words were my own, and my arms abandoned me, and clawed past the ceiling, until I could catch a glimpse of heaven.

When the worship concluded, I hadn't returned to my body, except for my electric trembling, my Our Father to close, a Hail Mary, and a *Glory be to the Father, to the Son, to the Holy Spirit* that we screamed in unison.

A man in a gray suit squeezed me. I tried to pull away. My body filled with my spirit. Your cologne strangled me.

"I'm proud of you, anak."

historic filipinotown, los angeles, 2020s

"How are you feeling?"

"There's parts that I can remember vividly," I said, collecting myself. The BLS thumping subsided. It had taken six weeks to get to this point: a brief three days' worth of coherent and unfragmented memory. My hands buzzed. "Everything from childhood, up to the seventh grade. Then sometimes, it goes blank. I can barely even remember high school. But for some reason, I remember a lot about playing music, about the Jesus Camps."

"How do those memories with music make you feel?"

I furrowed my brow. In my dining room, far from the Wi-Fi router and even further from my snoring roommate upstairs, the Zoom call oscillated between thick pixels and a crystal-clear rendering of Steve's face and salt-and-pepper beard, and the aloha shirt he had been wearing since we started working together before the pandemic.

"It made me happy, I think."

"Did it?"

"My dad was so proud of me," I blurted out. "It was another life. I really thought I'd grow up to play music for God. I can't even bring myself to touch my piano anymore."

"I never knew you stopped."

"I can't bring myself to do it." I paused, trying to find the right word. "I feel . . . guilty."

"Guilt. Let's go with that." Steve's eyes wandered to the top of the screen, searching for a button to start the BLS thumping again. "Ready?"

DUNG-AW

THE NIGHT THAT Nanay's father died, another language crawled out of my crypt. It wasn't Spanish, the language of your childhood, the one that rang in your ears while our clan scrambled to make meaning out of scattered parcels of land, the one whose loss you secretly mourned for yourself. It wasn't even Tagalog, which you and Nanay had discouraged me from speaking when my accent skewed too consonant, and which had naturally faded to bare comprehension, my responses back in English, the quintessential immigrant child's linguistic landscape, for which I forgave you years later. You came home and went straight to the basement to sit at the computer. Nanay walked to the master bedroom, and I retreated to mine, and I heard a choked sob from another room. Nanay's steps followed, and you were still downstairs. I wanted to practice piano, or use that excuse to eavesdrop, I forget which, and crept down the hallway so I could peek into Lola Pet's room. Nanay had wrapped her arm around Lola's shoulders, the mother weeping into the daughter's chest, the two chanting to each other in a rapid-fire staccato between tearful hiccups, in a language that sounded kind of like Tagalog but whose words I didn't recognize. Unlike Tagalog, which was loud and bouncy, this language was harsh and subdued at once, breathed out in secret, each string of consonants tumbling with the pitter-patter of fugitives in a thick forest. The language was Ilokano, from the northern Philippines, which Lola Pet would use to pray in the solitude of her bedroom, or mutter to herself before meals or under her breath when she was clearly pissed at you. Years later, I learned that this kind of outpouring of grief, the one beyond the purview of the Tagalogs, was called a dung-aw, a mourning chant, and that it lived in every Ilokano because of the frequency with which we lose our homes and one another. But before that, I learned that you forbade her from speaking the language in front of you. You followed me to the kitchen when I didn't greet you, and I snapped, *leave me alone, I don't want to talk to you,* and I didn't want to say another word, not in any of the languages that you had wanted me to learn. To your credit, you offered me grace, or perhaps Nanay reminded you that, no matter how anglophone or francophone or Filipino nationalist you had wanted me to become, I was an Ilokano at heart and I had every right to grieve Nanay's late father, my newest ancestor. What I was mourning, instead, was the chasm between the perch where I stood and the mountain lookout where my mother and grandmother held each other. It's a naked feeling, to have no language to bring me home, a wander through a wilderness without a knife, a vestigial weapon I wielded through its absence. I hated that feeling, of being an unarmed guerrilla, and resented you for disarming me before I could even learn how to use the blade right. And if I could help it, from then on, no language to which I had a right would be denied of me.

You were made "redundant," you announced one day, and I immediately understood that it meant you were laid off. You carried a tenuous kind of strength, one that I had misinterpreted as resignation but now know as your habit of adaptability. To cultivate my optimism, you and I would sit at the dinner table, and you showed me printouts of your new business ideas, such as a shop selling healthy fried chicken, the "broasted" kind, that we could, as an ailing family, both indulge in and sell to make ends meet. Sometimes, outside your bedroom, I could hear, behind the muffling wall, you wallowing in shame to Nanay that you couldn't do your part to support the family, and that you couldn't make good on the promises that Canada made you when you left the home country and the desert. The truth is, I never begrudged you for losing your job, or for the ways that you tried to keep us above water, even when the abyss of your heart health gripped you back into its depths. And thus a sunk cost, a redundancy. You were redundant because that's all corporations do, they absorb us into their labor force and promise that we are all a family, and like a family, they belittle you until they toss you out but promise that they care for you. You were redundant because you dreamed a little too close to the sun and mastered the computer, which the company had encouraged you to do, and you got so good at it that you built an entire system to replace you and make you redundant. You were redundant because, like every son who looks up to his father, I knew you to be singular and radiant, and sure, there were a hundred million suns in this arm of our galaxy, and a hundred million more clusters of a hundred million suns in the entire Milky Way, but none of them ever flare the same, and none of them boast the vivacious planets that ours does, and none of them have led the life that you did, the kind that took you into the deep sea and atop the scorching sand and atop the clouds, only to collapse on your work carpet clutching your chest, and then imagine our futures as small business owners after you were made redundant. I wanted to broast the chicken with you even if I had never heard of a broaster before, if it meant that we could live out our days like our neighbors did, the ones that owned the short-lived pizza joint with longganisa slices instead of pepperoni, and feed our neighborhood the way that it fed us on Sundays when you and Nanay were too tired to cook after church. I missed the treats you brought back from your office parties, the tiny butter tarts, the sticky kinds I've never found living in America as an adult, and so because I missed them, and I missed your everyday return migrations, I began to eat nonstop and fill the black hole that was my stomach, maybe because Stephen Hawking promised us that black holes radiate, too, and I didn't want any kind of economic recession to extinguish your light, and I started to grow and swell like a red star at the end of its life, because supernovae become new solar systems and, to the untrained eye, explode like bright suns in the night sky.

historic filipinotown, los angeles, 2020s

The beats stopped. My body buzzed. When I opened my eyes, they stung shut. I touched my cheek. It stuck to my fingertips.

Steve and I sat in silence. I sniffled away the stream pouring from my nose. My body trembled, its unsettled energy radiating from my abdomen.

"Right here." I rubbed my stomach.

"That's where you hold it. All in your gut."

I suppose it made sense. For most of my life, my stomach was notoriously upset. Whenever I felt nervous, I found myself leaning over a sink and vomiting until the quivering faded. As I ballooned to 335 pounds, I would suck my belly in all day, to the detriment of my breathing, in order to feel small. I told all this to Steve, who could only nod at me. For a seemingly unshakable white man, he seemed to palpably beam his pity through the screen. Did I seem that pathetic?

"I'm not a good person," I blurted out. "I don't think I'm a good person."

His eyes flashed, a pixelated occasion, a father's gaze, then a friend's, then mine.

"Let's . . ." He hesitated.

I nodded. *Keep going.*

"Let's go with that."

TATAY

I woke up to a rancid room
banana peels and chicken bones
and burnt rice and brown-streaked napkins and phlegm
the smell of tanyag

I forgot to take out the garbage
so you kindly reminded me
and dumped the compost all over my floor
I'm a fucking idiot how could I forget

fuck you

"I'm sorry, anak."

fuck you

our family swelled
and our spare rooms packed
nanay's cousins first
my inaugural guitar teacher
the man who taught me how to read
and reminded me how fat I was

then the cousin
who waited her turn
to see her husband
and her only son again

without her son around
the cousin rummaged
through my room
and dug out my latex secret
and threw them at you
because I'm your son

they aren't mine, I said
so I snatched them
and snuck her back
and barricaded my door
and wrapped the secret
around my cock

pitied
behind
my back
father
bruises
I wish
I knew

at church
we wailed
for unborn sons

in the assembly
we prayed
for rapture

on the streets
we screamed
at womb killers

at home
we fucked
and fucked
and fucked

I'm addicted
to collective
(to Christian)
panic attacks
my strings
induce

the hymns
of brimstone
apostates
burning alive
their tiyanak
their unborn
ghouls
eat their flesh

a million will kneel
before God
I told anyone
who would listen
a million sinners
a million me's
will bend
and release

iron
you smithed
into a parable
he'd become
my punishment
if I didn't stop
what you knew
I did behind
the barricade

if I didn't stop
I'd forge
my child

my other secrets
the vaults
you never met
every inch
of them
of me
in them
in me

we bellowed murder
we waved murder
we prayed murder
to murderers

by the river
in a québécois town
the summer I left you
for a world
of new words
I learned
under their weight
the french
for impure
was *immonde*
unworldly

on the stage
garbanzo raised her fist
a thousand roared
the rally
of the born-again
untouched
"true love waits"

we were the ark
we wanted to love
so hard
to escape the end
that two by two
the lines
along the strip
glowed red

I wasn't ready to raise it
I wasn't ready
to learn
how to overcome you

(downcast eyes
in the morgentaler)

after our future three
became two again
we huddled at the pews
st. martin candles
and begged our lord
to spare us hell

when they left
I understood
I was inferno

our corner house
the one that drained you dry
a blast radius
for our warheads
destroying you
nourished me

nanay begged
for an armistice
to fly the flag
across the front
we sat to talk
I lost my friends
(I had no friends)
the only ones
that tried escaped
my shrapnel

you smirked
a seasoned warrior
spotted an opening

you deserved to lose your friends

and I came to.

historic filipinotown, los angeles, 2020s

"I don't want to be a father," I blurted out.

I repeated this, until it rippled into a whisper, into the oblivion behind my eyelids. The orange glow from the sun, crystalline behind the gathering water. Pierced by the flickering candles of St. Martin's sanctuary. The clinical bulb of my childhood bedroom. The umbras of bodies against mine. The darkness of a worship session, the spotlight of the bully pulpit, its brightness marking my hypocrisy like acne scars.

The faded face of a child I never met.

"Let's come back here—you can open your eyes now . . ." I heard Steve murmur, his voice tinged with concern.

They stayed firmly shut. A torrent flooded against them, knocking against the crack, the capsizing saltwater seizing me into its depths, washing me ashore, tumbling into the estuary. Memory, an involuntary typhoon, the pleasure of self-inflicted punishment, my water cure.

Beat.

RIVERS

A CREEK THAT FANS OUT into branches, the streams sometimes winding into each other, tumbling into a river from an accumulation of sources, then a split into three, each a glimmer of a different direction. It appears to me as a bird's-eye view and a first-person landscape at once, an estuarial triptych across an ocean to which we, the salmon, swim home.

wolf and saint

The first branches from the Leading Sea, the southern shoreline where Morningside drops into a bluff, where the water gathered in the western escarpments flows northeast, where two empires cleaved the land into warring tongues, where they hate you for skin and speech, a place named for wolves. You sent me here against my will, funded by the feds, a culmination of your forlorn campaign to forge me into a bilingual citizen. You and Nanay and Balong and Lola Pet followed the river to its maritime gasp, and left me in a dormitory, six weeks sans anglais, after which I'd come back and leave the city again. On my floor, I was one of a handful of boys, and the only one with his own room, and own sink, and I learned how to cross-stitch a relation in a foreign language. I crafted many, unfurled a few, and tightened others. I learned that *fucking* wasn't only an expletive but a transitive verb, sometimes but not always of love, sometimes but not always to completion, sometimes not always to mess. I learned that redheads exist, and that they could be gay, and that they could be the most amazing weekend trip roommate, and that they could stay up with you all night and teach you about a love that made you want to burn the Bible preachers. I learned that you could steal from Quebeckers if you took off the tags in the changing room, that you could make a quick buck pawning the clothes off, that your after-class game could spawn a generation of kleptomaniacs. I learned that I could learn a new language on my own terms, that it was worthwhile work, that I could sing and write songs and do battle-shits and catch a whine at the reggae concert and strip somebody and come at the same time and tell a joke and swim and prank-call people back home in French. I learned that my heart could break in French, and I could break someone's heart in English. I learned that the river wasn't for swimming, but diving into Lake Pohénégamook revived you like a baptism, and that group showers were best enjoyed high and horny and with Black Eyed Peas bumping in the background. I learned that your first friends could grow up to be religious nuts, and that your religious nut self could grow up to be a great friend, and that the most unexpected people in that camp could be your ride-or-dies as adults, in Toronto and San Francisco and New York, that you could cry together at the final dance, the one where you made out with the girl with two boyfriends, where you learned how to straighten your hair into an emo aesthetic, where you learned how to hate your curls but love your people, that you could cry when you all graduate college and get your first jobs and your best jobs and when one of you marries the love of her life and you can't believe that you're all thinking about having kids when Black don't crack and Asian don't raisin fifteen years after a beautiful summer in French. I learned that I didn't want to stop living in French, because it meant that I could escape you, and it meant that I could open my mouth and write in my notebooks in a language all my own, and it meant that I could reinvent myself if I just kept learning a language and leaving you to do so, and that you would love it because it made me cosmopolitan and studied and you could show me off to your friends. And that if I spent enough time by the St. Lawrence, and the lupine village at its banks, I might, for a brief moment, miss seeing you again.

red and assiniboine

The second river, to the far west, above Toronto where the farmland gashes into Shield, where the air is so clean that you sneeze out all your accumulated urban sputum, where lakes glimmer with the blue I'd only seen in cleaning product labels, where the road creeps into the spindly evergreen forest, where we would die quietly if we tumbled down the cliffs with no cellphone signal, where our bus touches the greatest lake, where the bedrock rolls down into a plain, and the horizon flatlines wheat brown. At the fork of Red and Assiniboine, an oblique city where a lanky boy I met at Rivière had come from, who walked with me along the banks and tried to bond with me by talking shit about "natives," so I wrapped his doorknob in condoms in retaliation. On the Greyhound up, at the back of the bus, we summoned demons and convulsed as the wheels wiggled, and imagined ourselves as monstrous sinners, on a pilgrimage to Winnipeg, where God could cleanse thousands of us of our sins. Our splinter youth group had grown enough to assemble with everyone else on the continent, and we'd sleep in the creaky dormitories, wake up for stale sausages and crumbly eggs, worship God, listen to virgins whining about love, or more commonly hypocrites like us proselytizing virginity. You wanted me to lead the youth to God the Father, God the Son, and God the Holy Spirit, *no hanky-panky*, you'd repeat, *no hanky-panky* with a shaking finger to my face, at calloused gunpoint, an interrogation of my deviant behavior. Garbanzo calls us hypocrites, we hypocrites, the inclusive we, then the exclusive, and ascends the stage, and we raise our fists, her assistants hand out bracelets, the pure Christian cry, "True Love Waits," because no one should have to canoe up the river without the portage partner that God had picked out for them. We hypocrites stole away to the riverbanks, smacking away mosquitoes with the wingspans of golf balls, swarms that darkened like a prairie cloud, vivacious along the meeting place of the grasses and the two channels, we hypocrites crying pestilence. Winnipeg taught me how to hate myself because if you hate yourself you are raw and fresh enough to love God and love thy neighbor, even if that love should be turned back on yourself, and thus your love is Christian love, the purest expression of postmodern hate. Along the rivers we dreamed a heaven glimmering blue between infernos licking at our genitals, an austere paradise if we could wade through the ecstasy of burning alive, a promised land that crept away from us hypocrites locked in an orgiastic expression of Christian love, punching into the air, "True Love Waits," an exhortation by leaders too advanced to be hanging around teenagers, too old to be crushing on minors, too Christlike of an example to be lingering around our dormitories and hanging around half-naked teens past 2:00 a.m. after they had vowed to our parents to bring us home safe. They brought us home safe. If you ever wondered why, after I got back home from Winnipeg, I told you that I hated being Filipino, after we had come back from a Couples for Christ assembly, and you and Nanay stared at me on the verge of tears, and my face contorted itself, biting past the brown skin and freckles, your heirlooms, know that it began from a place of love, a waterborne convergence between heaven and earth, when hellfire was not a punishment but an escape from that theology of our bodies—the prisons of our flesh.

was the river I first met in your dreams, the leeches sucking your blood, the quack doctors cleaving your foreskin, the guava leaves you chew and spit as an antiseptic, the dreams in which I, too, feared the afflictions of my penis, the dreams in which I swam away, among the leeches, where the water bled purple, past the bridge, and into the open sea. Tenejero was your hometown, the one that you reprimanded me for forgetting, even though the only memory I have of it was a picture of your mother and aunt, where it was implied that I was behind the camera, a five-year-old who had yet to learn what it meant to become diaspora. Tenejero was your homeland, where you'd return for a month, days after you kicked me in the gut and left me on the basement floor and made sure that I knew—*that you really knew, anak*—that I was a stupid boy. It was the past conditional, the future return, the subjunctive punishment if I misbehaved, and then, that summer of 2009, the place to which we would inevitably travel after you and Nanay got married. After Winnipeg, after I told you that I hated being Filipino, and reminded you again at the Costco parking lot at Warden and Ellesmere, you told me that I had no choice but to come back to the Philippines with you, a family trip, a balikbayan, my first balikbayan, an opportunity to dig my feet into the soil again. As a child, you had wanted to answer God's call and become a priest, but when you had your first two kids, the Roman Catholic God said no, because priests can't be married, and so in 2009, you announced that you would study to become a deacon instead, the pastoral understudy for wedded men, the closest you'd get to serving our Lord Almighty. You needed a Catholic marriage certificate, and Nanay needed to actually convert to Catholicism, so I asked you why she needed to, if she had been going to church for years, and you said it was because she and Lola Pet had been raised in a sacrilegious congregation, the parish founded at the crossroads of two Filipinos you had little tolerance for, Ilokanos and Marxists, and the secret was that I always thought it was cool that we might have been little commies in another life. A fortnight after Winnipeg, we flew to our home/land, down past the orange clouds into the metropolis I had left over a decade prior, except we didn't have to grab a jeepney or a cab because you hired for us a private driver. It was a privilege to have Freon blow in your face and run your skin dry, for it shielded you from the humid air. Balong was the only one in the apartment who didn't need to run to the bathroom every ten minutes to take a shit, and mid-diarrhea, I learned that the home/water wasn't mine anymore, because my body rejected it in the way I rejected the motherland. The wedding was beautiful. I played keys for you, a traditional set list, the kind you'd bow your head to at St. Martin, nothing too rowdy, nothing too Youth for Christ. The pastor baptized Nanay in the name of the Father and of the Son and of the Holy Spirit amen, and at last, our family would finally receive the full blessings of the Lord. You'd never had a honeymoon because, after the courthouse and after the conception, the desert called you back. In a twelve-seater, we drove as far south as we could go, then on a boat, where vendors brandished their bags of peanuts, and you shouted at them to leave us alone because Balong was deathly allergic, and the patient sunset glowed across the ocean, and Mindoro approached in the horizon like a Werther's candy from afar, round and gold. On the road to the belated honeymoon, which cut through thick jungle, the van teetered and you worked the clutch pedal, your hand gripping the stick because our lives depended on it, except that you hummed to yourself while we clung to our seats and peered over the window, a cliff of certain death just inches away. After dark, we pulled into a town, Puerto Galera, and the black horizon drowned out all lights that the resort had put out for the beachfront, and one by one the whole family took turns taking a dump in the single bathroom, because not even the bottled water could save us from bacterial damnation. That night, I wandered the Mindoro shoreline and bellowed into the waves for no good reason. The next day, we hopped onto bangka and I flutter-kicked off of the outrigger, my face in the water, the fish darting across my chest and feeding on my skin, the corals braining along the seafloor. Back in Manila, you yelled at me for falling asleep in the front passenger's seat, and I didn't know what to tell you except that I was dizzy, but you said something about families sticking together and if I fell asleep it was just as bad as abandoning you, and I wondered why I ever agreed to come to the Philippines in the first place. In a sedan your cousin lent you, we drove to Bulacan and stopped at a Jollibee and Nanay insisted that you buy eight overflowing bags of Yumburgers and chicken and rice and palabok and everything else on the menu, even if it meant that our trip budget ran thin the rest of the way, and after a half hour of protest, you resigned to her splurge. I didn't understand why you were so nervous, or why Nanay drew the line in the sand, but we pressed on, and I thought that we would visit some relative or another in the subdivisions, but you veered hard into a wooded path, and I thought we'd drive into jungle again, but I saw a scattering of corrugated metal and sago and taho peddlers and open sewer drains next to shanty homes, and we turned into one of their lots, and you stepped out of the car and yelled *Mamá, dito na kami*, announcing our arrival to a short old lady with curly hair like mine, and I realized that this was the woman in the picture, your mother from Bataan. The first thing she did was scream at you for the food, reprimanding you for not bringing more, even though Balong and I were helping carry out the plastic bags, which were already hefty as fuck, and I knew then that I would never love your mother. Then she cried in the corner, and Balong and I stared at each other, and I noticed his anime T-shirt with hiragana and remembered that Lola Isabella had survived the Second World War, so he should probably wear his top inside out, and he understood. We sat inside the shack and some cousins two decades older greeted us, and I didn't want to ask why they had to take on the responsibility of taking care of this bitter old woman, but Nanay whispered to me that, in your family, no one wanted to deal with Lola Isabella, so she was passed around other reluctant family members until, at last, two generations removed, these cousins hesitated enough that by the time they considered saying no, Lola had already dumped her things inside. This was no hacienda, I thought, and Balong and I walked over to the sago man and bought a plastic bag of sugar water with pearls, into which he poked a straw, and when we walked back, you implored us to give our grandmother a kiss on the forehead, and so we did, and she twitched and skulked away, and I suddenly felt conscious of my dark lips, wondering what affliction had befallen them, and I told Balong that I hoped we never had to meet this lady again, and he nodded. Before we left the islands, you kept driving north and west, around the bay, and promised that you would show us that river you loved so much, even though the leeches were gargantuan and would probably chase us around, so we shouldn't dive in unless the water was absolutely clear, and you drove north on the freeway and reminded me of your stories, and I closed my eyes and conjured up the river you sang to me at night, but when I opened my eyes, and you had paused by the riverbanks, it was a hollow crevice, and the only water that was left was a trickle in the mud. I wish I could have told you that I was sorry.

was our odyssey, our second birth, our sacred text. To mark us for a lifetime of ~~membership~~ damnation, the Catholics drench us with its effigial waters, a pantomime of the prophet's first baptisms along its banks, in the years of our wailing animalhood, the years before we might have come to. I was Catholic before the fire ants bit my toes, I was Catholic before I was Canadian, I was Catholic before I convinced myself that I loved Catholicism and could speak about little more than every knee bending to God. I used to believe that, to make my Tatay proud, I should devote my life to the Almighty Father, the Tatay of Tatays, the Creator and the Destroyer at the same time. That devotion took form in the posters of computer-generated dead fetuses, in screaming expletives at the heretical leftists, in stretching my hands out to the heavens while inferno licked my heels. What I didn't understand, not then, in the nonlinear stupor of my adolescence, and not even after, when I no longer deified you, was that your faith, a quiet and devoted one, unlike mine, refused to conquer and dominate. As a Christian, you reached for the shepherd's cane, and I, the crusader, armed myself with the halberd first, then the bayonet, and then the submachine gun. At home, the cane would strike me, but to the world, its adornment gathered the forlorn and the wayward around you, save for your own son. First, it was our gym, in your starched uniform, and the cadence of your voice that carried both retribution and restoration, the two ingredients of sovereign power. Then it was the Couples for Christ assembly, in your crisp blazer, tailored to your shape by Lola Pet, and the way that you could exhort an entire church hall with nothing but your guitar and your pastor's instincts. And then your first departure, the exalted one, when you mistook the call of God for one into the diaconate, the Catholics' lesser ministry, the one reserved for the lackeys of the voluntary celibates, and you loved your work and your education, but the director hated you and your accent, and kicked you out of the program. And then your next departure, when you discovered that Rome did not have a monopoly on Catholicism, and that your childhood dream to join the priesthood was not incompatible with having a family. You found a man in the Netherlands, leader of an older order, one that broke away before Martin Luther nailed his complaints on that door, where they practice Catholic rites but their priests can marry, and he was charmed by you, and in short order, after your devoted study, ordained you as a priest. The Filipinos, who had once shared space with us, who brought their kids over to raise them alongside yours, dwindled until a trickle, and they called us heretics because you were no longer (Roman) Catholic, and they called me a devil when I called it quits and hated the church, and we, the sacrilegious family, no longer proper Catholics and therefore no longer proper Filipinos, paddled downstream, you at the rudder, Nanay and I navigating alternately with two different maps, forking into the tributary less traveled, and at the horizon, a sea beyond the brackish water, not the one where Jesus and his kinfolk live under empire's duress, not the one where the water died and the brine corrodes the possibility of fauna, but maybe an ocean, the shared one, the apathetic blue, where borders wash into its depths.

rouge

is my origin point, my creek, upon the cornucopia of bejeweled leaves in that shade, a touch more earthen, that greets the 116 bus as it soars down into the valley. It's the river, sometimes just a trickle, but vivacious enough for the salmon to skim down the water, watched by the rouge eyes of the hikers on the shoreline. It's the language that you once forced me to learn, to euphemize the color of blood. It's the only place where our neighbors would fish, and we'd watch out for each other if the cops were on their way, so everyone could book it back to their cars and stow away their gear. The summer after would take me back to this river, not as an occasional place to visit but as the place where I'd spend almost every day for four years, in a brutalist marvel overlooking the valley, the campus its own faraway place, even though it was literally on the other side of the street from the high school. Along the Rouge was where I first doubled over and learned that I was too fat and asthmatic to hike back up the escarpment, and so I gave up walking altogether and declared a biology and math double major so all I'd have to do was think, but the asshole from Frosh Week told me I was too stupid to do math, so I told him to fuck off and tried anyway. Along the Rouge was where I almost failed college, because I couldn't wake up on time and I used every excuse I could not to be home, and for the first time in my life you never questioned me, because I was, at last, a legal adult, and I knew from my other river trips that the best thing for our relationship was to be as far away from each other as possible. Along the Rouge was where I first realized that maybe the love of my life was half a world away and that I could meet her on Tumblr and try to make it work even if round-trip tickets to Honolulu would cost me a month's worth of wages at my first part-time job at the IT helpdesk. Along the Rouge was where I realized the guy from the Jesus Camp could no longer be in my life, and eventually decided that we would be better off as strangers, even if it meant that it would split our entire group apart, the one that had coalesced over the years, and I finally figured out that I could be popular at school if I stuck to my principles and learned how to be a student activist. And it was along the Rouge that you and I learned to give each other grace, after you couldn't help yourself from screaming at me and Nanay hugged you tight, and I told you that you were an abusive piece of shit, and that because you were sick I was supposed to be able to handle your abuse, and you apologized by letting me figure my own shit out and switch to the humanities even though neither of you saw any utility in studying the liberal arts. When you stepped aside, I learned to love you for your flaws, that you had done your best and these were my years to commandeer my own life, and so I wrote poems, and more poems, a poem for each subway station on the Toronto Transit Commission, and my bearded literature professor with the fabulous ties encouraged me to compile them into a book. When you stepped aside, I knew that I wanted to be a writer, and not only did you let me, but you encouraged me, because all you and Nanay wanted me to feel was happiness, and even if you didn't apologize for convincing me that I was an idiot for years, I knew that the gift you had given me wasn't only an education but a chance to learn that maybe, just maybe, I wasn't really stupid after all. And maybe that your struggle would pay off, even if I wouldn't become the medical doctor that you once wanted me to be, or wouldn't do anything that would put food on the table right away, because I could come home yapping about how much I loved my friends, how the Somalis and Egyptians invited the Filipinos to the Ramadan parties after a couple of us decided that we wanted to fast with them, and an entire geography opened up that we Catholics never knew about, the halal Trini store with the amazing doubles across from the masjid, and the midnight runs to PizzaLand, and that at the end of my degree, I learned that I didn't have to carry the weight of a chasm in my memory into my twenties. When I graduated, you insisted that I invite all my friends over to the house, and I asked you if you were sure because we'd be cussing into the night, and you and Nanay said that it was okay, and you'd drive people home if needed. What I never told you was that half of the friends that came over I'd cull from my circles within a year, and the ones I'd keep I'd call my best friends in the entire world, even if I often lived too far from them and missed them and you every single day. What I never told you was that, after that party, we gathered along the banks of the Rouge and chain-smoked some blunts that Italia's dealer had rolled up that day, and in the distance, flopping down the trickling stream, a single salmon greeted us to say goodbye, because we never gathered to smoke there again, and the little perch we always sat at, the makeshift sanctuary, had finally eroded into the river below.

historic filipinotown, los angeles, 2020s

Steve's eyes flicked to the corner of the Zoom screen. Our session had come to an end.

"That's all the time we have today. We're still good for next Friday?"

PART FOUR

SPIRIT

2010–2021

TONGUES

WHEN I LEARNED Tagalog again, I rehearsed a respectable story to explain why. I nearly failed college, for no better explanation other than untreated sleep apnea and severe depression (which I learned much later), but because I didn't want you to think I was stupid, I held off on telling you until professors handed me back my tests, circled Fs in red pen, zeroes throughout. The story grew so desperate that I brought myself to finally tell you, and to my surprise, you and Nanay offered a winter vacation, in a timeshare deep in Pennsylvania's mountains, where I could purge myself of those semesters and watch *Diners, Drive-Ins and Dives* and play *StarCraft II* and read Emily Brontë's *Wuthering Heights*, a book that I had skipped in high school. For some reason, that combination worked, and after a full season of Guy Fieri's frosted tips and failed space-era campaigns, I made my way through that novel, and the nested story—at one point, told as a narration within a narration within a narration—gripped me, and by New Year's Eve, I told you that I wanted to be an English major.

"So long as you finish, anak," you said, not to encourage my newfound passion but to resign yourself that the five career choices you'd given me (doctor, engineer, lawyer, accountant, priest) would never materialize. The irony was that we *did* manifest them for ourselves. Both of us: you, a priest, even if not in the congregation of your first faith; and me, a doctor, even if my ideas couldn't puncture flesh and save a life.

I loved my English major, and the reward was that I could come home excited about my classes, thrilled to sit on the stairs in a crowded auditorium listening to the tall, bearded poetry professor opine about the mathematical precision of Dionne Brand's lyric, and delighted that I, too, could take poetry classes, not because it was any sort of ambition of mine but because it was such a treat to pay tuition to express myself. When the bearded poet told me that I was good at writing critical essays, I learned to love research, too, and on the April of my junior year, after a full term in student politics, which I wouldn't renew because I didn't want to run a slate of candidates that my colleagues wanted, I told you that the university would pay me six thousand dollars to read and write and travel to pursue my own project. I told you, too, that I wanted to study Philippine literature, and right on cue, you lectured me about the great writer of our nation, José Rizal, and why my translations, the ones I bought on Amazon, were pathetic renderings of the country's foremost luminary, whose words could only be understood in the original Tagalog, even though Rizal himself actually wrote in Spanish. The added gift was the opportunity to tell you that I had learned enough Tagalog to keep studying it, and you nodded, as if it were your idea, "Keep exploring our history," you'd say, like that was my marching orders.

But if this is an epistolary of emotional truths, it might behoove me to punctuate it with some actual truth-telling. I didn't learn Tagalog to study Philippine history. It was the other way around: I convinced myself to study our homeland because I never forgot Tagalog in the first place. I left the Catholic Church right around the time the rest of our family did, when the director of your diaconate program pushed you out for some bullshit about your accent, and you still felt God's call to serve as His priest, and you and Nanay moved into a different denomination altogether. When I left, I hated being Filipino even more, not because you were Filipino but because the only expression of Filipinoness I knew was Catholicism, and when we left, the Couples for Christ people used to call us all kinds of names, heretics for the two of you, devil-spawn for me. A lot of those people in the youth group, even some of the ones in band with me, went to the same school, though most of us started ignoring each other in the hallways, especially when I didn't want to go to the Filipino Club anymore and had no interest in joining the Asian Christian unions. I even stopped bringing my guitar to school, that tradition of Filipino masculinity I had once proudly participated in, and told nobody for four years that I played music.

For my nineteenth birthday, I saved up my wages for a month and rented a suite in the Pantages Hotel in downtown Toronto, the bougie one right across the street from the Eaton Centre, and invited as many friends as I could, including the ones who had left Youth for Christ with me, to celebrate the first year of legal drinking age. Before I left, you reminded me that you and I had to have our first drink together, so you brought out two shot glasses and poured tequila into them, excited to show me the ropes. We clinked our glasses, and I slammed the shot down on the tabletop and knocked back the drink, "Thanks, Tatay, I'll see you tomorrow," and you always tell that story in the most hilarious way, because it was then that you knew that I had, indeed, been up to a ton of hanky-panky. I took the train downtown and got into the suite, a fancy unit with ample couches for everyone to mingle and make out on, and a California king bed for the foursome later that night, when Italia would dap me up, high as shit, "Happy birthday, bro," and the entire suite smelled like vaginas and Backwoods and stale champagne.

The following year, for my twentieth, the year I was on the student union, I wanted to use my income to host an even better party, so I booked the largest hotel room I could on Church Street, with its own kitchen and balcony, and my coworkers and my friends brought a cornucopia of bottles and joints, but we had no shot glasses, so we passed around a pot of jungle juice and sipped from the chalice like it was the blood of Christ. At some point, some uninvited friends of friends stumbled inside and tried to pick a fight, but by that time, I was already faded as shit and was on the verge of knocking out on the couch. I took a hit of the bong, the shared one that I stashed in a safe, and it was the next morning, I woke up entangled with a mass of bodies on the mattress, and we decided to do away with our grogginess with some brunch.

Up north on Church was a Sunset Grill, one of a local chain of brunch spots with greasy eggs too expensive for Toronto in the early 2010s, and when we got our order, Keto and Jellyfish—the same Jellyfish from the fourth grade—told me that they all had a video to show me. *Oh shit*, and my stomach lurched at the thought of something incriminating. Instead, Jellyfish produced her phone and pressed play on a video of me standing over Keto and Lasagna and everyone else lounging on the bed, deep in a freestyle rap battle. The rap cipher was a Scarborough tradition, and as I watched a couple of my coworkers get half naked and try to rhyme the words "rocket launcher" with something elegant, I was ready to dismiss the video, but Jellyfish said "*Keep going*," so I watched until it was my turn, and there I was on the screen, spitting bars, not in English, but in Tagalog—in metaphors and braggadocio, the kind of swagger that only fluency could achieve, the rhyme schemes that were only possible because of Tagalog's agglutinative syntactic structure. I kept watching the video while everyone chatted over eggs Benedict, and still hungover, I dumbly said, "I think I know Tagalog," and my friends cackled and said, "No shit."

That Tagalog rap battle was enough to give me the confidence to take up the bearded professor's call and learn how to become a researcher. That summer, with my first grant, I flew to the Philippines and tried to find whatever I could in the university and state libraries and heritage sites about the Filipino migrant writers who had left the home country and kept writing far away from our motherland, and my girlfriend at the time, whom I had met online, suggested that I go visit her in Hawaiʻi to do interviews there, because she was taking a Filipino literature class. Later that summer, I went to visit her and studied everything I could about where Filipinos there lived, especially the neighborhood of Kalihi, and the bus routes they took to work in the hotel industry in Waikiki, and I wondered why those workers were always out of sight wherever the tourists went, and there was my project. One of those nights, jetlagged as hell, I stared at the ceiling at five in the morning and realized that white people did this for a living, they got to read and write and talk about dope shit, so why couldn't I?

GETTING INTO graduate school took two tries. The first was a misguided application, and I had just learned what the Rhodes and Gates scholarships were and that the medieval literature professor I had a crush on had received one of those, so I asked her what it took and she bluntly told me that I didn't have what it took to get them. Neither did the department chair, even though I had gotten straight A's in almost every English class I took. When I tried anyway, I felt like I'd wasted your money again—the same feeling that I got when

I almost failed school—but you told me that it was okay, I could try again, and you would support me in whatever way I needed, even though I started to drop hints that I wanted to move out of the house.

When it didn't look like I would get in anywhere, I vowed that I would finish my English major as strong as I could, and so I wrote two theses, a critical one based on the Hawai'i research I'd done on Filipino American writers and the settler colonial tourism industry, and a creative one, where I spent my spare time writing poems in every single station on the subway. I wanted to commemorate a shooting in our neighborhood, the one where that clown-ass mayor that you loved stood across the street and told reporters that, for "these thugs," "the best social program is a job," and a Black senator agreed with him in front of hundreds of people and I yelled at him at a town hall, and I finally figured out that everything we had been through living in Scarborough, from the YFC people we lost, to the times I booked it into the ravine to run away from the cops, to your bankruptcy and your losing your job after your heart attack, to the times you couldn't put fresh food on the table except for the cheap mashed potatoes and Ikea meatballs, could be expressed in poetry.

On the second try, I felt like I had gotten my bearings. I had settled into my new apartment, and figured things out with my roommate, a Japanese ecologist, and met Focaccia, whom I loved but who had planned to move to Guyana for work, but we would try to figure things out until then, and we grew to love each other's friends, too. I had gotten into a groove with my college friends, the ones who stayed behind, with whom I could go on strolls in Kensington Market and wonder what it would be like to grow old and live past forty. I had a new set of mentors at school, two Americans with ambitions to build a food studies center, and they promised me that they would advocate for my admission into the program so I could go work with them and learn all about a new field of inquiry. All I wanted to do was get into graduate school, and when I did, I could have moved to the Pacific Northwest but stayed home because you were too sick to teach at the gym. I could take over as instructor, and grow old with the gym, and grow old at home.

At the University of Toronto, the downtown campus where all

the white people went and I finally knew what it was like to be a racial minority, I found a historical project all my own. It was something that would take me to Nanay's and Lola Pet's ancestral region in the north, even though my original mentors hated that I was going too native, and one of them tried to pawn off my work as his own and the other would give it his best shot to kick me out of the program when I called it out. I got really good at applying for grants and won a major federal scholarship and a Fulbright, which would take me to the United States for a year, where I could do my research, so I chose to spend terms in Honolulu and Seattle, the two places I had always wished I could live in if I was going to America to study. You asked me why I wasn't going to the Philippines to study real Filipinos if I had picked up Tagalog already, and I told you that I didn't want to study your kind of Filipinos but Nanay's kind, the ones who blessed me with my skin and my unruliness, who left home to pose naked in front of cameras and eat dogs in world's fairs and worked on sugar and pineapple plantations and wrote incredible novels without speaking a lick of Tagalog. You pressed again why I wasn't studying more Tagalog, and there was a whole world outside of Manila Bay, spoken in Ilokano, the language of dictators and revolutionaries, and in the language of Nanay and Lola Pet, who grieved in the realm beyond my comprehension, the night when my grandfather died.

In Honolulu, I spent my mornings between the sugar plantation archives and Ilokano language classes, and learned the differences between regional dialects, and took the bus after class to Chinatown and Kalihi just to keep exposing myself to the language as much as possible. I wrote Lola Pet a letter in Ilokano, too, not a good one, and probably littered with way too many archaic noun choices, but at the end of that letter, I figured that I should probably try speaking to her, too. Halfway through autumn, I flew back east to go to a conference at Harvard, my first time on that weird red campus, and then popped up to Toronto to visit everyone, and I stayed near campus and took the subway as far east as it could go, and the 116 bus east on Eglinton, up on Kingston, and down into the Guild and up Morningside, and walked to your house. Neither you nor Nanay were home, and neither was Balong, who was at music school downtown. But when Lola Pet answered the door, I blurted out *kumusta ni lelangko*, and without skipping a beat she switched into fluent Ilokano, and I could understand about 70 percent of her words, enough to ask her to repeat once so I could understand, and if she couldn't explain a word, she'd translate it to Tagalog and go back to Ilokano. We sat at the dining table together, and she microwaved a bowl of scrambled eggs and fish, and she told me all the gossip about the family in her native language, and I noticed that she told them with extra snark, instead of her usual muted personality in the colonial tongue of Manila.

An hour later, the rest of you arrived home, and we sat together at the dinner table, and I continued to talk in Ilokano, and Nanay and Lola Pet froze in shock, and shook their heads, terrified that you would yell at them to shut up with their savage speak, and I told them that of course I was going to speak in Ilokano, I had chosen to devote my life and career to this language, and left home to learn it, and damn this man's bullshit if I couldn't live my heritage and celebrate my maternal side. You turned your face away and Lola Pet kept talking to me, and Nanay kept watching the two of us to see if we'd blow up at each other, but you sat in silence and ate your dinner. Balong looked on in shock, and asked me how the hell I learned the language so quickly, and I told him it was way too much work but this moment was worth it.

Ilokano was worth it because I knew that it would irreversibly transform our family, and you would never be able to shut Lola up again. And Ilokano was worth it because, for once, language was no longer my escape from you but my sanctuary in a space that was just for me and Nanay and Lola Pet. Each time I speak Ilokano, I come home.

AFTER HONOLULU, I moved to Seattle. I was slated to do an internship at a fifty-year-old archive in a Catholic school basement, staffed by a single nonagenarian archivist, Auntie Dorothy Cordova, who offered unfettered access to the collections in exchange for my help transcribing interviews with Filipino elders she had done in the 1970s. Auntie was at once my mentor and my dear friend. We loved to bump heads over whether or not the oral histories she did were more Philippine history or American history. We debated the stakes of the civil rights movement over microwaved fish sticks and hot green tea, in the sanctuary of the ghosts of the Filipino American past, and reveled in the fact that we both had grandparents who hailed from the same region in Northern Luzon, even though she was older than Lola Pet herself.

A month into the internship, Auntie handed me a box of unorganized photographs from the 1930s, all taken by a single photographer in Reedley, California, and I offered to catalog them for her, because I had gotten really good at studying photography. At first, the photos were easy to work with: portraits of young men in tailored suits, dancing with their dates; family photographs around a single matriarch; landscapes of the grape farms in the Central Valley; Filipino hoboes grinning atop a rundown pickup truck. And then, nonstop, images of dead bodies, corpses in fields, corpses in open caskets, babies shriveled and sunken with rigor mortis, families in funereal white, their eyes swollen from tears. I gathered them up and turned them face down, packed my things, and called out to Auntie to tell her I was done for the day and that I'd come by tomorrow. She told me to take the next day off since I had been working myself to death, and I knew that she sensed something was wrong.

I stepped out of the archive and walked as far as I could go. I blinked, and I was trying to keep myself upright walking down the slippery incline from Central District into Capitol Hill. I blinked again, and I was under the I-5, moving through storage units and rusty fences, the starry lights of the port gleaming from behind the brownstones by the water. I blinked yet again, and I was in the International District, standing by the Japanese grocery store, and my phone buzzed against my thigh, and I opened it, and you texted me that Lola Isabella, your mother, had died. I sat on the curb, my ass damp from the rainy cement, and I texted back that I was so sorry. I didn't know how to feel, because the last memory I had of Lola Isabella was that she flinched when Balong and I tried to kiss her forehead to say goodbye.

Another buzz from my phone, and my cousin, your niece, the one who used to dig through my backpack for condoms and snitch on me, sent me a picture of Lola Isabella's face, and I puked out my fish sticks, a slurry dragging down my crewneck sweater, and I threw my phone against the ground, and miraculously it only cracked along the edge of the screen, but it was still at maximum brightness, and the image of Lola Isabella's lifeless face, sunken and pale, dressed up for a funeral, stared back at me from the open casket. I deleted my chat history with Ate and told Nanay to tell her never to contact me again.

Somehow, I ended up back home, a dingy student apartment in the Wallingford neighborhood I'd found on Craigslist, and I didn't leave for a week. Auntie Dorothy called me and told me that she missed me in the archive and that she had a surprise for me if I could come today, and that lifted me out of my stupor, and I ran to the bus stop by the University of Washington and rode down to the Central District. There, she was sitting with a group of elderly women who were half-Ilokano and half-Indigenous from all the different nations in the Salish Sea, and we talked about how much we loved fancy pens and the sound of the Ilokano language, which all their fathers had spoken as migrant workers before the war. Auntie Anna, with a short haircut and fabulous square glasses, exchanged contact information with me and made me promise to reach out to her again, because she enjoyed our conversation so much. After they left, Auntie Dorothy sat at the computer, which I interpreted as a signal that we were back on our same routine. I sat by the stacks of tape cassettes, which she had laid out for me next to my backpack, and I found the audio of a man with the last name Agbayani, unmistakably Ilokano, and I began to write.

What poured out onto my word processor wasn't a transcription of an interview but a single word: *dung-aw*. I texted a friend of mine back in Toronto that your mother had passed away, and I didn't know how to process the fact that I hated what that woman had done to my father, who still loved her stubbornly, and that my only memory of her was that she recoiled at my brown skin against her pale forehead. *Write in the broken language of the diaspora*, she messaged me back, the literary scholar, and I stared at my single word again. Dung-aw. The Ilokano mourning chant. I had learned the form in

Honolulu from my teacher, Professor Agcaoili, who demonstrated it to us. The person closest to the dead wails and chants a lyric, and someone responds, and adds their own. It ripples out to the whole family, and then the entire village, and when it's time to hold the funeral, the whole town has collectively composed a song to honor the kin they lost. My Ilokano was broken. But I could write my own dung-aw, maybe in that savage language that you had suppressed at home, maybe in a mongrel tongue of English and Spanish and Tagalog and Ilokano and however the proverbial Holy Spirit moved me to speak, a dung-aw for that kiss, when Lola Isabella's flinch taught me to hate my skin, and I wanted to learn to love it back:

beso-beso

bleached &
        leathered forehead

the afterimage
        of cordovilla
sun

        & fold

creasing
        a disenchantment

For the next two years, I kept writing dung-aw, for my aunties in Seattle whom I loved, and kept writing even when I learned Spanish in Middlebury that summer, or came back home to Toronto and danced with you and Nanay on the twentieth-anniversary gala of our gym, when you tried to salsa with the one I loved, and Nanay and I, skilled dancers both, spun each other until we teetered from dizziness, and I knew that it would be the last time I would really live at home, and kept writing dung-aw when you and Nanay cried in my arms after I told you that I got a job offer in Los Angeles and I'd be leaving Scarborough forever, and kept writing dung-aw when the world shut down and people died from that virus and I had to leave California to go back home, because I couldn't stop thinking about the fact that you, who had devoted yourself to caring for others, insisted on working on the hospital's front lines, even if it cost you your life.

CAESURA

"WE'RE OKAY," you repeated over FaceTime.

The border was closing in on us. Escargot, the friend I met in Quebec who had since moved to New York, was visiting me in Los Angeles when the news announced that the invisible scourge had become a pandemic. We had planned to chill out in Silver Lake and eat sushi, and maybe watch the Golden State Warriors game, when San Francisco announced that all public events would be canceled and the city was going on lockdown. LA, in its typical fashion, took longer to close up, but Escargot and I, Canadians both, couldn't stop thinking about our families back in Toronto. In my tiny Koreatown apartment, we frantically called home and figured out if we should leave.

You were the first thing on my mind. After years of unemployment, and after finding yourself in the priesthood, you had taken on a job in the palliative care unit at Scarborough General Hospital, which meant that you were right on the front lines. On video, you reassured me that you worked in a completely separate wing of the hospital, and that the Covid wards were far from your unit. But we knew nothing about the virus. I imagined you walking through a cloud of certain death clinging to your clothes, then bringing it home and infecting you and Nanay and Lola Pet and Balong, and all of you were immunocompromised in some way. I, the healthiest member of our immediate family, was halfway across the world in California. Should I come home? I kept asking. Did you want me home?

"We're okay, anak. Don't worry about us."

How could I not? Your ministry placed you right in the crosshairs of the global pandemic. Before you were a priest, you were a volunteer at the hospital where Balong was born, the one near our Silver Springs apartment, and when you were ordained, you stayed on and brought your guitar, and sang songs to comfort the patients who were in their final days. I couldn't fathom the thought that you would die on the job, even if it's what you always did, the consummate shepherd, sacrificing your own well-being for the sake of the flock.

You insisted that I stay in California and that you'd take care of everyone. And like the bad son I always was, I did the exact opposite. I came home.

In my half-furnished living room, with Justin Trudeau's livestreams on the TV and Donald Trump's on the laptop, Escargot and I charted out our itinerary. She reached out to her uncle, who owned a spare condo in downtown Toronto, where we could isolate for two weeks until it was safe enough to return to our childhood homes. We wrapped ourselves in as many layers as we could—even our wrists, because I was afraid of Covid sneaking into my pores—and headed straight for the airport, shirking away from the other bodies, since they packed us into the plane like sardines. We traveled like automatons, executing every step of the plan, and we brought you two into the logistical planning, and at the condo, you dropped off two weeks' worth of dry goods and some Costco rotisserie chicken. *I'll see you soon*, we kept saying to each other, half promise and half prayer, and I watched you drive off in your brand-new Toyota RAV4, that quintessential Filipino immigrant vehicle, and we hauled everything upstairs, not knowing if the condo would be our sanctuary or our tomb.

Over Zoom, Escargot introduced me to all of her friends in New York, DJs and designers and writers who had made her feel at home in that city. Every evening, we gathered online and played games, and occasionally I'd host my own with some Scarborough folks, spirited campaigns on *Animal Crossing* and *Among Us*, all the virtual simulacra of public spaces that the pandemic had deprived us of. We cooked together with the government's reports on in the background, and I sent you pictures of all the things that Escargot and I whipped up together, delectable improvisations of pastas and toasts that we elevated into haute pandemic cuisine.

After two weeks, you picked me up downstairs, and I took my place in my childhood bedroom, which you had converted into your personal office but was mine again. The same bedroom where I would lock myself in during a depressive stupor, the closet where I'd slap myself across the face until I calmed down enough to sit at dinner with you, the bed I'd sneak my paramours into after school, the floor where I kept my bag and our extended family would invade my personal space. During that first week, I locked myself in the room, coming out only with a mask, because you kept going to work and came home and sprawled out on the couch, and I visualized a cloud of virus around you following wherever you went.

Your pandemic livestream of choice was not the federal government's but Doug Ford's provincial updates. I rolled my eyes every time he appeared on screen. He looked like a sloppy Photoshop edit of his late brother, Rob Ford, the nepo baby who had made a mockery of our neighborhood when he was the city's mayor. During the early lockdown, Balong introduced me to TikTok by way of a resurfaced viral clip about Doug, in which a fourteen-year-old called him a Timbit, which I thought was an insult to those delicious donut holes that we used to buy from Tim Hortons for kuntaw classes. In those early weeks, Doug seemed to communicate updates to the lockdown mandate with genuine concern, except that, when it came to your colleagues on the front line, he reserved particular disdain for the nurses who demanded better wages for their work.

The report cut to an interview of a nurse who described the horrid conditions that they faced at work while isolating themselves from their families. You sneered at the screen.

"These ungrateful nurses. They get paid so much already—and to do what? To keep complaining?"

"They have every right to complain. They're swimming in that virus. And unlike you, they actually care enough about their families to isolate from them."

That shut you up. You switched the TV over to Netflix and aimlessly scrolled through the menu, before resigning yourself back to the bedroom. I sat at the dinner table and pulled out my laptop and opened a Word document, and cranked out the sketches of an op-ed about Donald Trump's preferred term for Covid, the "China virus."

Over lunch, while you were at work, I demanded to know why Nanay hadn't encouraged you to isolate, too. She had no answer but promised that she would bring it up with you. Sensing my bubbling anger, Balong excused himself and retreated to the basement to play *Call of Duty*.

"Tatay is so goddamn irresponsible," I kept repeating, my voice shaking. "I came home to huddle up with all of you, and he's putting us at risk?"

"Please, anak," Nanay said quietly. "The hospital said that things were okay."

"Really? With that death toll? Even with that dumbass on the TV announcing how many people were dying every day?"

"Please, anak."

The next morning, Nanay woke me up and told me to bid you farewell. You packed your things, two luggage bags' worth, and told me that you had found an Airbnb in Whitby, a half-hour drive to the east, where you would isolate yourself as long as you needed to. "Take care of our family," you said and reached over to hug me, but stopped when I didn't move from the stairs. You kissed Nanay goodbye and closed the door. I took my place at the dining table to work on my essay. Nanay set up shop across me with her own laptop and didn't look up from the screen until her shift was over.

For three months, you kept us company over FaceTime, and sometimes over Zoom, and you would wave at Balong and me to tell us that you missed us, and that the hospital reassured the staff that the pandemic was under control, thanks to your work. Sometimes, I thought about urging you to retire and come back home. But you loved your job too much, and I coveted my isolation from you too much, that it felt like an insult to both of us to tell you to leave.

At home, the lockdown was the most productive period that we'd ever had. Nanay was killing it at work, and in her off-hours she researched what it would take to rebuild her credit score and learn how to make some money outside of her salary. You were on the cusp of getting an insurance payout for some work injury you'd never told me about, and you and Nanay discussed putting that money into some investments. Lola Pet was thriving with her frequent phone calls to her family around the world, and when she wasn't yelling into her phone and reprimanding her distant grandsons for their attitude, we watched Korean dramas together in the living room.

When Balong grew tired of yelling expletives in the *Call of Duty* lobby, he joined us upstairs in the dining room and taught himself how to produce music. And when I wasn't staring at my dissertation and beating myself up over my inability to do any academic work, I wrote more dung-aw poems.

At the end of May, an officer in Minnesota choked a Black man to death over a supposedly fake twenty-dollar bill. Over the next few hours, the world exploded in protest, even north of the border, and I watched over the livestreams and mulled the possibility of wearing a double mask and a face shield and commuting downtown to join, but I remembered that I lived with three immunocompromised people and stayed put. You texted me that evening to see if I had been keeping up with the news. Expecting some contrarian debate about how right the officers were, I ignored your texts. You followed up with another set of texts. At work, you asked your Caribbean colleagues what they thought of the situation, and they reminded you that this kind of shit happened in Toronto, too, especially if you were Black. You told me that you pondered their words, and they resonated with you, and that you concluded that if these cops could keep getting away with brutality, the police should be dismantled altogether.

You asked me if I had any readings that you should check out to inform you of the situation. It was the first time that you ever asked me for recommendations, a year after I received my PhD in a field that you begrudgingly acknowledged my expertise in, Philippine studies. I sent you some basic essays, and when you asked for more readings even if it was too complicated for someone without a humanities degree, I emailed you PDFs of *Golden Gulag*, written by a pioneering abolitionist geographer, and the punchy theory book *Carceral Capitalism*, whose author brims with poetry. You read them voraciously. I marveled at the fact that, out of all people, it was my own father who was asking me for an abolition reading list.

On Twitter, I started to follow the protests in Los Angeles, and obsessively watched the virtual town halls with city council, hundreds of testimonies hurling expletives at the inaction of politicians, while the Los Angeles Police Department swarmed and kettled protestors along Wilshire Boulevard. Over Discord, I organized my own study group, sticking close to my expertise in Asian American studies, and we gathered every week to close-read a selection of anticolonial texts. You would update me on how it was going at the hospital, and your evolving thoughts on the murder of Mr. Floyd, and you asked what you could do to help. My first instinct was to tell you to keep studying, but a friend reminded me that study was nothing without action. With the reading group, I discussed what it might mean to do solidarity work, whether it was in the streets or otherwise, and for those of us who couldn't be outside, we could wire money to some bail funds and keep pushing our politicians to give a shit.

One of the movements I found was emerging in LA's Historic Filipinotown, a really incredible leaderless initiative, local artists and cooks preparing free meals for the Filipino nurses working overtime at the hospitals, and extending the same meals for Black folks in the neighborhood. I asked if I could make regular donations, and if I were to come back to the city at some point, I offered to help out at the kitchens. Filipino poets, too, wanted in on the action, and organized fundraisers through their virtual readings, which drew attendees over Zoom from around the world.

It was around that time that I heard from my real-estate agent, whom I had recently hired, and she texted that she'd found an interesting property that had been sitting on the market for months, a three-story townhouse with a garage and laundry room in the basement, a modest living room and kitchen, and two bedrooms. The pictures online made it seem as if the walls were yellow, so I asked her if she could tour it for me. To my relief, the walls weren't jaundiced after all, and she speculated that it might have been the bad photographs that were sinking the house's price. And the best part of that house was that it was along Temple Street, the main artery of Historic Filipinotown. I put in an offer right away, but because I was in Canada, and the American embassy was closed for the pandemic, I had to return to LA to close the deal. And even though I had left home a year prior, this felt like the moment in which, finally, I would be free of you and my life in Toronto. And unlike the first move, in which I felt nothing but relief, this move was one that we preemptively mourned at home.

"You'll have to learn to drive!" Nanay said. I had deliberately chosen a neighborhood in LA that was a bus ride away from my office in South Central, but because public transit was a health risk, it was time to take that final step to millennial adulthood: getting my license and buying my first car.

The week before I left, my college friends came to see me off. Focaccia, who'd come back from Guyana to work in the city, offered to get us doubles from a Trini restaurant and have a picnic in the park. Lasagna pulled up in his Subaru, and we sat on the hood of the car and talked about all the ways that our lockdown experiences were roughly the same. Satoru, my friend and a far better poet than me, left her car windows down and taught me how to drive in the Rouge Valley parking lot. Minolta, the wholesome skater boy from grad school whom I loved to death, did the same in the park by the lake. As the sun went down, he thought I looked beautiful in the twilight and snapped a picture of me in front of a concrete wall. And Balong, not wanting to miss his turn, suggested that we walk to the convenience store and buy some Freezies, for old time's sake.

THE BOOK OF dung-aw was almost complete. Assembling a handful of poems I had written over the years, I crafted a first draft with dung-aw for anything and everyone I wanted my mourning to reach. Poems about the transcontinental railroad, where a Chinese worker struck a stake into Shoshone land, and poems about the slave trade, the antecedent of our sufferings, and about Lola Isabella's and Nanay's relatives and the millions and millions that swelled as unnamed death counts during the pandemic.

In the days before I was to leave for Los Angeles and close on my house, I told Minolta about an article I'd come across in a video game magazine about the fourteenth main installment of my favorite franchise, *Final Fantasy*, and how a community had emerged around a player who died of the coronavirus. Over a thousand people had logged in to the servers to pay their respects. Their sprites were dressed in black, and they marched across the map to a tree, which was to be the character's virtual resting place. I watched the YouTube video of the procession, the entire stream, and wept on the couch. At that point in the pandemic, Nanay no longer asked why, at any given moment, it seemed like I was on the verge of tears. We all were.

Minolta suggested that we hang out before I go west, and he'd teach me how to drive and prepare me for my test. He brought his parents' RAV4, the same model as yours, and picked me up for the day. I got behind the wheel, and because the streets were empty, I could take my time and make sure that my steering was crisp. We got food from a nearby Hakka restaurant and I blasted my favorite Drake songs while he rolled his eyes, even when I tried to convince him that *If You're Reading This It's Too Late* was a masterpiece of an album.

"Hey, do you want to drive to the beach?" he asked.

I had never driven there before, but I knew the way. From our neighborhood, where we were practicing left turns, I drove north on Morningside Avenue, past our first apartment on Danzig Street, north of the St. Martin schoolyard, and turned right on Lawrence Avenue East, as far as the road would go, toward the shadow of the nuclear power plant, east of the end of the bus route, down a gravel road, past the marshlands, underneath the rusty pedestrian bridge, near the overpass where the screaming GO Train runs, into a parking lot along the banks of the Rouge River's main tributary. Some families had braved the outdoors and cast their fishing lines off the rocks, while others sparked bonfires along the sand. He brought his film camera, and we took turns snapping pictures of each other, like we were models in the lingering summer twilight. The shoreline had retreated inland, victim to the increasingly aggressive tides of the last few years. The power plant's domes, silhouettes in the darkening sky, peeked from the horizon.

We climbed up the bridge and took some pictures of each other along the graffiti-rich railing. Over the Rouge's marshlands, the ancient village a murmur in the distance, the ripples glowed in the last of the sunset. Minolta handed me the camera to take one last picture before it was completely dark. I pointed the lens into the gap in the metal and peered into the viewfinder. I wondered, in the dread of the pandemic, when I would see this view again, the soft shimmer of the urban river that gave our family solace, the waters where you taught me how to snag and release the sunfish. This place, Scarborough, which had cared for us for over two decades, half a world away from that archipelago.

One night, at four in the morning, I took my place at my dinner table. Instead of reaching for the laptop, I grabbed my notebook and pen instead. In the flicker of the kitchen light, twenty-two lines, in eleven couplets, poured out of me. My mind's nose scrunched at the rancid stench of the garbage bags you'd leave out for me when I forgot to do the chores. Another odor punctured that memory, the clinging air of Manila, the sheet metal of my childhood, the roasting quail eggs by the concrete steps, the same ones where, in my first memory, my toes seared from the bite of the fire ants.

And you hobbled up the concrete steps, your eyes prematurely wizened from your Homeric sojourn, your suitcase still dusty from the desert air, your roughened palms against my cheek, your lips pressed to my forehead, and in that gentle baritone murmur:

I'm home, anak.

PHILIPPINE STUDIES

On a fresh week for rage, my father scattered
open garbage cans across my bedroom floor.

I had dreamed that I was back in Taguig, sifting through
sheet metal in the alley behind the quail egg stand;

a rusty corrugated corner pierced a bag of rancid chicken
before my eyes stung open from the same stench.

Years before, leather lashed at my flesh & I reveried
bloody-knuckled ways to forgive each crack; instead,

I supposed that it was the rattan of alabaster
nuns beating me through the Father's wrist,

or the hooks whipping welts on the spine of Christ,
raw repentance into clotting, dirt-dyed skin.

When the lashes stopped, new punishments,
creative labors all, sprung from his mind:

guilt-gilded yardwork in the parish I never asked for;
lifelong labor taxes for the upkeep of the pastor indoors;

or this morning, kitchen compost dispersed like us
across my floor: the burden of sensing the homeland.

Later that week, we gathered written scraps of property
around the dining table to stitch into my parents' will.

I inherited his freckles, but couldn't distinguish
which came from Father & which came from Sun.

PRODIGAL

AT THE END of our relationship, as in the beginning, we had no words left. In that chasmic absence, we spoke a battleground instead.

Until your constitution started to fade, martial arts was the language you were most fluent in, not out of any natural gifts, but by hard work, often against your own body. "Martial arts is a mediated relationship to violence," my friend Totoya, a proud son of the Rio Grande Valley, told me. In the West LA neighborhood of Palms, over a hearty plate of nachos, I entrusted this letter to him. Like me, Totoya was an outsider to Los Angeles, still madly in love with the place he called home. In the faint glow of a propane space heater, two immigrant professors of language arts struggled to put words to the memories of our fathers. At dinner, as I compulsively picked at the nachos and guacamole, his theory made sense. What else could describe a paternal relationship in crisis, a patriarchal inheritance of empire, except for violence?

For all the mastery of the English language you coveted for me, the one person I could never address was you. Whenever I tried to speak, and we weren't arguing, you policed my speech mannerisms—so I stopped talking to you. Whenever I tried to show you my stories, you corrected my grammar like I was doing an assignment—so I stopped writing to you. And whenever I tried to love you as a son, you loved me back with the divine justice of a Christian patriarch—so I stopped trying to love you.

Maybe I could write to Tatay one day, I thought once. A real letter, in the clearest language, unfiltered by self-censorship, unfettered by bitterness, unencumbered by the silence of family secrets. A letter, a gift born out of the stillness of paper, the softness of cursive, the quietude of script. To train, it took me fifteen years, a literary anthology, two books of poetry, and two historical tomes. Lyric, art, archival analysis, polemic, documentary, essay—any and every medium that would prepare me for the inevitable time when writing about you would consume me.

THE GYM WAS the one place where you and I found peace, at least enough of it that we could converge on some common language. This is in spite of having lived with you for two decades; in those same twenty years, our times together were organized around the dojo. We hardly overlapped at home, and—for many reasons—less so as I grew older. In this absence, what parts of you did I come to know? A Google search might have revealed your exploits and accomplishments on a makeshift HTML website I designed as a teenager. Some news reports, perhaps, of your accolades from your martial arts peers. A blog post or two about some ongoing spat between grandmasters. Or otherwise it might have been another website, this time for your religious congregation in a makeshift basement church, the aftermath of a tempestuous collision between chronic unemployment and midlife crisis: Tatay the Pastor.

Even though I lived with you for sixteen years, and even though I have devoted my professional life to writing about our family's historical inheritance, I am no authority over the story of your idiosyncratic life. Your siblings didn't give me consistent details, either. For starters, they all called you different names. Some called you a rascal, while others emphasized how studious and disciplined you were. Everyone disagrees over your political loyalties, especially when you joined the military during the dictatorship. And everyone still maintains different silences about your relationship with them and with your parents. Still, I managed to piece together something like a teleology. It goes like this:

You were born along a river on the Bataan Peninsula, over a decade after the Philippines' independence. You were the sickly eighth child of nine, often interred to your bed with respiratory issues. But your full given name predestined you for a life of combat: *little warlike one.* Little, nicknamed as such by your family after the diminutive part of that name. Child of the Ingkong of Mariveles, the elder of his community, freedom fighter against the Japanese Occupation, survivor of the 1942 Death March from his beloved Bataan to the wartime prison of Tarlac in Central Luzon. You were the youngest son of a proud Spanish mestiza from Bicol—another peninsula—at the base of the sacred mountain Mayon, far-flung from her ancestral Iberia. Reluctant emigrant to Manila and scholarship kid, proud captain in the Philippine military, rebel against the dictator Ferdinand Marcos Sr. Almost-Father in the Roman Catholic seminary, now archbishop in a different church. Migrant worker in the oil fields of Saudi Arabia, champion of the Middle Eastern tournament circuit. Then grandmaster, proud inheritor of the Mindanawon martial art, kuntaw, bestowed to you by a revered master. And always, Tatay.

BUT THIS TIMELINE doesn't capture the texture of the father I knew, the one who lived a life in an east-end community. Rarely with them or among them, but always at the front of a dojo or some bully pulpit. You could command a room with a stern look alone, or three booming claps before class. You boasted a charisma anointed by God, a presence that could (literally) stop a fifty-person brawl in a community center. A smile that could lighten the roughest of folks, and a glare that could make anyone cower in shame.

Your two other gifts, oration and pedagogy, made you a beloved figure in Scarborough's Filipino community. You're a beautiful storyteller, with a natural gift for linear time and narrative arc that I, a historian, never could master. Like those of your favorite man, Jesus Christ, your stories were always parables, no matter how mundane or out of left field they began. A story about your time as a deep-sea fisherman, when a shark got caught in the net, became an allegory for compassion, even for the scariest members of society. A tale about circumcisions and quack doctors on the riverside was the model for your bildungsroman on how to become an upstanding man. And your stories always riveted your audiences; your favorite way to tell them was cross-legged, on the gym mats, seated in a circle with your listeners, even if your ramblings took up the rest of the class.

Most of all, you loved to teach. With the students in our gym, you understood their growth in the long term, and invested in their training and development over many years. To this day, in remarkable detail, you remember every student you ever taught, their parents' names and marital statuses, their history of run-ins with the law or foster care, and their particular strengths and weaknesses as martial artists.

Away from the bully pulpit, in the fold of a social gathering or a crowd or an extended-family party, you struggled. Absent of taking over a conversation with your stories, or your poor sense of Canadian humor that always fell flat, you never learned how to make casual small talk, in the dainty way that North American society demanded of its newcomers. And despite your best efforts, Nanay was always the funny and charming one. Balong and I (but especially Balong) inherited her jocular demeanor and her ancestral heritage of shit-talk. People laughed politely at your jokes but guffawed at Nanay's. At parties, I often watched you fade into the background, masking anxiety behind a belabored nonexpression, until an opportunity presented itself for you to be the center of attention once more.

At home, I think you struggled the most. Under your regime, the home could only function in languages you understood, English and Tagalog, never Ilokano, my maternal language. Your standards of excellence and middle-class respectability needed to be met, from the school grades down to the sterile smell of the home, which could never be tainted with the smells of ethnicity—no garlic, no ginger, no onion, no fat.

Gone was the warmth of the teacher and storyteller, or the meekness of the awkward partygoer. In its place, an array of technologies. First the belt, then the shoe. Choreographed punishments that began with an incarceration to the bedroom, moved to the verbal judgment and testimony of guilt, and then the corporal punishment. Eventually, the fist or the palm took the place of these objects. And then, to inaugurate my teenage years, the sole or the heel of the foot. The choreographies of self-defense, turned against your son.

As I grew older, we became mirror images of each other. In our many quarrels, you called me "stubborn" and "aggressive" as pejoratives. For me, those qualities were superpowers that I could use to claw my way out from underneath your shadow and into the limelight.

Outside, this garnered us endless respect. But in the comfort of our home, we waged an endless war, the collateral damage of our clashes lodging into our family like shrapnel.

I could not deliver a counterattack effective enough to knock sense into a grandmaster of martial arts. No amount of physical impact could substitute for something like conversation. I wanted to block or parry, or evade the line of attack just enough to break open a quiet space to talk.

IN ANOTHER LIFE, perhaps another homeland, we might have had a fighting chance. Bataan is a land of crypts, most of them unmarked, stories interrupted by slaughter upon slaughter upon slaughter. And you, the proverbial medium, lived with the whispers of the dead at every waking moment. They crowded your dreams, infected your throat, curdled your screams, and energized every blow you landed on me. You heard these poltergeists, so intensely and so rudely, that not a single decibel was left to listen to your son.

But if you couldn't give me your ear, you offered me something else, even if every part of me wanted to reject your gifts. You insisted that you help pay for my education, until the money ran out and I had to take over the bills. You threw me into the linguistic worlds of the colonizers, if at the expense of the languages of our own, the colonized. You nurtured my music the way you did my armed combat, even when God demanded that I sharpen those songs into blades. You choreographed for me self-defense, even in the moments when I could not perform the steps, even when you were the assailant. You taught me to teach, if not to listen and learn. You gifted me gentleness, however rare yours was, as tender and hard-won as the flesh you whipped. And you gifted me a father, an imperfect but present one, when all you inherited from your father was his trace.

You, the aspiring shepherd, had hoped that you could show me a path to an exemplary life. Instead, out of your offerings, I fashioned my own, a life that I don't always believe was good, a hurtful one that lost me friends, a sinful one in the eyes of your Christ, but it was mine nonetheless. And on the curbs of that makeshift road, I foraged whatever words I could find, poems and stories and histories of our country, even if that country wasn't yours but Nanay's. I foraged those words, and I harvested them in abundance, and with trial and error, I could speak a banquet, even if now I can't stop cooking, to the point of obsession. But for all those delectable words, no ingredient, no metaphor, no enjambment, no image, would suffice to make a plate for you.

Like every good Asian American studies professor, I wanted to believe in the discursive power of therapy, the kind of magical thinking that better writers than me had sought out to give them language. My first therapist, the one I never told you about, I used to see in college, and for a year, she thought I was perfectly fine, until I broke down in tears on our last day, and my student insurance ran out. It took another six years before I tried again. I started seeing Steve, my university's faculty counselor from Marina del Rey, almost immediately after I got to LA, for a different set of reasons altogether, and only for a limited number of sessions at first, because American health care sucks.

And then, toward the end of those sessions, we started talking about you. He left the university and started his own virtual private practice, and I decided that I wanted to keep seeing him, even if it meant that my health insurance bills doubled. We talked about our love of fishing, and how you loved fishing, too, even if your sojourn in the open ocean was for work and his was for weekend pleasure. Over the first four years, we chipped away at everything I felt about you, the whole spectrum of things, the anger and the love at once.

At the end of the fourth year, we hit a block. My chest—or, more accurately, my solar plexus—tightened every time I thought about the possibility of being a father. On video, Steve watched as my face convulsed and my eyes flitted about, replaying something implacable that had happened to me in the seventh grade and knocked out not only my capacity to remember but my sense of time altogether. Steve's collaborator, my psychiatrist, diagnosed this later as a cocktail of maladies, post-traumatic stress disorder and anxiety disorder and dissociative disorder ad nauseam, and to live with them was to numb them with another cocktail of drugs. Over the course of two years, I depended on that medication, and then weaned myself off it altogether, when I tried to write this letter to you at first and couldn't muster anything but clichés. Now, I carry these traumas as my personal archive, my repository of past silences, my windows into a glimmer of a fatherland aglow from a blood-red sun.

I'm still scared of being a dad. I was terrified back then, when I was almost one, when the heavenly father (really, the Couples for Christ) breathed down my neck. And I'm still scared now, still afraid that I'll fuck up so hard and become another you, without any of the masculine craftsmanship that you tried and failed to teach me. But in those five years, and through every kind of creative maneuver that Steve pulled out, eye-movement desensitization and reprocessing or whatever the technical term was, the dam finally cracked. From the crevice, these eighty thousand something words. Each one of them, for you.

ACKNOWLEDGMENTS

FOR MY PARENTS. This is not the book you wanted, but this is the book that let me piece myself together. Thank you for reading these wounds, and for tending to the ones you didn't realize you had. Thank you for wanting to suture with me.

For Nanay in particular, and always in the universal, it's an honor every day to be your son, in this life and the next.

For my grandmothers. The one who flinched at our touch, and the one who cradled us to sleep. Thank you for your hands.

For my grandfathers. Both haunted and haunting, even in diaspora. Thank you for surviving, and for trying to live.

For my brother. My example of freedom and kindness all at once. Thank you for your stubbornness and your kinship.

To my Canadian editor (and fellow child of Scarborough), Janie Yoon at Bond Street Books, and my agent, Johanna Castillo at Writers House, for taking a chance on me so early into my literary career, when I didn't realize that I could craft in prose outside of the scholarly mode. Thank you for the patience and guidance, both as I waded through the seas of genre and as I journeyed across the oceans of living.

To my American editors, Catherine Hodorowicz, Kiese Laymon, and Deesha Philyaw, and the entire team at Great Circle Books and the University of North Carolina Press, for the support and faith in the work, and for shuttling this project through the process as quickly and as kindly as possible. To my various readers, especially Anthony Ocampo, salamat for the encouragement and for reading this Filipino story from south of the parallel, and for recognizing that borders don't matter—our stories do.

To the Asian American Writers' Workshop and the Writer's Block literary residency in Las Vegas, Simon Fraser University and the University of British Columbia (especially Nadine Attewell, Joanne Leow, David Chariandy, May Farrales, Gym Pangilinan, Danielle

Wong, and JP Catungal), the University of Southern California (especially Viet Thanh Nguyen, Brian Bernards, Karen Tongson, Evelyn Alsultany, Sarah Gualtieri, Edwin Hill, Francille Wilson, Grace Ryu), and New York University (especially conversations with Martha Hodes, Steven Hahn, Rebecca Karl), for the intellectual and creative spaces that nurtured this work.

To those who made me feel at home in New York: Wynton, Maya, Julian, Ying, Spencer, Kodak, Shakil, Benny, Kevin, Jun, Jackie, Hika, Michael, Madina, Audrey, Irvin, Christy, Tomson, Rachel, Emily, Michael, Jacinda.

To Catherine, Carrianne, and David. Thank you for showing us the way.

To my first and last readers: Diriye, Hassan, Yusef, Jason, Natasha, Daniela, Patrick, Téa, Mel, Ariel, Jonathan, Jackie, Fiori, Jane, Ann, Wes, Jacinda, Alyssa, Karen, Joan, Joy, Paul, Ana, Oona, Dolly, Royce, Alex, Chris, Reyna. To the one who read with me through the pandemic until we couldn't read anymore. Thank you.

To Amine and Troy and Abel and Lilliana at Ali Mama in Los Angeles, and Layla and Mustafa and the family at Eastside Story in New York, for the second and third homes that felt safe enough to write this.

To Jason, fishing buddy and emotional Virgil, and this book's anchor.

To my love. At the end of these eighty thousand something words, and many more imperfect Odysseys, you welcomed me at the pier. Home is this voyage we've embarked on together.

Salamat. Agyamanak. Gracias. Merci. Thank you.